THE GREAT GLEN WAY

THE GREAT GLEN WAY

FORT WILLIAM TO INVERNESS
TWO-WAY TRAIL GUIDE

by Paddy Dillon

JUNIPER HOUSE, MURLEY MOSS,
OXENHOLME ROAD, KENDAL, CUMBRIA LA9 7RL
www.cicerone.co.uk

Third edition 2025
ISBN: 978 1 78631 127 6
eISBN: 978 1 78765 100 5
Second edition 2016
First edition 2007

MIX
Paper | Supporting responsible forestry
FSC® C010256
FSC www.fsc.org

Printed in China on responsibly sourced paper on behalf of Latitude Press Ltd.
A catalogue record for this book is available from the British Library.

Cicerone's EU representative for GPSR compliance is Easy Access System Europe, Mustamäe tee 50, 10621 Tallinn, Estonia. Email gpsr.requests@easproject.com.

Updates to this Guide

While every effort is made by our authors to ensure the accuracy of guidebooks as they go to print, changes can occur during the lifetime of an edition. Any updates that we know of for this guide will be on the Cicerone website (www.cicerone.co.uk/1127/updates), so please check before planning your trip. We also advise that you check information about such things as transport, accommodation and shops locally. Even rights of way can be altered over time. We are always grateful for information about any discrepancies between a guidebook and the facts on the ground, sent by email to updates@cicerone.co.uk.

Register your book: To sign up to receive free updates, special offers and GPX files where available, create a Cicerone account and register your purchase via the 'My Account' tab at www.cicerone.co.uk.

Front cover: A ruined barge lies beached beside Loch Lochy, just off the Great Glen Way outside Gairlochy (Stage 2 S/N or Stage 5 N/S)

CONTENTS

A whitewashed pepperpot lighthouse marks where the Caledonian Canal joins Loch Lochy near Gairlochy (Stage 1, S–N; Stage 6 N–S)

Symbols on the route maps

- route
- alternative route
- Ⓢ start point
- Ⓕ finish point
- † church
- castle
- railway
- railway station

Contour lines are drawn at 50m intervals and labelled at 100m intervals.

0 kilometres 1 2
0 miles 1
SCALE: 1:100,000

Relief data

Route map relief

>1100m
1000m
900m
800m
700m
600m
500m
400m
300m
200m
100m

Overview map relief

>800m
600m
400m
200m
75m
0m

See 1:25,000 map booklet for the key to the 1:25,000 maps

GPX files

GPX files for all routes can be downloaded for free at www.cicerone.co.uk/1127/GPX.

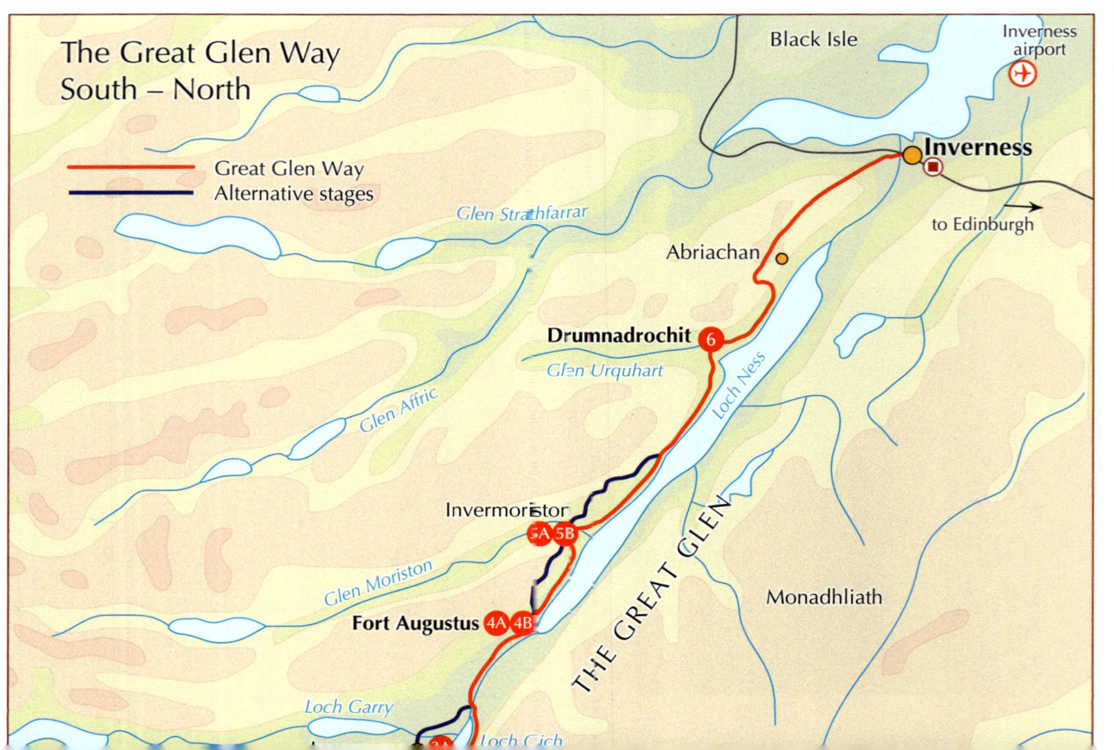
The Great Glen Way
South – North
Great Glen Way
Alternative stages
Black Isle
Inverness airport
Inverness
to Edinburgh
Glen Strathfarrar
Abriachan
Drumnadrochit
6
Glen Urquhart
Loch Ness
Glen Affric
Invermoriston
5A
5B
Glen Moriston
Fort Augustus
4A
4B
THE GREAT GLEN
Monadhliath
Loch Garry

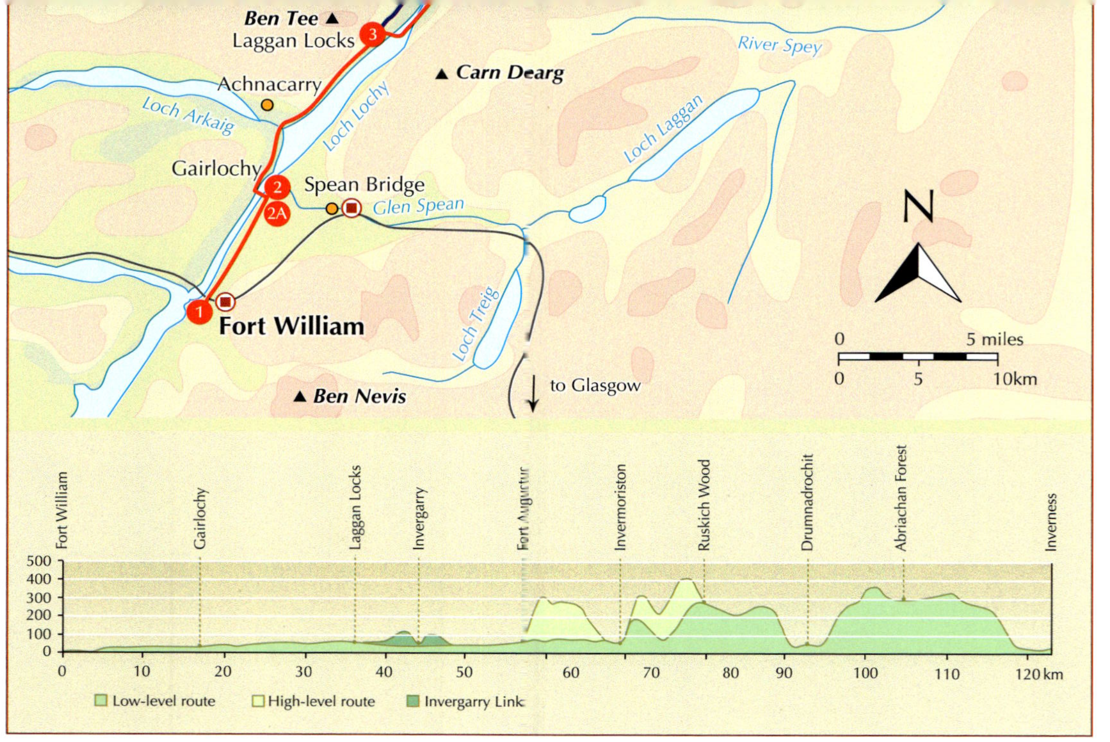

Ben Tee
Laggan Locks
3
Achnacarry
Carn Dearg
River Spey
Loch Arkaig
Loch Lochy
Loch Laggan
Gairlochy
2
Spean Bridge
2A
Glen Spean
N
1
Fort William
Loch Treig
0
5 miles
0
5
10km
to Glasgow
Ben Nevis
Fort William
Gairlochy
Laggan Locks
Invergarry
Fort Augustus
Invermoriston
Ruskich Wood
Drumnadrochit
Abriachan Forest
Inverness
500
400
300
200
100
0
0
10
20
30
40
50
60
70
80
90
100
110
120 km
Low-level route
High-level route
Invergarry Link

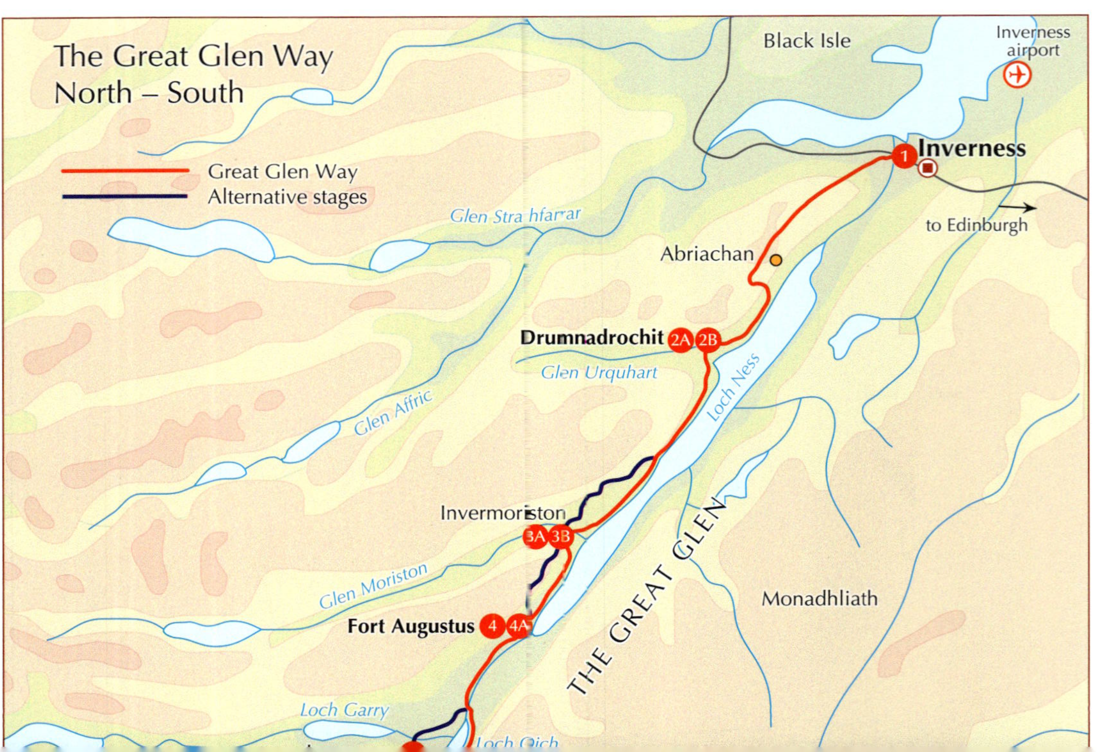
The Great Glen Way
North – South
Great Glen Way
Alternative stages
Black Isle
Inverness airport
Inverness
1
to Edinburgh
Glen Strathfarrar
Abriachan
Drumnadrochit
2A
2B
Glen Urquhart
Loch Ness
Glen Affric
Invermoriston
3A
3B
THE GREAT GLEN
Glen Moriston
Monadhliath
Fort Augustus
4
4A
Loch Garry
Loch Oich

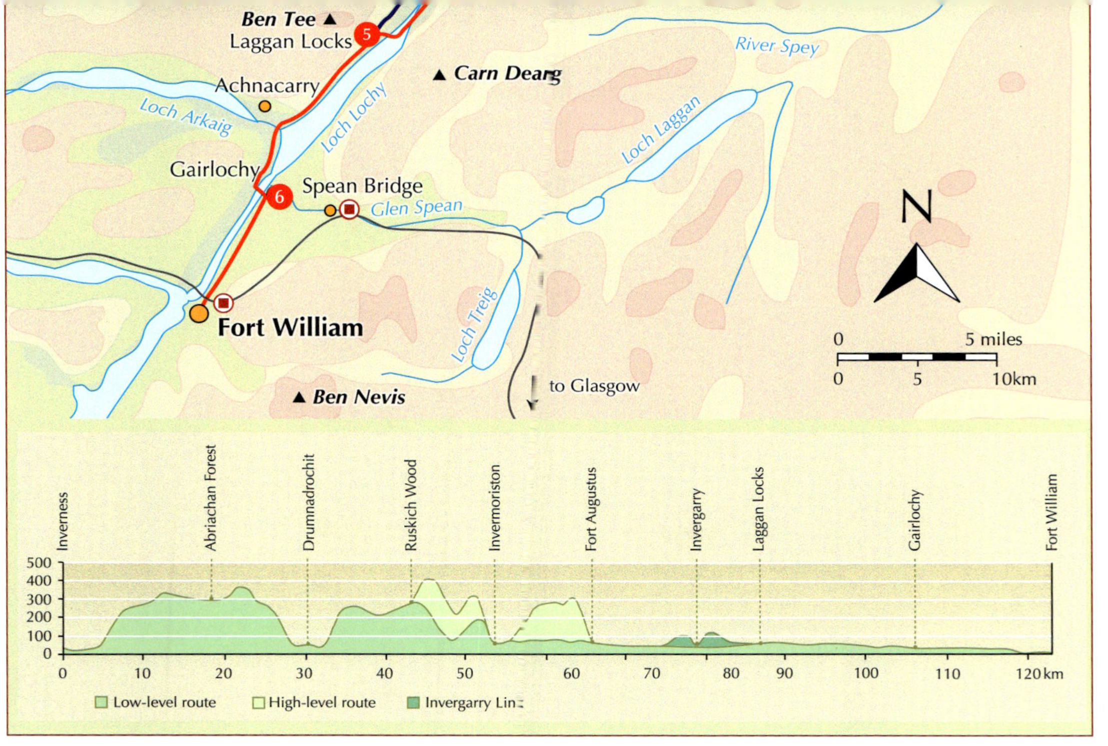
Ben Tee
Laggan Locks
Achnacarry
Loch Arkaig
Loch Lochy
Carn Dearg
River Spey
Loch Laggan
Gairlochy
Spean Bridge
Glen Spean
Fort William
Loch Treig
to Glasgow
Ben Nevis
N
0 5 miles
0 5 10km
5
6
Inverness
Abriachan Forest
Drumnadrochit
Ruskich Wood
Invermoriston
Fort Augustus
Invergarry
Laggan Locks
Gairlochy
Fort William
500 400 300 200 100 0
0 10 20 30 40 50 60 70 80 90 100 110 120km
Low-level route
High-level route
Invergarry Lin

The view from Inverness Castle, taking in the cathedral and River Ness (Stage 6, S–N; Stage 1, N–S)

ROUTE SUMMARY TABLES

The Great Glen Way – south to north

Stage		Leg distance km (miles)	Ascent m (ft)	Page
1	Fort William to Gairlochy	17 (10.5)	40 (130)	43
2	Gairlochy to Laggan Locks	19 (12)	330 (1080)	53
3	Laggan Locks to Fort Augustus	17.5 (10.75)	30 (100)	61
Invergarry Link		*+3.5 (2.25)*	*250 (820)*	*68*
2A	Gairlochy to Invergarry	26.5 (16.5)	480 (1575)	68
3A	Invergarry to Fort Augustus	13.5 (8.25)	100 (330)	71
4A	Fort Augustus to Invermoriston (high-level)	12.5 (7.75)	560 (1840)	73
4B	Fort Augustus to Invermoriston (low-level)	12 (7.5)	300 (985)	79
5A	Invermoriston to Drumnadrochit (high-level)	22.5 (14)	710 (2330)	84
5B	Invermoriston to Drumnadrochit (low-level)	23.5 (14.5)	600 (1970)	91
6	Drumnadrochit to Inverness	30.5 (19)	500 (1640)	99
Totals (low-level without Invergarry Link)		**120 (74.5)**	**1800 (5905)**	

The Great Glen Way – north to south

Stage		Leg distance km (miles)	Ascent m (ft)	Page
1	Inverness to Drumnadrochit	30.5 (19)	540 (1770)	110
2A	Drumnadrochit to Invermoriston (high-level)	22.5 (14)	580 (1900)	121
2B	Drumnadrochit to Invermoriston (low-level)	23.5 (14.5)	590 (1935)	128
3A	Invermoriston to Fort Augustus (high-level)	12.5 (7.75)	710 (2330)	135
3B	Invermoriston to Fort Augustus (low-level)	12 (7.5)	320 (1050)	141
4	Fort Augustus to Laggan Locks	17.5 (10.75)	40 (130)	147
5	Laggan Locks to Gairlochy	19 (12)	300 (985)	154
Invergarry Link		*+3.5 (2.25)*	*250 (820)*	*161*
4A	Fort Augustus to Invergarry	13.5 (8.25)	190 (625)	161
5A	Invergarry to Gairlochy	26.5 (16.5)	400 (1310)	165
6	Gairlochy to Fort William	17 (10.5)	10 (35)	169
Totals (low-level without Invergarry Link)		**120 (74.5)**	**1800 (5905)**	

STAGE FACILITIES PLANNER

Stage	Place	Distance (km)
Great Glen Way		
1	Fort William	0km
1	*Glen Nevis 4km off-route from Fort William*	
1	Lochyside	2.5km
1	Caol	1.5km
1	Corpach	1.5km
1	Banavie	1.5km
1	Moy Bridge	8km
1	Gairlochy	2km
1	*Spean Bridge is 5.5km off-route from Gairlochy*	
2	Glas-Dhoire	14.5km
2	Laggan Locks	4.5km
3	North Laggan	1.5km
3	*Well of the Seven Heads is 1km off-route from Laggan Bridge*	
3	Leitirfearn	5km
3	Aberchalder Bridge	4km
3	*Lundy View B&B and Jaggy Thistle restaurant lie 1km off-route from Aberchalder Bridge*	
3	Kytra Lock	4km
3	Fort Augustus	4km
4	Inver Coille	8km
4	Invermoriston	4km
5	Alltsigh	6.5km
5	Grotaig	8km
5	Drumnadrochit	9km
6	Abriachan	12km
6	Bught	16km
6	Inverness	2.5km
6	*Seaport Marina is 2km off-route from Inverness Castle*	
Invergarry Link		
2	Between Kilfinnan and Laggan Locks	0km
2	*Well of the Seven Heads is 750m off-route from a road junction near Laggan Bridge*	
2/3	Invergarry	8km
3	Aberchalder Bridge	5.5km

general accommodation · campsite · wild camping/biv · refreshments · grocery shop · outdoor shop · bus · train · ATM · tourist info

Cum. stage distance (km)	general accommodation	campsite	wild camping/biv	refreshments	grocery shop	outdoor shop	train	bus	ATM	tourist info
0km	✓			✓	✓	✓	✓	✓	✓	✓
	✓	✓								
2.5km	✓							✓		
4km				✓				✓	✓	
5.5km	✓			✓	✓		✓	✓	✓	
7km	✓			✓			✓	✓		
15km			✓							
17km			✓							
	✓			✓	✓		✓	✓	✓	
31.5km			✓							
36km			✓	✓				✓		
37.5km	✓							✓		
				✓						
42.5km			✓							
46.5km								✓		
	✓			✓						
50.5km			✓							
54.5km	✓	✓		✓	✓			✓	✓	
62.5km		✓			✓					
66.5km	✓			✓	✓			✓		
73km	✓							✓		
81km				✓						
90km	✓	✓		✓	✓			✓	✓	
102km		✓		✓						
118km	✓	✓		✓				✓		
120.5km	✓			✓	✓	✓	✓	✓	✓	✓
	✓		✓	✓	✓			✓	✓	
				✓						
	✓			✓	✓			✓		
								✓		

Looking across the Caledonian Canal at Cullochy Lock near Aberchalder (Stage 3 S–N or Stage 4 N–S)

INTRODUCTION

A path follows the wooded shore of Loch Lochy from Gairlochy towards Achnacarry (Stage 2 S–N or Stage 5 N–S)

The Great Glen is a remarkable geographic feature, running ruler-straight from coast to coast through the Scottish Highlands. Loch Ness, Loch Lochy and little Loch Oich are neatly arranged through the glen, while steep and forested slopes rise towards splendid mountains to north and south. Man has not missed the opportunity to run a road along this low-lying glen, and the Caledonian Canal was cut through the glen, linking its three lochs with the coast. Walkers are now blessed with the provision of a waymarked trail through the glen, running up to 124km (79 miles) from Fort William to Inverness via Invergarry and Fort Augustus. It was officially opened on 30 April 2002 by Prince Andrew, in his role as the Earl of Inverness. As a low lying trail, most walkers could complete it at most times of the year, and there is always ready access to accommodation, food, drink and transport services.

The Great Glen Way provides an easy and scenic route through the Highlands, where walkers can admire the rugged mountains without having to climb them. Although much of the route can be covered by mountain bike, some paths are only for walkers. Take the time to delve into the long and turbulent history of clan rivalry, strife and warfare. Marvel at the engineering associated with military roads, railway lines and the Caledonian Canal. Keep an eye peeled for a glimpse of the celebrated Loch Ness Monster!

PLANNING YOUR TRIP

A ruined barge lies beached beside Loch Lochy, just off the Great Glen Way outside Gairlochy Stage 2 S–N or Stage 5 N–S)

CHOOSING AN ITINERARY

The Great Glen Way can easily be walked within a week, and most walkers will aim to complete the route in five or six days. The daily stages are likely to be uneven, and while some will happily walk an occasional long day, others may prefer to split a long stage into two shorter days.

The first thing to decide is whether to walk from Fort William to Inverness (south to north), or Inverness to Fort William (north to south). From a practical point of view, walking from Fort William to Inverness means that you are more likely to have the sun behind you, with the prevailing wind, and hence the weather, at your back. Rainfall also tends to decrease markedly the further you go in this direction. However, the route becomes progressively more difficult, with the higher and more remote stretches coming towards the end.

Those who choose to walk from Inverness to Fort William can cover the hilly parts first, but should bear in mind that if bad weather is coming from the south-west, as it usually does, then they may be walking directly into it. The route does become easier and lower on the way towards Fort William, but the weather may become progressively wetter. Many walkers who have covered the route both ways are convinced that the scenery is better when walking north to south, or at least, they are more aware of it.

This guidebook describes the Great Glen Way in both directions; and given the connection with the West

Highland Way at Fort William, there is no reason why both trails shouldn't be walked together in one long journey between Glasgow and Inverness, or vice versa. Many walkers also find themselves drawn to climb Ben Nevis while based at Fort William.

WHEN TO WALK

Most walkers will choose to trek through the Great Glen in the peak summer period. This can be a splendid time, weather-wise, with as much as 18 hours of good daylight. However, it is also a busy time and there can be a lot of pressure on accommodation and services along the way. The advantage is that all services will certainly be in full swing and are there to be used. Those who walk in spring or early summer will be able to enjoy the added colour of wildflowers along the way, while those walking in late summer should be able to catch the purple heather at its blooming best.

Summer is also the peak breeding season for the voracious 'midge'; a tiny insect (*Culicoides impunctatus*) that can cause distressingly itchy bites. Midges favour still conditions in the mornings and evenings, and are unlikely to be a problem in the middle of sunny, windy or rainy days. Most walkers move at a pace that outwits the midge, denying it a chance to land on the skin, but at every resting point, they seize the opportunity to feed on your blood. There are a number of repellants on the market, which meet with mixed reviews from users: basically, the less skin that is exposed, the less skin will be bitten.

Autumn brings its own delights, as the days are often cool and ideal for walking, and most services are still operating, although under less pressure. As the deciduous trees and

Weather conditions can change rapidly, but the Great Glen Way is essentially a low-level walking route

bracken-clad slopes turn russet and golden, the scenery can be breathtaking. However, the weather can be wet, windy and misty at times, and some parts of the route may become wet and muddy.

Winter walking is possible, since the low-lying Great Glen is often free of snow even when there are deep drifts elsewhere. A thin covering of snow will not be a problem, but care should always be taken on icy slopes. Deep drifts, although short lived, can make walking very difficult. Camping might not be the best option in the winter months, unless walkers are particularly hardy and possess the right gear for it. The chance to finish the day by a blazing fire in cosy lodgings has much more appeal, but bear in mind that not all the accommodation will be open throughout the winter months. Also note that midwinter daylight hours are very short: maybe as little as six hours!

TRAVEL TO THE GREAT GLEN

See Appendix A for the contact details of transport operators and information services.

Air

The nearest airport to the Great Glen is Inverness Airport (tel 01667 464000, www.hial.co.uk/inverness-airport). There are direct flights to Inverness from major British airports such as London Heathrow, London Gatwick, Luton, Bristol, Manchester, Belfast and a few small Scottish airports. Most flights are operated by Loganair, www.loganair.co.uk, and Easyjet, www.easyjet.com. Direct flights to Inverness are also available from Amsterdam with KLM, www.klm.com. Stagecoach Highlands number 11 bus and local taxis operate from the airport into the centre of Inverness, which is very handy for the northern terminus of the Great Glen Way, or for onward bus services to Fort William. A much greater number of flights operate to Glasgow and Edinburgh, with most budget flights landing at Prestwick. All three airports have good public transport links to the cities for onward transport to the Great Glen by train or bus.

Rail

Long-distance rail services to Scotland are operated by Cross Country Trains, www.crosscountrytrains.co.uk, Avanti West Coast trains, www.avantiwestcoast.co.uk, and LNER trains, www.lner.co.uk. ScotRail, www.scotrail.co.uk, operates the long-distance Caledonian Sleeper, www.sleeper.scot, services into Scotland, and also provides onward rail services to Fort William and Inverness. Walkers travelling from continental Europe can take advantage of combined Eurostar and Caledonian Sleeper services from Lille, Paris or Brussels in order to reach Fort William or Inverness refreshed and ready to start walking.

Scottish Citylink buses run regularly through the Great Glen

Coach

National Express coaches, www.nationalexpress.com, from all over England and Wales converge on Glasgow and Edinburgh to link with Scottish Citylink coaches, www.citylink.co.uk, to Fort William and Inverness. Walkers from around Europe can book coach travel through Flixbus, www.flixbus.com, that will include onward travel with National Express and Scottish Citylink coach services.

Car

Use the M6 and A74/M74 to travel north to Glasgow, then skirt the city on the M8 to follow the A82 north to Fort William. The A82 runs roughly parallel to the celebrated West Highland Way. Alternatively, use the A1 to reach Edinburgh and cross the Forth Road Bridge, then follow the M90 and A9 north to Inverness. Walkers who require safe parking for a week could have problems, but might be able to negotiate space with an accommodation provider.

TRAVEL THROUGH THE GREAT GLEN

Bus

Shiel Buses, www.shielbuses.co.uk, and Stagecoach Highlands, www.stagecoachbus.com, operate many services in and around the Great Glen. There are comprehensive town services around Fort William and Inverness, as well as a few buses through the Great Glen each day. Most of the buses through the Great Glen are operated by Scottish Citylink, www.citylink.co.uk. All bus services through the glen follow the main A82 road, serving Fort William, Spean Bridge, Laggan, Invergarry, Aberchalder, Fort Augustus, Invermoriston, Alltsigh, Drumnadrochit and Inverness. On average, buses operate every two hours, and the full journey through the Great Glen takes two hours.

With a careful study of current bus timetables, walkers could operate from a single base in the Great Glen, commuting to and from sections of the route each day. However, as the A82 is a busy road, drivers may insist that you use only the recognised bus stops, and they may not be able to stop at all on some parts of the road.

Car

The A82 is the main road through the Great Glen from Fort William to Inverness. Anyone accompanied by a back-up vehicle will find access to the Great Glen Way at several points, including Fort William, Inverlochy, Caol, Corpach, Banavie, Gairlochy, Bunarkaig, Clunes, Laggan, Invergarry, Aberchalder, Fort Augustus, Allt na Criche, Invermoriston, Alltsigh, Balbeg, Drumnadrochit, Abriachan Forest, Ladycairn, Blackfold and Inverness.

Cruises

The Caledonian Canal and the lochs it links create a coast-to-coast navigable waterway through the Highlands. Two barges – *Fingal of Caledonia* and *Ros Crana* – are operated by Caledonian Discovery (tel 01397 772167, www.caledonian-discovery.co.uk), which sail back and forth between Banavie, near Fort William, and Inverness. These barges are equipped with berths for a dozen guests, offering unusual floating lodgings with a full meals service. Furthermore, passenger/guests may join week-long cruises and walk or cycle along parts of the Great Glen Way, returning to the barges further along the trail. It's also possible to paddle canoes alongside the barges. Alternatively, feel free to mix any possible combination of 'boot, bike or boat' through the Great Glen.

More expensive and more luxurious cruises are available aboard two hotel barges operated by European Waterways: *Scottish Highlander* and *Spirit of Scotland* (tel 01753 598555, www.europeanwaterways.com/destination/scotland).

Shorter cruises are available on Loch Ness, where the Caledonian Canal runs into it from Fort Augustus. These are operated by Cruise Loch Ness (tel 01320 366277, www.cruiselochness.com). *Spirit of Loch Ness* carries up to 210 passengers and has an on-board bar. Smaller vessels include *Legend of Loch Ness* and the speedy *Deborah Leah*. Two RIBs, *Ness Express* and *Ness Explorer*, each carry 12 passengers.

Traveline Scotland

Any public transport service, anywhere in Scotland, whether it is by bus, train or ferry, can be checked or confirmed simply by contacting Traveline Scotland (tel 0871 200

Looking along the length of Loch Lochy, where the Great Glen Way largely follows the shoreline (Stage 2 S–N or Stage 5 N–S)

2233, www.travelinescotland.com, or download its smartphone app).

Familiarisation with the Great Glen

Walkers can easily familiarise themselves with the Great Glen by driving along the main A82 road. The budget method of familiarisation simply involves catching a bus between Fort William and Inverness, watching the scenery passing by for two hours. For those with more time and money, travel at a more sedate pace through the Great Glen on one of the Caledonian Discovery cruises mentioned above.

FIRST/LAST NIGHT: FORT WILLIAM

While the Highlands and islands of Scotland can boast a long and proud Pictish and Gaelic history, the bustling town of Fort William is a relatively new development. There was little in the way of settlement up to the 17th century, until a wooden fort was built by General Monck in 1654, on the orders of Oliver Cromwell. A stone fort replaced it in 1690, built by General Mackay, who named it Fort William in honour of William of Orange. The town that grew alongside the fort was named Maryburgh. The Gaelic name for the town has always been An Ghearasdan, which means The Garrison. The Jacobites mounted a siege in 1746, but the fort stood fast. Maryburgh was rebuilt with wood in 1750, so that it could be quickly burnt and destroyed in the event of a further siege, rather than fall into enemy hands.

Fort William prospered following the arrival of the West Highland Railway Company in 1889, allowing early tourists to reach the Highlands more easily. However, this led to most of the stone fort being destroyed. Most of the buildings seen around town are 19th and 20th century, and the West Highland Museum on Cameron Square is worth a visit (tel 01397 702169, www.westhighlandmuseum.org.uk). Tourist information is available at the Fort William iCentre, 29–31 High Street (tel 01397 701801, www.visitscotland.com).

Facilities around Fort William include plenty of accommodation options, with a campsite and youth hostel available in nearby Glen Nevis. There are banks with ATMs, a post office, toilets, plenty of pubs, restaurants, cafés and take-aways. There are plenty of shops, too, including several gift shops and outdoor equipment shops. Fort William proclaims itself the 'Outdoor Capital of the UK', www.outdoorcapital.co.uk. After a quick exploration of the town, most active visitors will be keen to head for the hills, or set off along walking routes such as the West Highland Way or Great Glen Way.

Fort William is served by good road and rail links, while town services are operated by Shiel Buses, www.shielbuses.co.uk.

LAST/FIRST NIGHT: INVERNESS

The origins of Inverness stretch back some 7000 years, and while Inverness Castle is basically an 18th-century edifice, it occupies a strategic site that has been fortified throughout the millennia. In AD565 St Columba visited the Pictish king Brude nearby. Shakespeare had Macbeth murder Duncan here in the 11th century, but the play is not a true record of history. Inverness was made a royal burgh in the 12th century and granted several charters, quickly establishing itself as a centre for trading and shipbuilding. The first bridge over the powerful River Ness was built in the 13th century, and a Dominican Friary was established.

Centuries of Highland strife saw Inverness suffer a succession of attacks and burnings, with peaceful interludes allowing for rebuilding, and its story throughout the Middle Ages was one of slow growth and increasing prosperity. When Cromwellian troops occupied Inverness in the middle of the 17th century, they built a garrison, of which only one tower survives. Jacobites occupied the castle in 1746, leaving it in ruins. Following the Rebellion, a huge fortified barracks was constructed outside the town, known as Fort George. Inverness continued to expand, and wooden buildings with thatched roofs were gradually replaced by more substantial stone structures. The town developed a thriving port and gained several splendid buildings and new industries. While bridges over the River Ness proliferated, the Kessock Bridge between the Moray and Beauly Firth dates only from 1982. In the year 2000, Inverness was granted city status to take it into the 21st century. The city proudly proclaims itself as the 'Capital of the Highlands'.

Facilities around Inverness include plenty of accommodation, including

A winter view from Laggan Locks, across Ceann Loch, at the head of Loch Lochy (Stage 2 S–N or Stage 5 N–S)

a campsite and youth hostel, both handy for the city centre. There are banks with ATMs, post offices, toilets, plenty of pubs, restaurants, cafes and take-aways. There are also shops of all types, including gift shops and outdoor equipment shops. The Inverness Museum and Art Gallery is on Castle Wynd, below the castle.

There are plenty of bus services around Inverness, as well as into the surrounding countryside and further afield. There are also rail services, as well as a nearby airport.

BAGGAGE TRANSFER

Walkers who require their luggage to be transferred between overnight stops should contact the following operators: Loch Ness Travel (tel 01463 832566, www.lochnesstravel.com); Ticket to Ride (tel 01463 419160, www.tickettoridehighlands.co.uk); Piggyback Baggage Transfers (tel 01687 460167 or 07909 640907, www.piggybackbaggagetransfers.com).

ACCOMMODATION

It is essential to book accommodation well in advance if you plan to walk during the peak summer season, as lodgings are very sparse in some places. If an address is some distance off-route, it may be possible to arrange to be collected in the evening and dropped off the following morning, but ask about this when making a booking. Accommodation can be booked while on the move, either through tourist information centres along the way or through Visit Scotland by telephone or through their website, www.visitscotland.

The Great Glen Way passes canal-side moorings above Fort Augustus (Stage 3 S–N or Stage 4 N–S)

com. Other accommodation search and booking sites could also be used, such as www.airbnb.co.uk and www.booking.com.

Always remember that when you make a booking with an accommodation provider, a contract exists between you. If you fail to show, then you could lose any deposit paid, or even the full amount if already paid. Also, failure to show could cause concern for your well-being, and the rescue services might be alerted unnecessarily. If you think you will not be able to take up accommodation you have booked, please contact the provider and tell them.

Camping

While there are no commercial campsites actually on the course of the Great Glen Way, a few can be reached by walking a short distance off-route. Commercial campsites are located near Glen Nevis, Fort Augustus, Drumnadrochit, Abriachan and Inverness. There are small, basic, free canal-side pitches available for single night use at Moy Bridge, Gairlochy, Aberchalder, Kytra Lock and the Seaport Marina at Inverness. There are also a couple of basic 'Trailblazer Rest' sites at Dhoire-glas and Leiterfearn. Some of these basic pitches provide toilets, for which a key must be obtained in advance, for a small payment. Apply to the Caledonian Canal office at the Seaport Marina in Inverness, or tel 01463 725500. Wild camping is possible in many places, subject to the provisions of the Land Reform (Scotland) Act 2003 and the Scottish Outdoor Access Code. Those who establish overnight wild camps should do so discreetly, well away from habitations, and leave their pitches scrupulously clean.

Hostelling

There are just two Scottish Youth Hostel Association (SYHA) (www.hostellingscotland.org.uk) properties, located at either end of the Great Glen Way in Glen Nevis and Inverness. Three more hostels are affiliated to the SYHA, located at Invergarry, Fort Augustus and Drumnadrochit. There are also independent hostels and bunkhouses (independenthostels.co.uk), located at Fort William, Corpach, Banavie, Laggan, Alltsigh, Lewiston and Inverness. Together, these places offer enough budget indoor accommodation to cover the whole of the Great Glen Way.

Hotels and B&B

There are plenty of B&B establishments through the Great Glen, as well as hotels in some places, offering a higher degree of comfort and privacy, at a higher price. If evening meals or packed lunches are required, please tell your accommodation provider when making a booking, since these may be difficult to organise at short notice. Some providers, while unable to offer meals, may be willing to take walkers to nearby restaurants for a meal, but again, ask about this when booking.

FOOD AND DRINK

There are plenty of places offering food and drink along the course of the Great Glen Way, but they are very unevenly distributed. In places such as Fort William, Fort Augustus,

A tempting sign near Abriachan Forest (Stage 6, S–N; Stage 1, N–S)

Drumnadrochit and Inverness, there are plenty of shops, bars, restaurants, cafés and take-aways available. In places such as Invermoriston there are only a couple of restaurants, while around Laggan and Gairlochy the choice is even more limited, and when places are closed it might be necessary to catch a bus elsewhere if you are not carrying food. Shops and places offering food and drink are mentioned throughout this guidebook, and if there are lengthy stretches where nothing is mentioned, then assume that nothing is available and be sure to carry some kind of drink and snack with you to cover the distance.

In certain places, the facilities on offer are numerous!

MONEY

Most accommodation and food providers along the Great Glen Way accept payment by credit/debit cards, although a few only take cash. There are a few ATMs along the way, at Fort William, Spean Bridge, Fort Augustus, Drumnadrochit and Inverness, but bear in mind that some of these may be inside shops and may not be available on a 24-hour basis. Those who have never visited Scotland before will find that banknotes are issued by the Bank of Scotland, Royal Bank of Scotland and Clydesdale Bank, and these are used alongside Bank of England notes, so your wallet may often contain quite a variety of banknotes. Study them carefully if you are unfamiliar with them. Scottish banknotes are legal tender throughout Britain, although the further you travel from Scotland, the more difficult it can be to spend them, although banks are always willing to change them.

WHAT TO TAKE

Unless you sort out baggage transfers along the route of the Great Glen Way you are likely to be carrying everything you need for a week's walk, so it goes without saying that you will need to pack essential kit only. Bear in mind that surfaces are generally hard tarmac or gravel, so light, comfortable walking shoes may be better than boots, but use something that you know works for you. If staying indoors, a small pack need

An idyllic loch-shore pitch, but is it legal to camp in the wilds? Refer to the Scottish Outdoor Access Code to find out

only contain your usual walking kit, plus a change of clothes. Naturally, waterproofs should be packed, along with sufficient food and drink each day, plus a basic first aid kit for minor cuts and grazes. Full mountain walking gear is not necessary as the trail is essentially low-level and easy underfoot. The high-level routes created in 2014 are more exposed, but feature firm and obvious paths.

If backpacking, it makes sense to pack lightweight and low bulk. A lightweight tent and sleeping bag will be fine for low-level pitches, outside of the winter months. Some campsites have showers and toilets, but there are also basic 'Trailblazer Rest' sites where a key has to be obtained in advance for the toilets. There are also a couple of sites with no facilities at all. If cooking meals, then pots, pans, stove and fuel need to be carried, but it is possible to buy food at shops along the way, to save carrying too much. If camping wild, pitches must be left spotless, and if relying on water from streams either satisfy yourself that it is drinkable, or treat it before drinking.

PLANNING DAY BY DAY

Walkers pass a small loch that was incorporated into the Caledonian Canal near Kytra Lock (Stage 3 S–N or Stage 4 N–S)

USING THIS GUIDE

The route is described both from south to north (starting from Fort William) and north to south (starting from Inverness) in this guidebook. The Great Glen Way is split into six stages, with high- and low-level options given for two of these. An alternative route past the northern side of Loch Oich (via Invergarry) is also described.

For each stage start and finish points (with grid references), distance in miles and kilometres, and total ascent in feet and metres are given. A note of the terrain to be encountered is included, and the relevant maps listed. Places to grab a bite to eat along the way, and details of public transport options relevant to the stage, are also included.

ADDITIONAL MAPPING

The linear extracts reproduced throughout this guidebook, showing each stage of the route in overview, are extracted from 1:100,000 Ordnance Survey data and the map booklet included at the back contains the full route on 1:25,000 OS® mapping.

If you wish to consult additional mapping, the Ordnance Survey covers the Great Glen Way on three Landranger® maps at a scale of 1:50,000. The sheet numbers are 26, 34 and 41. Three Ordnance Survey Explorer® maps also cover the route at a scale of 1:25,000, and the sheet numbers are 392, 400 and 416 (www.ordnancesurvey.co.uk).

Harvey Maps produce a specific detailed map of the Great Glen Way at a scale of 1:40,000 (www.harveymaps.co.uk). The maps that are appropriate for each stage are listed at the start of the route description.

In addition, all these maps are available in digital formats that can be downloaded and used with GPS-enabled devices and a full set of GPX files, for each stage described in each direction, are also available to download from the Cicerone website once you have bought this guidebook at www.cicerone.co.uk/1127/GPX.

WEATHER FORECASTS

Walkers on the low-level Great Glen Way do not need to be concerned with specific mountain forecasts: it is sufficient to check the ordinary local weather forecast every evening after the news. What you hear might influence your choice between high-level and low-level options.

A joint Great Glen Way and cycle route 78 marker post

WAYMARKING AND TERRAIN

Walkers will encounter easy terrain and splendid waymarking along the length of the Great Glen Way. However, do not rely entirely on the markers, which can disappear for all sorts of reasons. If you have not seen one for a long time you may have left the route at some point and will need to turn round and walk back until you regain the waymarked route.

SCOTTISH OUTDOOR ACCESS CODE

The Land Reform (Scotland) Act 2003 has established a statutory right of access to land and inland waters for outdoor recreation. The *Scottish Outdoor Access Code* gives guidance on your responsibilities when exercising access rights. The Act sets out where and when access rights apply. The Code defines how access rights should be exercised. The *Scottish Outdoor Access Code* is available on leaflets that can be obtained from Scottish Natural Heritage, tourist information centres and local government offices, as well as on the website www.outdooraccess-scotland.scot.

The Great Glen Way is a waymarked trail so there are no access issues along the route. If you explore around the route, then normal provisions of the Scottish Outdoor Access Code need to be followed. You have a right of responsible access, subject to the Code:

A new path has been created above Fort Augustus (Stage 4A, S–N; Stage 3A, N–S)

- Respect the interests of other people: be considerate, respect privacy and livelihoods, and the needs of those enjoying the outdoors
- Care for the environment: look after the places you visit and enjoy. Care for wildlife and historic sites.
- Take responsibility for your own actions: the outdoors cannot be made risk-free for people exercising access rights; land managers should act with care for people's safety

The responsibility of recreational countryside users is to:

- Take responsibility for your own actions: the outdoors is a great place to enjoy, but it is also a working environment and has many natural hazards. Make sure you are aware of these and act safely, follow any reasonable advice and respect the needs of other people enjoying or working in the outdoors.
- Respect people's privacy and peace of mind: privacy is important for everyone. Avoid causing alarm to people, especially at night, by keeping a reasonable distance from houses and gardens, or by using paths or tracks.
- Help land managers and others to work safely and effectively: keep a safe distance from any work and watch for signs that tell you dangerous activities are being carried out, such as tree felling or construction. Do not hinder land management operations and follow advice from land managers. Respect requests for reasonable

limitations on when and where you can go.

- Care for the environment: follow any reasonable advice or information, take your litter home, treat places with care and leave them as you find them. Don't recklessly disturb or damage wildlife or historic places.
- Keep your dog under proper control: it is very important that it does not worry livestock or alarm others. Don't let it into fields with calves and lambs, and keep it on a short lead when in a field with other animals. Do not allow it to disturb nesting birds. Remove and carefully dispose of dog dirt.
- Take extra care if you are organising an event or running a business and ask the landowner's advice. Check the full version of the Code for further details about your responsibilities.

RESCUE SERVICES

The Great Glen Way is essentially a low-level route and is usually close to roads and habitations, so there are few dangers. Obviously, common sense dictates that walkers should take care next to canals, rivers and lochs, as well as when crossing or following roads. The waymarking system is good, so route-finding difficulties are unlikely. If a marker has not been seen for some time, you may be off-route and it might be a good idea to retrace your steps. If the emergency services are needed at any point, police, ambulance, fire, mountain rescue and coastguard are all alerted by dialling 999 (or the European emergency number of 112). Be ready to give full details of the emergency, and give your phone number so that the emergency services can keep in touch. Members of the public cannot request direct helicopter assistance; their call-out and use will be determined by the emergency services based on the information you provide. A small first-aid kit should be carried to deal with any minor cuts, grazes and injuries along the way. Aim to be self-sufficient for each day by carrying food and drink in your pack.

GREAT GLEN WAY RANGERS

Should any problems be noticed along the course of the Great Glen Way, a team of rangers are ready to address them. Contact the Great Glen Way Ranger Office, Auchterawe, Fort Augustus, Inverness-shire PH32 4BT, tel 01320 366633, email greatglen@highland.gov.uk. The Great Glen Way website is www.highland.gov.uk/greatglenway.

PHONES AND WI-FI

Mobile coverage is, as is usual in mountainous areas, patchy in places. When sorting out overnight stops in advance check with the accommodation provider about the provision of wi-fi and mobile coverage.

ALL ABOUT THE GREAT GLEN

A straight stretch of the Caledonian Canal between Kytra Lock and Fort Augustus (Stage 3 S–N or Stage 4 N–S)

GEOLOGY

If the Great Glen has a fault, then it is the Great Glen Fault! Even a casual glance at a map of Scotland reveals the true scale and extent of the Great Glen; a suspiciously ruler-straight trench running north-east to south-west. The underlying cause is geological, as the Great Glen lies on a major fault line. The fault has an incredibly long history, having become active some 400 million years ago. However, the rocks either side of it are considerably older. The fault is termed a 'strike-slip fault' and the land on either side has been displaced over a staggering 105km (65 miles) or more. It is an interesting exercise to trace out a map of Scotland, cut with scissors along the Great Glen, then slide the northern half of the map that distance along the line of the fault. All other geological events being equal, that is what Scotland would look like if the Great Glen Fault had never existed!

Geologists have studied the granite bedrock near the villages of Foyers and Strontian, and although there is some dispute, many have concluded that they are essentially the same. However, these ancient granite emplacements lie on opposite sides of the Great Glen far distant from each other, ripped apart by the Great Glen Fault. The line of the fault is still considered active and it can give an occasional slight judder. Minor shock waves have been known to disturb the surfaces of the lochs, and structural damage has been caused in the past in Inverness. Earthquakes include one in 1816 that was felt throughout Scotland, with other notable events recorded in 1888, 1890 and 1901.

The power unleashed during such incredible movements has crushed an enormous band of rock along both sides of the fault, in places up to 1.5km (1 mile) broad. During the Ice Ages, when huge glaciers formed in the Highlands, the already weakened line of the Great Glen Fault was deepened considerably by the inexorable power of slowly moving glaciers. The broken rock along the line of the fault was more easily ground, crushed and moved than the solid rock of the mountains alongside, so that the Great Glen was carved considerably deeper than other Highland glens. As a result, low-lying hollows flooded when the ice melted, some 10,000 years ago, and have remained so ever since. The highest part of the Great Glen is occupied by the relatively shallow Loch Oich, while heading south-west Loch Lochy is broader and deeper. Heading north-east, Loch Ness is broader and deeper again, with its lowest parts being around 180m (600ft) below sea level!

View from the Laggan Swing Bridge, where the Caledonian Canal enters or exits Loch Oich (Stage 3 S–N or Stage 4 N–S)

The Commando Memorial occupies a splendid site between Gairlochy and Spean Bridge, with rugged mountains leading the eye to Ben Nevis

ANIMALS AND PLANTS

The Great Glen Way starts and finishes on tidal inlets, and often runs within sight of broad lochs, stretches of canals and rivers. However, the glen is flanked by steep and rugged slopes, well forested for the most part, although there is some farmland on the floor of the glen. As there are a variety of wildlife habitats, there is plenty for an observant walker to see along the way.

The largest wild mammals are of course red deer, although there are also smaller sika deer and hybrids of both species. Deer are generally stalked from mid-August to mid-October, and anyone leaving the course of the Great Glen Way and heading for more remote places should be aware of this. The best places to observe deer are around the margins of woodland and forest at dawn and dusk, although they can be seen anywhere throughout the day. During the autumn, or 'rutting' season, red deer stags emit a deep-throated call known as 'belling', while sika deer make more of a whistling sound. The woodlands and forests of the Great Glen are strongholds of the red squirrel and pine marten, both in serious decline in many parts of Britain.

Scotland's native woodlands have been decimated over the past couple of thousand years. The most notable tree is the Scots pine, which is Britain's only native pine, and once formed extensive Caledonian forests. The Forestry Commission is playing a leading part in re-establishing this species. When growing close together, Scots pines form tall and straight trunks, with branches that die off, leaving a green crown. In isolation, the lower limbs of a Scots pine will often grow almost as thick as the main trunk, and are often bent into grotesque forms. Oak, birch, hazel, ash and rowan will be seen from time to time, but with so much land planted with imported conifers, deciduous woodlands are of limited extent. Beech trees flourish in many places, although these were introduced to the Great Glen.

While seabirds will doubtless be noticed at either end of the Great Glen, they are also found at many points along the way, using the low-lying, loch-filled corridor as they cross from coast to coast. Gulls, geese, ducks and even cormorants or shearwaters could be spotted at any point where they are attracted by water. Also look out for grey herons as they patiently wait for fish, or more rarely, ospreys as they dive dramatically for a catch. Other birds of prey include golden eagles, buzzards, kestrels and merlins, while owls are also present. All seek small mammals such as mice and voles. Speak to a fisherman if you want to know what is in the lochs and waterways, or look out for salmon as they work their way inland to spawn late in the summer.

The growing season at such northerly latitudes is short, but summer days are very long and the abundance of water is an advantage for many species. While flowering plants may start to bloom late, they can continue to bloom long after the same species further south have set seed and died back. Few things compare with the sight of rampant flowery watersides in

Heron fishing on the River Ness near Inverness

early summer, or the purple heather on moorland slopes later in the season. Ling heather is dominant, but there is plenty of bell heather too. While red grouse can be spotted on heather moorlands, the rarer black grouse is most likely to be spotted on the Dochfour Estate near Inverness. In the autumn months, when the deciduous trees turn russet and gold, the scenery through the Great Glen can be astonishingly colourful.

THE LOCH NESS MONSTER

The year was AD565 and a follower of St Columba was swimming across Loch Ness to get a boat for his master. Suddenly, 'with a great roar and open mouth', a monster rose from the loch and bore down on the swimmer. St Columba swiftly intervened, commanding the monster, 'think not to go further, nor touch thou that man'. The monster sank back into the loch and caused barely a ripple of concern throughout succeeding centuries.

The whole world has seen the grainy black-and-white image that seems to show a tapering neck and head above the waters of Loch Ness. It is generally referred to as the 'surgeon's photograph' and was taken by the Harley Street consultant RK Wilson in 1934. Since that time there have been several 'sightings' of 'Nessie', as well as a number of amateur and professional 'hunts' around and within Loch Ness.

Some photographs are easily dismissed as fakes, while others have enjoyed a period of notoriety before an admission of foul play is made.

Some people believe the Loch Ness 'monster' to be an ancient plesiosaur, marooned in the deep water

Vast sums of money have been sunk into the dark and murky depths of the loch, and while some might say that there has been little return for the investment, it has been great for tourism. One only needs to observe the coaches rumbling alongside the loch, or the cruisers that take trippers out onto the water, to say nothing of those who eagerly scan the surface for sight of something... anything. One man, Steve Feltham, www.nessiehunter.co.uk, has been living beside the loch since 1991, keeping vigil for Nessie. In 2015 he announced that the 'monster' was probably a Wels catfish, introduced to the loch for sport, but he remains open to other options.

There may or may not be a Loch Ness Monster, and in the absence of evidence one way or the other, visitors are free to believe what they wish. Two things are true: first, 'Nessie' does draw a lot of visitors to the area. Second, human beings have a proven capacity to believe almost anything, no matter how bizarre, and scientific proof is not always necessary.

Those who are wavering in their belief are amply catered for at Drumnadrochit, where Nessieland and the Loch Ness Exhibition Centre clamour for attention. Shops throughout the Great Glen sell a variety of 'monsters', some smooth and sinuous, others plump and furry, some ferocious, but most of them happy and smiling, wearing kilts or playing bagpipes. You pay your money and you make your choice!

HISTORY

The history of the Scottish Highlands often seems remote from the history of the Lowlands. The Highlands were often inhabited by people with distinct cultural differences from those found further south. The Romans pushed into the area, but retreated. The Picts held sway for centuries, but were later eclipsed by the 'Scots', who came from Ireland. A thriving Gaelic civilisation existed in the Highlands throughout several centuries when Scottish history was wrought largely in terms of strife and warfare against England. Cromwellian troops subdued the Highlands in the 17th century, but there were notable rebellions in the 18th century, before the region was finally 'tamed'. The timeline history in Appendix C focuses on events in the Great Glen and the Highlands.

The Caledonian Canal

The low-lying Great Glen, with its three convenient lochs, was considered an ideal location for a coast-to-coast canal as early as 1726. However, Scotland was quickly embroiled in strife, and no further plans were considered until well after the Jacobite rising of 1745. Following a number of surveys, a serious proposal was put forward in 1802, and Thomas Telford was engaged to design and oversee construction. Although the Caledonian Canal is said to measure 96.5km (60 miles), only 35.5km (22 miles) is actually man-made. The cut sections of the

A fishing trawler passes from Loch Oich towards Laggan Swing Bridge on its way through the Caledonian Canal (Stage 3, S–N; Stage 4, N–S)

canal were engineered between 1803 and 1822; the first government-funded transport project in Britain. There are four aqueducts, 10 bridges and 29 locks.

The Caledonian Canal was created primarily to allow safe passage for naval vessels at the time of the Napoleonic Wars, but was not really used by the military until the Great War. As a through route for trading vessels, allowing a short-cut through Scotland, the canal boosted the local economy. Large commercial craft still use the canal, but these days most vessels are leisure craft, plying through some of the most splendid canal-side scenery anywhere in the world. As the locks are operated by employees of British Waterways Scotland, they have set daily operating hours. Also, as there is a five-knot speed limit on the canal, even the most determined cruisers should allow a minimum of 14 hours sailing, spread over two-and-a-half days, to negotiate the Caledonian Canal.

Anyone interested in canoeing through the Great Glen should visit www.scottishcanals.co.uk/visit/things-to-do/paddling/discover-the-great-glen-canoe-trail, while those interested in cruising through should contact: Caledonian Canal Office, Seaport Marina, Muirtown Wharf, Inverness IV3 5LE (tel 01463 725500).

THE GREAT GLEN WAY
SOUTH TO NORTH

The original gateway to the garrison at Fort William was rebuilt at the entrance to a cemetery on Belford Road

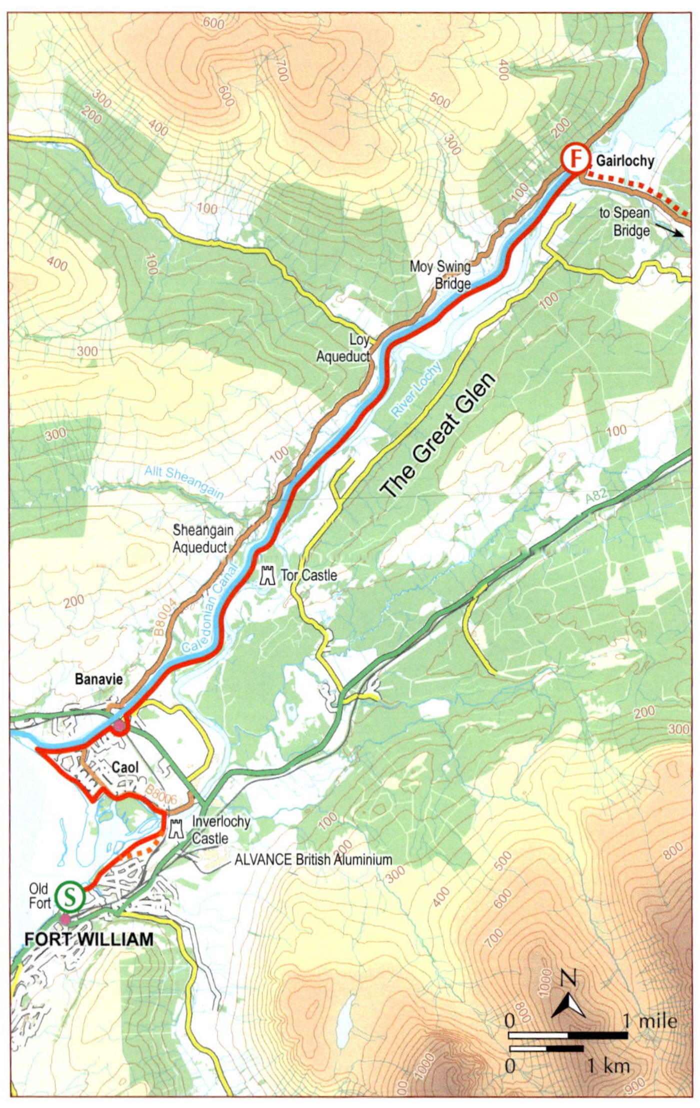
Gairlochy
to Spean Bridge
Moy Swing Bridge
Loy Aqueduct
River Lochy
The Great Glen
Allt Sheangain
Sheangain Aqueduct
Tor Castle
Caledonian Canal
B8004
A82
Banavie
Caol
B8006
Inverlochy Castle
ALVANCE British Aluminium
Old Fort
FORT WILLIAM
N
0
1 mile
0
1 km

STAGE 1

Fort William to Gairlochy

For 1:25K route map see booklet pages 6–10.

Start	Railway station, Fort William (NN 105 742)
Finish	Gairlochy Bottom Lock (NN 176 842)
Distance	17km (10.5 miles)
Total ascent	40m (130ft)
Time	4hr 30min
Terrain	Low-level paths, tracks and roads near the coast, followed by a long, clear canal-side track.
Maps	OS Landranger 41, OS Explorers 392 and 400, Harvey Great Glen Way
Refreshments	Bars, restaurants, cafés and take-aways around Fort William. Shops and take-aways at Caol. Shops and bars at Corpach. Bar and restaurant at Banavie.
Public Transport	Shiel Buses run the town bus services around Fort William, and also serve Caol, Corpach and Banavie. Trains between Fort William, Banavie, Caol and Corpach, as well as between Spean Bridge and Fort William. Shiel Buses run a limited schooldays-only bus service linking Fort William, Gairlochy and Spean Bridge.

The Great Glen Way starts near the coast in the busy Highland town of Fort William, in the shadow of Britain's highest mountain. This is an easy day's walk, largely along a canal-side track. There is very little climbing, and most of that comes in very short stages alongside canal locks. Most of the walk is on a long and narrow 'island', flanked on one side by the Caledonian Canal and on the other by the River Lochy.

Bear in mind that facilities decrease as the route unravels, and at the end of the day Gairlochy only offers a small wild campsite. During school termtime there is a limited bus service linking Gairlochy with Spean Bridge and Fort William, but be sure to check the timetable carefully. Alternatively, ask in advance whether your accommodation provider is able to offer pick-ups and drop-offs.

Walkers starting at either the railway station or bus station in **Fort William** have immediate access to town centre facilities by way of an underpass. To find the start of the Great Glen Way, however, avoid the underpass and walk across Morrison's supermarket car park, then keep left of McDonald's restaurant. Note that the **Old Fort** is located on the far side of a busy roundabout, where a few low walls stand above the shore of Loch Linnhe. A stone monument marks the start of the Great Glen Way, and the route is marked throughout with signs bearing a 'thistle' logo. Note the design of the monument – two rock types joined at an angle, to mimic the Great Glen Fault.

The original '**Old Fort**' was a timber structure built by General Monck to house 250 men. He referred to it as 'the fort of Inverlochy' in 1654, when writing to advise Oliver Cromwell of its completion. A stone fort was constructed in 1690 by General Mackay, housing a thousand men and defended by 15 guns. It was named in honour of King William, a member of the Dutch House of Orange, who fought a decisive battle against King James in that year. William ruled Britain jointly with his wife, Mary, the daughter of James II of Scotland. General Gordon attacked the fort during the 1715 rebellion, then in 1746 Sir Ewen Cameron attacked it. The fort was largely dismantled and the land bought by the West Highland Railway Company in 1889. They pushed a railway through the site, leaving only the small portion of the original walls seen today, which includes a sally port.

Leave the Old Fort and double back round the roundabout to find a tarmac pathway on the left side of McDonald's. This is signposted with the 'thistle' logo and markers for the number 78 cycle route and soon passes a 'shinty' pitch (shinty is a popular Gaelic sport that resembles hockey). ◂ Briefly follow a brick-paved road past a few houses and cross a bridge over the River Nevis. Ben Nevis rises far inland to the right, while the waters of Loch Linnhe are a short distance downstream.

The number 78 cycle route links Fort William and Inverness, largely following the course of the Great Glen Way to Fort Augustus.

Turn left as signposted for the Great Glen Way and follow a gravel path that swings right, running roughly parallel to the tidal **River Lochy**. Alder trees tend to screen both the river and the Inverlochy suburbs of Fort William from sight. ▶ The path crosses a couple of small footbridges, then emerges from the wood into a rushy meadow. Go through a kissing gate and follow the riverside path past a sports pitch, then drift right to reach a narrow road. Turn left to cross a bridge over the tailrace from the ALVANCE British Aluminium works. Soon afterwards, consider a detour beneath the railway line to visit **Inverlochy Castle**.

At peak high tides, there is an alternative route through the suburbs to the ALVANCE British Aluminium tailrace.

INVERLOCHY CASTLE

The Comyns were a powerful Scottish family with two branches, the Red Comyns and the Black Comyns. The Red Comyns built Inverlochy Castle (*Gaelic* – Inbhir Lòchaidh) in 1280 and surrounded it with a moat connected to the River Lochy. The four-square thick stone walls are protected by drum towers at each corner, the largest being Comyn's Tower. There was probably a timber-built Great Hall inside the walls. The castle is always open and there is no entrance charge.

The Red Comyns and Black Comyns supported John Balliol's claim to the Scottish throne, and therefore attracted the enmity of Robert the Bruce. The MacDonalds supported Bruce, and in 1297 their vessels engaged Comyn vessels off Inverlochy, resulting in the sinking of two ships. The Comyns were later defeated in battle at Inverurie in May 1308, and Bruce granted Inverlochy Castle to the MacDonalds.In the 15th century the MacDonalds were often in conflict with the Stuarts, who sat on the Scottish throne. Following a MacDonald raid on Inverness, James I sent a force commanded by the Earl of Mar to Inverlochy in 1431. As the army camped by the river they were picked off by MacDonald bowmen from the strategic hill of Tom na Faire, losing a thousand men. In 1645 there was another battle, this time between the Royalist army of Charles I, led by the Marquis of Montrose (with MacDonald support), and a Covenanting force led by the Marquis of Argyll (with Campbell support). Again, the strategic hill of Tom na Faire was put to good use by the Royalists; despite their smaller force they suffered only 20 casualties, while their opponents suffered 1500.

A plan of Inverlochy Castle, displayed beside the ruins, shows how it was originally surrounded by a moat

Following the construction of a fort at Fort William in the late 17th century (see above), Inverlochy Castle fell from favour. Military might was further consolidated when General Wade built a road from Fort William to Fort Augustus, passing Inverlochy Castle and completed in 1727. The castle was abandoned and was used by the Invergarry Ironworks from 1729 to 1736 as a store for pig iron.

Cross the Soldier's Bridge near Inverlochy Castle. This long footbridge, opened in 2018 to replace a wooden structure, runs parallel to the railway bridge over the **River Lochy**. Walk up to the **B8006 road** and turn left to follow it downhill to a bus stop. Continue along a shared footpath and cycleway beside a flood defence wall. Cross the B8006 road and follow it as it bends left into the village of **Caol**. Turn left along Glenmallie Road, then turn right to follow a broad coastal path beside a green, running parallel to Erracht Drive.

Caol (Gaelic – *Caol Loch Abar*) is a village close to The Narrows, where Loch Linnhe turns a right-angle corner and becomes known as Loch Eil. There are a couple of shops, pubs and take-aways, a post office, toilets and regular daily bus services to and from Fort William, Corpach and Banavie.

At the end of Erracht Drive continue walking along a coastal path hemmed in between the shore of Loch Linnhe and a sports pitch. (Note that a cycleway on the right offers a short-cut directly to the Caledonian Canal.) Cross a footbridge and follow the path up onto the stout embankment of the **Caledonian Canal**. At this point, either turn right to follow the Great Glen Way onwards, or turn left to explore the nearby village of Corpach first.

CORPACH

Corpach (Gaelic – *A' Chorpaich*) is an interesting little village, well worth a visit, overlooking the western sea terminus of the Caledonian Canal. There is public access to the Corpach Sea Lock and Corpach Basin, where boats may be moored while they wait for a favourable tide. The Narrows nearby are dominated by a huge sawmill, which chews up trees from the surrounding forests. A popular attraction for those with an interest in geology is 'Treasures of the Earth', which focuses on mines, minerals, gemstones and fossils. February and March 10am–4pm; April, May, June, September and October 10am–5pm; July and August 10am–6pm. Limited opening in winter (tel 01397 772283, treasuresoftheearth.co.uk). There is an entrance charge.

Corpach has a couple of bunkhouses and B&B establishments. The Co-op store has a post office inside and an ATM outside. Toilets are available in the Kilmallie Hall, when open, while canal users have access to toilets near the canal office. The Tradewinds pub offers meals. There are regular daily bus and train services to and from neighbouring Banavie and Fort William.

Follow the course of the Caledonian Canal inland, climbing beside the Corpach Double Lock. A broad gravel track is followed, flanked on the left by grassy, flowery waterside banks, with fine trees on the right. Note the overspill weir, where excess water from the canal flows down into Loch Linnhe. The canal describes a broad and graceful curve to the left, with tall beech trees alongside, often obscuring views of Caol. Simply follow the canal-side track until directed by a marker post down a path on the right, not far from a little pub restaurant called The Lochy. Walk along a road, over a level crossing near **Banavie Station**, and turn left to follow the busy A830 towards Banavie Swing Bridge.

Banavie (Gaelic – *Banbhaidh*) is a little village with only a few facilities, but take note of them as there is nothing else after this point. The Moorings Hotel, a couple of guest houses and a hostel are available, along with a canal-side restaurant and ice cream shop. There are regular daily bus and train services to and from Corpach and Fort William, as well as a schooldays-only service ahead to Gairlochy.

Cross the road without crossing the bridge, then climb uphill in stages beside the celebrated rise of locks known as Neptune's Staircase.

Neptune's Staircase is an inspired name for the tightly packed series of eight canal locks at Banavie. The arrangement is difficult to see in its entirety, and the best views are those seen in the aerial shots used for postcards. Canal cruisers can pass from top to bottom in about ninety minutes, including the road and rail swing bridges at the bottom, but the time taken can almost double if craft pass through in the other direction at the same time.

The upper part of Neptune's Staircase is Banavie Top Jetty. Follow the broad gravel canal-side track onwards, passing through a gate beside tall pines. The canal curves gently right and left and for brief periods there are no signs of habitation. A splendid variety of trees flank both banks. It is quite possible to cross the **Sheangain Aqueduct** without noticing, but take a few minutes to have a proper look at it.

Use a narrow path to descend from the embankment to gain a view of the three arched tunnels. Two carry water from the **Allt Sheangain**, while the third covers a stone-paved passage for man and his animals.

Not far from the Sheangain Aqueduct, **Tor Castle** overlooks the River Lochy. It was built by the MacIntoshes, who vacated it towards the end of the 13th century. Some time later it was occupied by the Camerons, sparking a feud between the two clans that spanned some 350 years, continuing even after the Camerons abandoned the property in 1660 and went to settle in Achnacarry. There is a B&B near the castle.

Continue enjoying the variety of trees alongside, and look across the water to spot a stream feeding water into the canal. Pass a cottage where the track rises gently, then falls gently, passing abundant birch trees on the little hill of Druim na h-Atha. The track later crosses an overspill weir, where excess water flows down into the River Lochy. Look across the canal to see a knoll crowned with a few pine trees, which is an old burial ground. Further along, the canal crosses the **Loy Aqueduct**, built over the River Loy.

To see the **Loy Aqueduct** properly, you must drop down a track on the right well beforehand, then retrace your steps. It is a splendid structure; the River Loy flows through a large central arch, while smaller arches on either side allow passage for man and beast.

Continuing along the canal-side track, the trees diminish, allowing views across small meadows near the River Lochy. The attractive white **Moy Swing Bridge** comes into view.

The **Moy Swing Bridge** simply allows the farmer from Moy to drive tractors and trailers down to his riverside meadows. Canal traffic, meanwhile, relies on a keeper to open and close the bridge on

A yacht navigates the Caledonian Canal above Banavie

demand. However, the bridge is not mechanised, and only one half can be opened manually at a time; hence the need for a small boat so that the keeper can row across and open the other half. Basic camping, with no facilities, is permitted on level grass beside a cabin.

Just beyond the bridge, look across the canal to spot another inflowing stream. Also, look out for another knoll with distinctive pine trees on the far bank, which is another old burial ground. Tall beech trees again grace the canal-side. Follow the track across an overspill weir and enjoy a fine view of the broad and shingly River Lochy. Looking back you can see Ben Nevis rising majestically from the Great Glen. Climb past Gairlochy Bottom Lock to reach a swing bridge on the narrow B8004 road at **Gairlochy**.

Walkers with time to spare can cross the road and continue along the canal-side track. A slight climb leads past Gairlochy Top Loch, where the canal broadens into a mooring basin. Continue beyond a gate and follow a grassy path along an embankment to reach a small white lighthouse where there is a fine view along the length of Loch Lochy. Steps must be retraced to the road afterwards.

GAIRLOCHY

Gairlochy (Gaelic – *Gèarr Lòchaidh*) has won, or come runner-up, in the 'Waterway Length Competition' on several occasions. Note that Gairlochy isn't a village, but merely a scattering of houses, and if anything can't be obtained in the locality, then it is necessary to move far off-route.

Basic camping is permitted near the Gairlochy Top Lock, but a key for the toilet at the canal lock must be obtained in advance via the Great Glen Way website or Caledonian Canal office. The nearest lodgings are a hotel and guest house located towards the far end of the B8004 road, near the Commando Memorial. Any further facilities are well off-route at Spean Bridge. Shiel Buses run a very limited schooldays-only service linking Gairlochy with Spean Bridge and Fort William. The nearest taxi service operates from Fort William.

A broad path runs alongside the Caledonian Canal as it passes Moy Swing Bridge

SPEAN BRIDGE

Spean Bridge (Gaelic – *Drochaid Aonachain*) is 6km (4 miles) away from Gairlochy. The High Bridge, built by General Wade in 1736, was the first bridge to span the rocky gorge beside the village. The West Highland Railway, built to serve Fort William from 1889, was equipped with a station at Spean Bridge. Outside the village, at a junction with the Gairlochy road, is the celebrated Commando Memorial, dating from 1952.

The Commando Memorial lies off-route, but can be visited by those who head to Spean Bridge for accommodation (Stage 1, S–N; Stage 6, N–S)

There are a few accommodation options around Spean Bridge, including hotels. There is a post office shop, with an ATM inside, as well as a restaurant, café and take-away. Regular daily Scottish Citylink bus services run to and from Fort William, Fort Augustus and Inverness. Sheil Buses link Spean Bridge with Fort William, while schooldays-only buses link Spean Bridge with Gairlochy and Fort William. Trains run to Fort William and Glasgow. Some accommodation providers in Spean Bridge offer lifts to and from Gairlochy, if given due notice.

STAGE 2

Gairlochy to Laggan Locks

For 1:25K route map see booklet pages 10–17.

Start	Gairlochy Bottom Lock (NN 176 842)
Finish	Laggan Locks (NN 286 963)
Distance	19km (12 miles)
Total ascent	330m (1080ft)
Time	5hr
Terrain	Clear, firm paths, minor roads, forest tracks and canal-side path
Maps	OS Landranger 34, OS Explorer 400, Harvey Great Glen Way
Refreshments	Café and the *Eagle* bar/restaurant at Laggan Locks
Public Transport	Schooldays-only Shiel Buses linking Fort William, Gairlochy and Spean Bridge, which will divert to Achnacarry on request to the driver. Regular daily Scottish Citylink buses link Laggan with Fort William, Fort Augustus and Inverness.

This whole day's walk runs close to the northern shore of Loch Lochy. The slopes rising from the loch are often well wooded or forested, so that the water is only glimpsed from time to time. Timber harvesting and replanting in the forests ensure that, over time, views will change. Detours from the Great Glen Way can be considered around Achnacarry, either to see St Ciaran's Church, tucked away in the woods, or to visit the Clan Cameron Museum. This is essentially Cameron country (or at least it became so after the Camerons concluded a 350-year feud against the MacIntoshes!). The land around Achnacarry was once used as a training ground for commandos.

Bear in mind that once you leave Clunes there is no exit from the long, forested loch-side track until the end of the stage. Laggan Locks on the Caledonian Canal concludes the day's walk, where nearby facilities are very limited. Some walkers might prefer to follow the Invergarry Link instead (see Stages 2A and 3A).

Leave **Gairlochy** by crossing the swing bridge, then turn right to follow the **B8005**, which is signposted for Loch Arkaig. Keep straight ahead at a junction, then turn left as marked up a gravel path. This path undulates across a forested slope just above the road, then later drops down to cross it. A short, steep descent leads to the shore of **Loch Lochy**. Look back towards Gairlochy to spot a prominent little lighthouse and signs that indicate where the Caledonian Canal joins the loch.

The level of **Loch Lochy** was raised 3.65m (12ft) during the construction of the Caledonian Canal. Its surface level is now 28.5m (94ft) above sea level, and its maximum depth is 40.5m (133ft). The loch is just short of 16km (10 miles) in length and only exceeds 1.5km (1 mile) in width at one spot. It is said to be inhabited by a monster known as 'Lizzie', no doubt related to 'Nessie'.

Follow the clear, firm gravel path along the shore, which features fine beech trees. Cross a footbridge and

A winter day on the shore of Loch Lochy near Bunarkaig

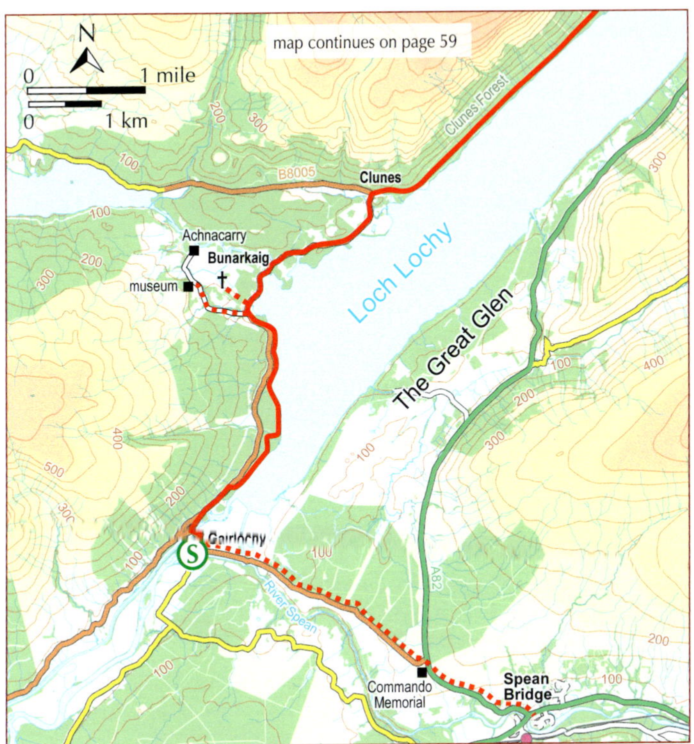

note how much moss thrives beneath the trees, covering boulders and fallen tree trunks in soft, bright green, rumpled velvet. Later, birch trees fringe the loch shore and densely packed conifers allow little light to reach the ground. The path drifts away from the shore. Cross a footbridge over the Allt Coire Choille-rais. Later, the shoreline path crosses two footbridges as it runs round a small bay, then climbs gradually across a slope of gnarled oaks, slender birch, beech and alder. Continue along the **B8005 road** to reach a cluster of houses, where a sign invites visitors to make a detour to the **Clan Cameron Museum** at Achnacarry.

CLAN CAMERON

The Clan Cameron has a long association with the Great Glen. Originally, there were three families: the McMartins of Letterfinlay, the McGillonies of Strone and the McSorlies of Glen Nevis. The first Chief of the combined families was Donald Dubh, born around 1400, and the most recent is Donald Andrew John Cameron of Lochiel, the 28th chief. Never shy of battle, the Camerons were described as 'fiercer than fierceness itself'. Their rallying cry was 'Sons of the hounds, come hither and get flesh!' The Camerons moved from Tor Castle to Achnacarry around 1660, and visitors will appreciate the attractions of the location, an easily defended mountain fastness with sheltered pasture.

The 19th Chief, the 'Gentle Locheil', supported Bonnie Prince Charlie in 1745, thus ensuring that many other clans rallied to the cause. Despite early military success, the Prince's forces were soundly beaten at Culloden and Charles was lucky to escape with his life. In retribution for Locheil's support, the Duke of Cumberland destroyed the original timber-built Achnacarry House in 1746, and Locheil fled into exile. The current stone-built house dates from 1802, and the Clan Cameron has distinguished itself by raising generations of soldiery for the Queen's Own Cameron Highlanders. Achnacarry House was occupied by the military for most of World War 2, when it was the Commando Basic Training Centre, featuring one of the most gruelling military training regimes in the world.

A detail from one of the stained glass windows in St Ciaran's Church, just off-route near Achnacarry

If you are a Cameron – and that includes members of nearly seventy 'sept' or sub-branch families! – then you should feel obliged to make a detour to the **Clan Cameron Museum**. The Museum, housed in a whitewashed 17th-century croft, is open from April to mid-October 11am–3pm. There should be a notice by the gates on the B8005 road if the museum is open. There is an entrance charge (07900 217975, www.clancameronmuseum.co.uk and www.clan-cameron.org).

Another short detour could be made to St Ciaran's Church, in a quiet woodland setting. Watch out for a sign showing the way along a track. Continue along the B8005 road, crossing a bridge over the River Arkaig at **Bunarkaig**. Later, a fine variety of trees grace the landscape. The most striking conifers are the giant redwoods, or sequoias, while the most impressive deciduous trees are the copper beeches. The most colourful are undoubtedly the rhododendrons when in bloom, but they do have a habit of choking out other species over time. The land near Loch Lochy is very wet and boggy, supporting profuse growths of bog myrtle. Pass a large white house and modest forestry houses at **Clunes**, then turn right along a forest track. This passes a couple of houses and some wooden cabins, one of which is the Clunes Forest School, arkaig.org. ▸

Occasionally, the Great Glen Way Rangers station themselves at the Forest School and welcome the opportunity to have a chat with walkers.

Go through a tall gate to leave a car park and follow the forest track parallel to the shore of Loch Lochy. The track undulates and passes commercial conifers, as well as self-seeded alder and birch scrub, along with bracken, brambles and tufts of heather. Pass a small waterfall and a gateway on the Allt na Molaich to walk through a more mature part of the forest. The track dips downhill, then climbs gently, passing another gateway before descending again. On the next gentle ascent and descent, clear-felling allows good views across the loch, then after crossing a bridge over the **Allt Glas-Dhoire Mór**, the track passes through another area of mature forest. There is a stretch at a lower level through younger forest, with a margin of alder scrub, where there are more views across the loch.

Walk among tall trees, again with no views. Cross a bridge over the **Allt Glas-Dhoire** and drop steeply downhill a short way. Just off-route, beside the loch near the ruins of Glas-Dhoire, is a basic 'Trailblazer Rest' campsite. ▸ The track continues close to the shore of the loch and the trees are remarkably mixed, with conifers, alder and birch. When the track climbs markedly uphill, it is almost exclusively flanked by birch. A junction of tracks is reached near a communication mast, where a right turn is made. Go through a tall gate and continue straight ahead, passing the access for the Highland Lodges. Enjoy views over the head of Loch Lochy on the way downhill, then cross a bridge at **Kilfinnan Farm** to continue along a narrow tarmac road. When a junction

A key for the toilet needs to be obtained in advance from the Caledonian Canal office.

is reached, the route keeps right and crosses a cattle grid, but note that the Invergarry Link heads left (see Stage 2A).

When the road enters a forest, turn right along another narrow road to pass some wooden lodges, and keep right along the flat to walk along a causeway road, crossing boggy ground beside Ceann Loch, to reach **Laggan Locks**. These are double locks, and the Caledonian Canal needs to be crossed at the lock gates. Once across, the route turns left, but it is also possible to turn right to visit a café kiosk and wild campsite, or leave the route and head straight for the main road, where there are bus stops. Facilities around **South Laggan** and North Laggan are sparse, and some walkers might like to walk a little further by using the Invergarry Link.

Looking along the length of Loch Lochy from a wild campsite beside Laggan Locks

A conflict known as the '**Battle of the Shirts'** took place at Laggan in the 16th century. The seeds were sown, as was often the case among Highland clans, with a perceived insult. Ranald Galda, of

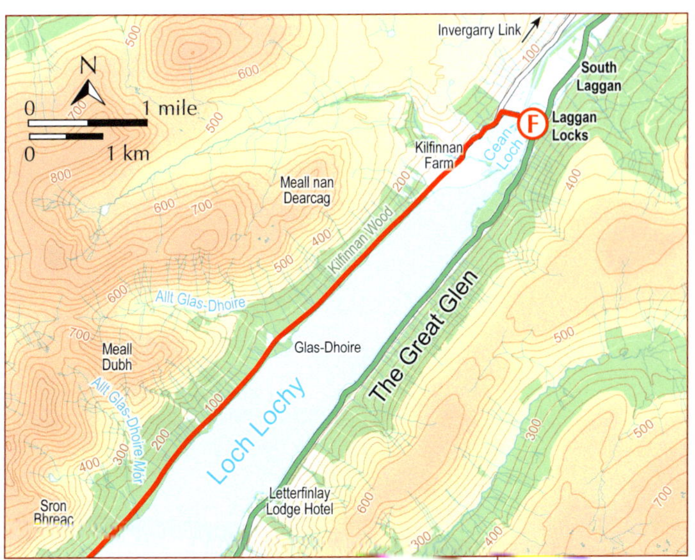

Clanranald, had been reared among the Frasers, and when he returned to his home a feast was prepared by way of welcome. As seven oxen were slaughtered, Ranald remarked that a few hens would have been sufficient, thus spurning the hospitality of his hosts. They called him 'Ranald of the Hens' and said that he could return to the Frasers if he didn't like it.

It was an uncomfortably hot day in 1544 when 300 Frasers faced a combined force of 600 MacDonalds and Camerons to settle the score. Both sides had to put aside their hot and heavy woollen plaids and fight each other wearing long undershirts; hence the name 'Battle of the Shirts'. Neither side scored a victory, since the carnage was so great that only four Frasers and eight of their opponents were left standing at the conclusion of the battle.

The 'Eagle' is also known as 'The Inn on the Water', offering a floating bar and restaurant at South Laggan

LAGGAN

Laggan (Gaelic – *Lagan*) is a sprawling settlement with no clear centre. South Laggan is the area near Laggan Locks, while North Laggan is closer to the Laggan Swing Bridge, over 2km (1.25 miles) away. Facilities are limited to the Great Glen Hostel and Forest Lodge B&B. A café kiosk and a wild campsite are available near the locks. The *Eagle* is a converted Dutch barge that operates as a floating bar/restaurant near Laggan Locks; another restaurant can be found at the Great Glen Water Park on the shores of Loch Oich (see Stage 3). Regular daily Scottish Citylink buses link Laggan with Fort William, Fort Augustus and Inverness.

STAGE 3

Laggan Locks to Fort Augustus

For 1:25K route map see booklet pages 17–22.

Start	Laggan Locks (NN 286 963)
Finish	Caledonian Canal Centre, Fort Augustus (NH 379 092)
Distance	17.5km (10.75 miles)
Total ascent	30m (100ft)
Time	4hr 30min
Terrain	A clear, firm track runs beside Loch Oich and a canal-side track leads onwards to Fort Augustus
Maps	OS Landranger 34, OS Explorer 400, Harvey Great Glen Way
Refreshments	Restaurant off-route from Aberchalder Swing Bridge. Plenty of restaurants, cafés, take-aways and bars around Fort Augustus.
Public Transport	Regular daily Scottish Citylink buses link Laggan and Fort Augustus with Fort William and Inverness

This is a splendid day's walk, starting with an easy stroll alongside the Caledonian Canal. The walls of the Great Glen rise closer to hand and there are often views of high mountains beyond. The Great Glen Way leaves North Laggan and continues along the southern shore of Loch Oich, where the richly wooded slopes are protected as a nature reserve. The course of an old railway trackbed is followed parallel to a stretch of General Wade's military road along the shore. At Aberchalder, there is an opportunity to admire the cunningly designed Bridge of Oich. Another lovely stretch of the Caledonian Canal leads onwards, gradually locking down until a steep flight of five locks drops down through Fort Augustus into Loch Ness. As this is a relatively short and easy stage, some walkers choose to pass straight through the bustling village of Fort Augustus and continue along the Great Glen Way to Invermoriston.

Leave **Laggan Locks** by following a track along the top of the canal-side embankment, passing the *Eagle* barge and bar/restaurant. The track reaches a slope of pine trees and dwindles to a narrow gravel path. The tree cover becomes

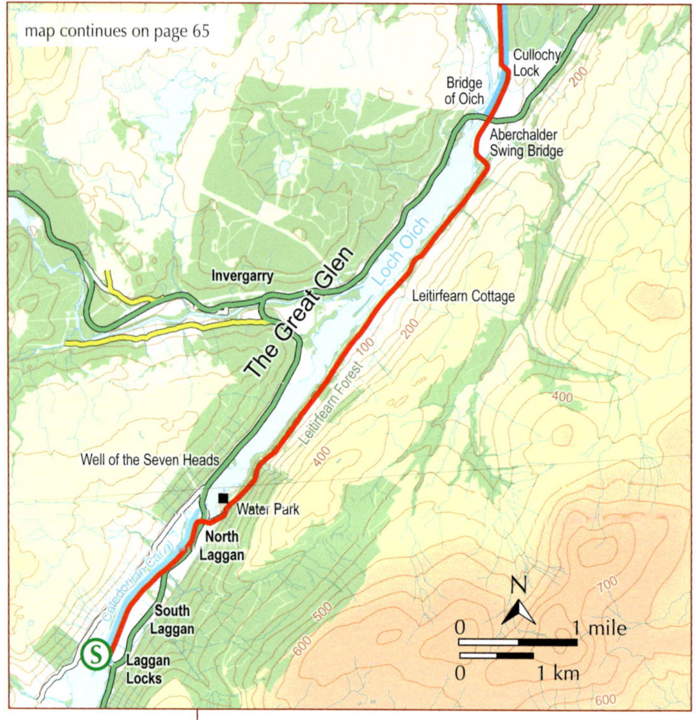

The Well of the Seven Heads Coffee & Take-away is over 1km (0.5 mile) away and the road to it can be very busy.

more varied, with rhododendron and broom becoming common. All of a sudden, there is access on the right to the A82 road, not far from the Great Glen Hostel in **South Laggan**. Take care if following the road there, as it can be very busy.

Continue along the path by crossing a footbridge over a canal feeder, the Allt an Lagain. There is later a good view along the canal, from high above a mooring stage, where broom, gorse and brambles grow. Follow the path through an area of bracken to reach the A82 road again, near the Laggan Swing Bridge. ◂

Loch Oich is the smallest of the three lochs linked by the Caledonian Canal. It measures 6.5km (4 miles) in length and is only 0.5km (0.3 miles) across at its widest point. Loch Oich's greatest depth is 40.5m (133ft), but it had to be deepened at both ends to accommodate traffic using the Caledonian Canal. The surface level of the loch is 32m (105ft), which is also the summit level for the canal.

Cross the main road to follow a quiet road past the **Great Glen Water Park**, on the shore of **Loch Oich**. There are several wooden holiday chalets here, and some of them can be hired to serve as a base while walking the Great Glen Way, commuting to and from each stage by bus.

The **Invergarry and Fort Augustus Railway Museum** (www.invergarrystation.org.uk) is being developed adjacent to the water park. A section of railway track has been restored.

An engine waits at the restored Invergarry Station near North Laggan

Head right up a track and pass the old Invergarry Station, where a short stretch of railway has been restored. The old trackbed is followed onwards, through cuttings on a steep and wooded slope. Look down to the left to see the remains of a military road constructed by General Wade.

Leitirfearn Forest Nature Reserve features a lush, damp, vibrantly green woodland: a mix of ash, birch, elm and hazel. The steep slopes support cushions of moss and delicate ferns, as well as flowers in spring and fungi in autumn. It has the appearance of a jungle, yet it has been cut back twice to accommodate a road and railway. General Wade pushed a road through the woods around 1725, while the Invergarry and Fort Augustus Railway Company opened a line here in 1903. Both routes fell from favour, the road switching to the other side of the loch and the railway being abandoned in 1946.

A basic 'Trailblazer Rest' campsite is available. A key for the toilet needs to be obtained in advance from the Caledonian Canal office.

There are views across the loch from time to time when the trees thin out, and the ruins of Invergarry Castle might be seen on the far shore. Pass the old whitewashed **Leitirfearn Cottage** and overlook a small meadow. ◂ The trackbed continues easily, losing views as it enters a deep rock cutting. Go through a tunnel and follow the trackbed onwards, eventually crossing an old railway bridge spanning the Calder Burn.

A restaurant and a B&B can be found by following the main road towards Fort Augustus, but they lie over 1km (0.5 mile) off-route and traffic can be very busy.

Turn left after crossing the bridge, then go through a gate and continue along a canal-side path. A mown grassy patch close to boat moorings offers a basic wild campsite, before reaching the **Aberchalder Swing Bridge** (from where the **Bridge of Oich** can be accessed). Cross over the busy A82 road with care. ◂

After crossing the A82 road, follow a clear track beside the Caledonian Canal. Look across the water to spot a large overspill weir feeding excess water into the River Oich. When **Cullochy Lock** is reached, cross over the lock gates to pick up and follow a track on the other side of the canal, passing several particularly tall and graceful birch trees. The canal broadens considerably where a small loch was incorporated into its course. An overspill weir has to be crossed later; this could mean wet feet if there is excess water in the canal, although this would be a very rare occurrence.

Pass **Kytra Lock**, where tall pine trees flank the canal on both sides. ▸ The pines soon give way to more mixed woodland cover; there are glimpses of the **River Oich** from time to time as canal and river pursue parallel courses. Hazel trees are abundant beside the track, while later a fine row of pine trees grows along the opposite bank, after the canal bends gradually to the left and passes a power line. Another covered overspill weir is passed, then the canal bends to the right and the buildings of **Fort Augustus** can be seen ahead. The village sits on either side of a fine flight of five locks stepping down towards **Loch Ness**. The Caledonian Canal Centre

A basic 'Trailblazer Rest' campsite is available.

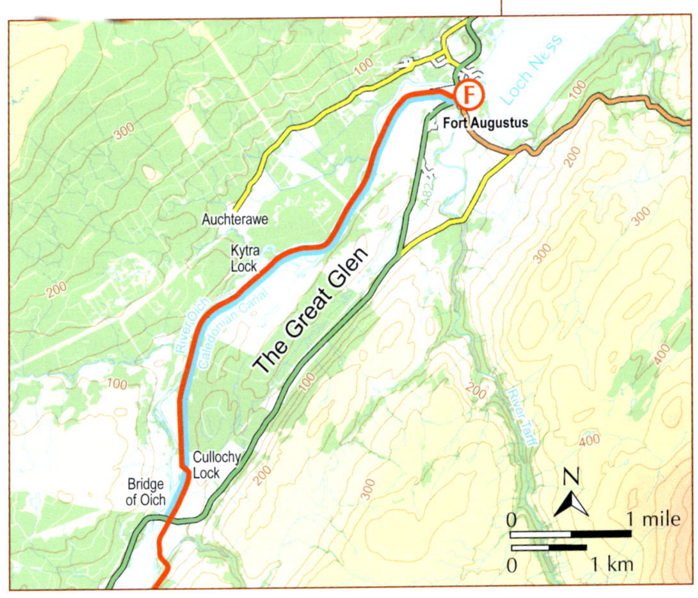

The Caledonian Canal is considerably broader after Kytra Lock

is reached, along with the A82 road at a swing bridge. If continuing onwards, turn left to follow the main road.

Walkers descend a flight of five canal locks through Fort Augustus. At the bottom is the **Caledonian Canal Centre,** which tells the story of the canal, its history, construction and use. The centre also incorporates a café and accommodation. Open daily, 9am–5pm, with free entry, tel 01463 725581.

FORT AUGUSTUS

The earliest settlement at Fort Augustus (Gaelic – *Cill Chuimein*) was founded in the 6th century by monks from Iona, led by St Cumin. Precious little else is recorded about the place until, in the aftermath of the Jacobite Rising of 1715, a fort was constructed on the site now occupied by the Lovat Hotel. When General Wade built a military road through the area in 1726, the fort was moved to where the Abbey now stands. Fort Augustus was named after William Augustus, Duke of Cumberland, and was destroyed at the beginning of the Jacobite Rising of 1745. 'Butcher' Cumberland had it rebuilt while engaged in a brutal campaign to suppress the Highland clans. In 1876 the site was given to the Benedictines who built the Abbey, vacating it in 1997. The Abbey has since been redeveloped and there is no longer any public access.

The bustling tourist village of Fort Augustus is halfway along the Great Glen Way. It offers plenty of accommodation, from luxury glamping, hostel and humble B&Bs to fine hotels. There is an ATM at the Londis store, a post office and a choice of food and gift shops, several bars, restaurants, cafés, take-aways and toilets. The Great Glen Way Rangers have an office in the forest at Auchtertawe, not far from Fort Augustus (see Appendix A). There are regular daily bus services to Fort William and Inverness. A variety of cruises on Loch Ness are also available. The Caledonian Canal Centre is worth a visit.

The Caledonian Canal cuts straight through Fort Augustus

INVERGARRY LINK

The Invergarry Link allows walkers to vary their journey along the Great Glen Way by passing through the village of Invergarry, instead of walking along the southern shore of Loch Oich. Invergarry offers slightly more in the way of lodgings and facilities than the main route. However, using the link route adds 7.5km (4.75 miles) to the distance covered from Gairlochy on Stage 2, while that to Fort Augustus on Stage 3 becomes 4km (2.5 miles) shorter. Overall, using the Invergarry Link means walking 3.5km (2.25 miles) more than the main Great Glen Way route, with 250m (820ft) of extra ascent.

STAGE 2A

Gairlochy to Invergarry

Start	Gairlochy Bottom Lock (NN 176 842)
Finish	Invergarry (NH 307 011)
Distance	26.5km (16.5 miles)
Total ascent	480m (1575ft)
Time	6hr 30min
Terrain	Minor roads, forest tracks and paths
Maps	OS Landranger 34, OS Explorer 400, Harvey Great Glen Way
Refreshments	Take-away at the Well of the Seven Heads. Hotel bar/ restaurant in Invergarry.
Public Transport	Regular daily Scottish Citylink buses link Invergarry with Fort William, Fort Augustus and Inverness

After spending a day walking beside Loch Lochy, there are few facilities at Laggan. Some walkers might prefer to switch to the Invergarry Link, which offers a few more facilities. An easy road walk leads towards the Well of the Seven Heads and a take-away. Forest tracks, including one good view of Loch Oich, are used to continue towards Invergarry. Limited lodgings and bus services are available, while the Glengarry Heritage Centre lies off-route.

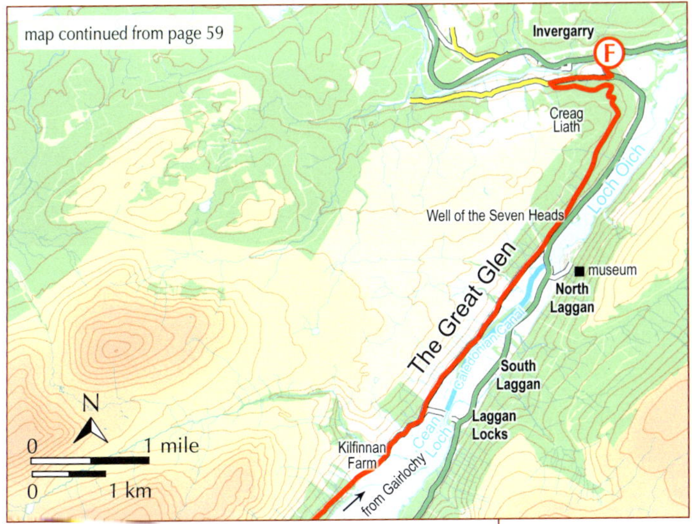

Follow the Stage 2 route description as far as **Kilfinnan Farm**.

After passing the farm, a narrow tarmac road reaches a junction where the main route heads right for nearby **South Laggan**, while the Invergarry Link heads left, marked for 'Invergarry Services'. The road rises gently, undulates as it passes a few houses, then descends gently to the A82 road near **North Laggan**. Turn left and follow the path parallel to the road, then turn left again onto a forest track, as marked. ▸

A take-away and the Well of the Seven Heads monument lie 750m further along the road.

The Well of the Seven Heads marks an historic and bloody act of retribution. On 25 September 1663, Alexander MacDonald, Chief of Keppoch, and his brother Ranald were killed by seven others during a clan dispute. While most of their kinsfolk seemed content to let the matter rest, Iain Lom, the Keppoch Bard, called for revenge, enlisting the support of MacDonald of Glengarry and Sir James MacDonald of Sleat. After two years, the seven culprits were

A little house beside the road on the way to Invergarry

tracked down to Inverlair, where they were slain and beheaded. The severed heads were washed in a well beside Loch Oich, then displayed at Invergarry Castle before being taken to Gallows Hill in Edinburgh on 7 December 1665. The Well of the Seven Heads is now enclosed in stone and bears a monument crowned with seven unhappy-looking heads, surmounted by a hand holding a dagger. The tale of murder and revenge is carved around all four sides in English, Gaelic, French and Latin.

Walk up the forest track and keep straight ahead at a couple of junctions, gently undulating and gaining a view of **Loch Oich** from a picnic table around 130m (425ft) on the slopes of **Creag Liath**. The track continues through the forest and swings left as it descends, later swinging right to join a narrow tarmac road. ◂ Turn right and follow the road past a couple of houses, and the Saddle Mountain Hostel. When the main A82 road is reached, turn left to follow the pavement, crossing a bridge over the River Garry. Turn left along the A87 into the village of **Invergarry**.

A short-cut is available across a nearby footbridge to Invergarry.

Invergarry (Gaelic – *Inbhir Garadh*) offers a small range of lodgings, including hotels, B&Bs and an independent hostel. Regular daily Scottish Citylink buses link Invergarry with Fort William and Inverness. Check opening times in advance for the Glengarry Heritage Centre, which can be visited free of charge (tel 01809 501424, **glengarryheritagecentre.com**).

For 1:25K route map see booklet pages 10–18.

STAGE 3A

Invergarry to Fort Augustus

Start	Invergarry (NH 307 011)
Finish	Caledonian Canal Centre, Fort Augustus (NH 379 092)
Distance	13.5km (8.25 miles)
Total ascent	100m (330ft)
Time	3hr 30min
Terrain	Minor roads, forest tracks and paths
Maps	OS Landranger 34, OS Explorer 400, Harvey Great Glen Way
Refreshments	Restaurant off-route from Aberchalder Swing Bridge. Plenty of cafés, restaurants, take-aways and bars around Fort Augustus.
Public Transport	Regular daily Scottish Citylink buses link Invergarry with Fort William, Fort Augustus and Inverness

Leaving Invergarry involves a short climb and traverse across a forested slope. Once the main road is reached near the Aberchalder Swing Bridge, it is worth making a short detour to inspect the older, elegant Bridge of Oich. Afterwards, simply re-join the main Great Glen Way, which follows the level track beside the Caledonian Canal. A fine flight of locks finally leads down into Fort Augustus.

To leave **Invergarry**, pass the Invergarry Hotel and a block of houses, then turn right at a telephone kiosk. Follow a winding path uphill, passing tall oaks and rhododendron bushes, which later give way to conifers and rhododendron bushes. Cross a forest track, later joining it again, turning left to follow it gently uphill past **Nursery Wood**. Later, there is a view down to the roof of the Invergarry Power Station. Follow the track downhill and keep straight ahead at a junction, almost reaching a gate and the main A82 road. However, turn left beforehand as marked, along a gravel path following a power line through a broad forest ride. The path rises and falls, crosses a bridge and makes

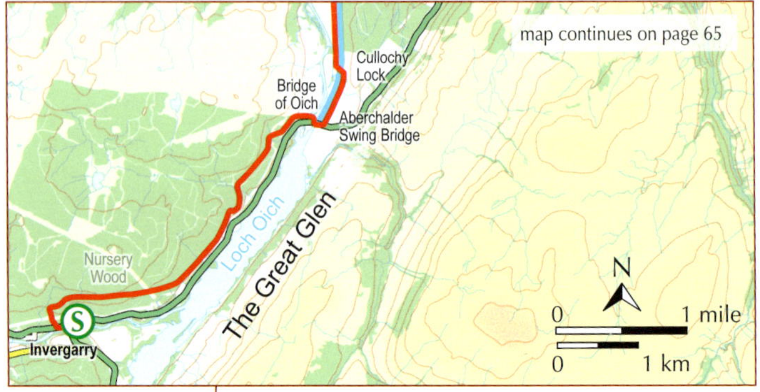

Alternatively, on reaching the swing bridge, turn left to visit the Bridge of Oich, then follow a track beside the Caledonian Canal to re-join the main route of the Great Glen Way at Cullochy Lock.

a loop as it crosses a clear-felled slope. Eventually, drop to the main road, turn left and follow the pavement to the **Aberchalder Swing Bridge**. Cross the road with care to use the safe pedestrian path across the bridge, then cross back over the road to follow a track beside the **Caledonian Canal**. This is the main route of the Great Glen Way. ◂

It is worth leaving the Great Glen Way for a few minutes to reach the **Bridge of Oich**. An older bridge was swept away in devastating floods during 1849, when the embankment of the Caledonian Canal was also breached. Five years elapsed before a new bridge was built, by a brewer-turned-engineer called James Dredge, from Bath. The Bridge of Oich looks like a slender suspension bridge, but was actually patented as a 'double cantilever', built on the 'taper principle'. The supporting chains gradually diminish as they spread outwards from the stout granite pillars that support them, and hold very little weight in the middle of the bridge. Apparently, if the bridge was severed in the middle, it would remain standing. The Bridge of Oich carried traffic until 1932, but the busy A82 road now crosses a more solid-looking stone bridge nearby.

Follow the Stage 3 route description to Fort Augustus.

Kytra Lock is on an island between the Caledonian Canal and the River Oich

STAGE 4A

Fort Augustus to Invermoriston (high-level)

For 1:25K route map see booklet pages 18–22.

Start	Caledonian Canal Centre, Fort Augustus (NH 379 092)
Finish	Glenmoriston Arms Hotel, Invermoriston (NH 420 168)
Distance	12.5km (7.75 miles)
Total ascent	560m (1840ft)
Time	3hr 15min
Terrain	Forest tracks and upland moorland paths with some short, steep slopes
Maps	OS Landranger 34, OS Explorer 416S, Harvey Great Glen Way
Refreshments	Invermoriston has a hotel with a bar/restaurant and one other café
Public Transport	Regular daily Scottish Citylink buses link Fort Augustus and Invermoriston with Inverness and Fort William

There are two options for linking Fort Augustus with Invermoriston. The high-level route should be open at all times, but in really bad weather it might be wise to take the low-level option (Stage 4B). It isn't particularly difficult, and some walkers might add it to the previous day's walk if they are trying to cover the Great Glen Way in a hurry. Alternatively, the morning could be spent exploring Fort Augustus, or taking a short cruise on Loch Ness in order to gain a greater appreciation of its vastness.

The high-level route of the Great Glen Way climbs above the forested northern slopes of Loch Ness, allowing far more expansive views than are gained from the low-level route. Invermoriston is a tiny village, which can be explored easily in the evening. Alternatively, it is worth looking for fine waterfalls on the lower reaches of the River Moriston. If planning to stay in the village, it is wise to book lodgings in advance, although it is a simple matter to catch a bus elsewhere in search of accommodation.

For 1:25K route map see booklet pages 22–26.

Leave the Caledonian Canal Centre in **Fort Augustus** by following the busy **A82** road in the direction of Inverness. Turn left up a minor road called Bunoich Brae (or more correctly short-cut up a tarmac path just beforehand). Follow the road uphill, past Morag's Lodge, an independent hostel, keeping straight ahead at a junction. ◀

A left turn at the junction, for Jenkins Park and Auchterawe, leads to the Great Glen Way Rangers' base.

The narrow road passes a few B&Bs and runs down towards the busy main road. Just before reaching the road, at Three Bridges, turn left along a riverside path. Cross a footbridge in a wood, then climb a steep slope covered in tall, stately pines. Turn right along a forest track and follow it gently downhill, crossing a bridge. There are good views from a noticeboard overlooking the head of **Loch Ness** and **Cherry Island**.

Follow the track downhill to a junction, where the high-level and low-level routes part, and turn left. The track rises gently and ends at a junction with the waymarked Allt na Criche Trail. Turn left up a gravel path, climbing beside vigorous little waterfalls, later joining another track. Turn right and cross a bridge over another waterfall on **Allt na Criche**, then turn left up another winding path, glimpsing yet more waterfalls. The path rises from the forest onto a rugged moorland slope of

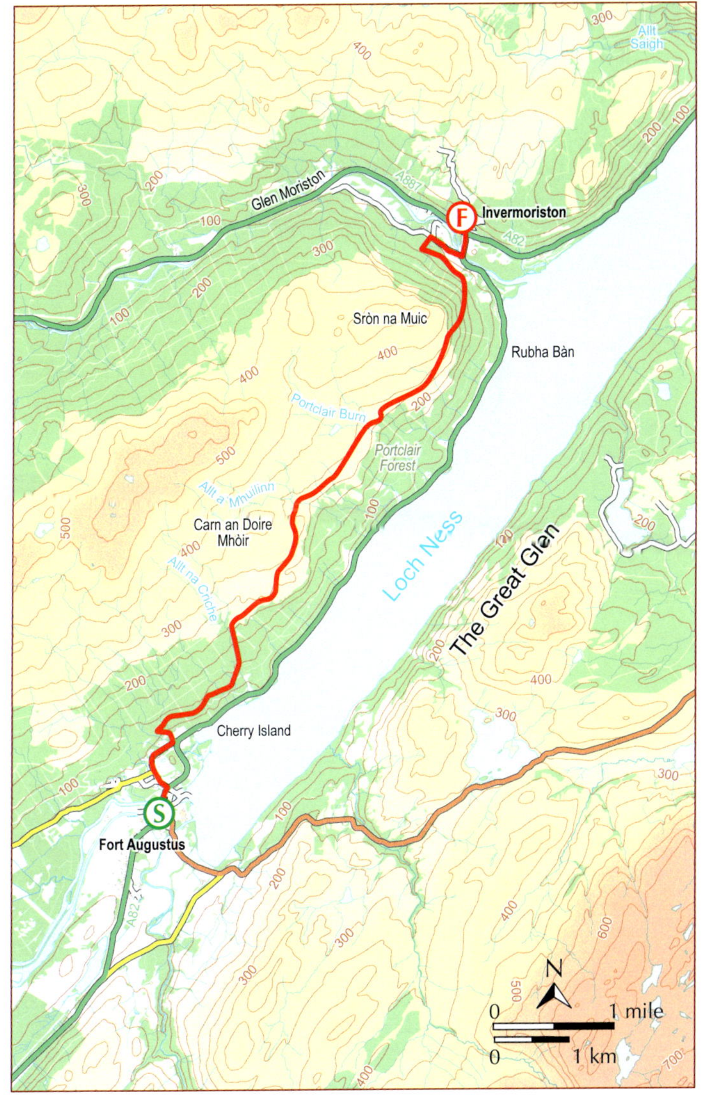
Invermoriston
Glen Moriston
A887
A82
Allt Saigh
Sròn na Muic
Rubha Bàn
Portclair Burn
Portclair Forest
Allt a' Mhuilinn
Carn an Doire Mhòir
Allt na Criche
Loch Ness
The Great Glen
Cherry Island
Fort Augustus
N
0
1 mile
0
1 km

LOCH NESS

Walkers see more of Loch Ness from the high-level route, especially when walking above the forest. The deep trough it occupies has been filled with water ever since the end of the Ice Age around 10,000 years ago, and it reflects enough light to brighten even the dullest days in the Great Glen. Six major rivers carry water into Loch Ness, from a part of the Highlands known for high rainfall, explaining why the River Ness flows so powerfully past Inverness. Here are some facts and figures to help appreciate its full extent:

- Catchment area: 1800km^2 (700 square miles)
- Surface area: 56km^2 (21.5 square miles)
- Length: 37km (23 miles)
- Width: 3km (2 miles)
- Shoreline length: 86km (53.5 miles)
- Volume: 7.5 cubic kilometres (1.8 cubic miles)
- Maximum depth: 230m (755ft)
- Surface level: 16m (52ft) above sea level

There is only one island in Loch Ness: the diminutive Cherry Island near Fort Augustus, which is actually an ancient man-made island dwelling, or *crannog*. More astonishing facts include oft-repeated statements that the volume of water in the loch exceeds that of all the lakes and reservoirs in England and Wales, and is sufficient to immerse the entire population of the world!

grass, heather and bog myrtle. The path surface is firm, easy and dry, with good drainage.

Reach a viewpoint around 225m (740ft), where there are good views of Loch Ness. The path ahead is very clear, undulating and winding, with a few stone steps leading up and down. Later, pass a stone-built windbreak shelter on a shoulder of **Carn an Doire Mhòir**, around 315m (1035ft), where views of the loch are more extensive. The path winds down into a valley to cross a footbridge over the **Allt a' Mhuilinn**.

The path continues easily across the rugged moorland slopes above the forest, crossing a couple more footbridges. Later, there are two footbridges close together, where there are waterfalls on **Portclair Burn**. Cross yet another footbridge and pass beneath a power line, then briefly touch the edge of the forest. The path traverses the slope and crosses a couple more footbridges, as well as passing a stone bench.

Eventually, the path enters the forest below the rugged face of **Sròn na Muic**, and winds steeply downhill. There are stone steps on some of the bends, then two forest tracks are crossed in quick succession above **Glen Moriston**, as the high-level route re-joins the low-level route, around 90m (295ft).

Turn left and follow an old track running just below the forest track, passing big beech trees, birch and alder, rather than conifers. Either track could be used, but whichever is chosen, it is important to watch for a waymarked path dropping suddenly on the right, winding down a clear-felled slope. Turn right along a road and follow it to a junction with the main A82 road. Turn left, but note the ravaged remains of Telford's Bridge spanning the River Moriston, and the splendid Moriston Falls that spill beneath it. The main road runs into the little village of **Invermoriston**.

The high-level route was constructed in 2014, crossing moorland above forested slopes

The ramshackle remains of **Telford's Bridge**, also known as the Old Bridge, could be crossed in preference to the main road bridge, but take care as the masonry is in a bad state of repair. Despite being nothing more than a standard double-span stone arch, its construction spanned several years from 1805 until 1813, owing to a 'languid and inattentive contractor' and 'idle workers'. The bridge is one of more than a thousand associated with Telford.

THE SEVEN MEN OF GLEN MORISTON

The date was 27 July 1746, when Bonnie Prince Charlie was on the run after the crushing defeat at the Battle of Culloden. Pursued by 'Butcher' Cumberland, and with a bounty of £30,000 on his head, Charles had not eaten for two days and was clad in rags by the time he reached Glen Moriston. Coming upon a crude hut and ravenously hungry, he was warned by his companions not to seek food or shelter in case he was recognised. Charles declared 'I had better be killed like a man than starved like a fool', and made his way to the hut. The seven men inside were mere outlaws, and one of them recognised him, but to their credit, they spurned the chance to claim the bounty and risked their lives to feed and shelter him. Meanwhile, on the road through Glen Moriston, an Edinburgh merchant named Roderick MacKenzie, who bore a passing resemblance to the Bonnie Prince, was shot at by troops. As he died he declared, 'Alas, you have killed your prince', and this ruse was sufficient to buy enough time for Charles to be smuggled out of the country.

Invermoriston (Gaelic – *Inbhir Mor Eason*) has only a few facilities, but at the end of the day these prove most welcome. The Glenmoriston Arms Hotel is very prominent. It was originally a drovers' inn, dating from 1740, and the oldest parts are around the bar and reception area. Johnson and Boswell stayed there while planning a trip to the Hebrides in 1773. There are a few B&Bs in and around the village, as well as the Invermoriston Community Shop, the Clog and Craft Shop, and further along the Skye Road, the the Glen Rowan café. Toilets are available inside the Glenmoriston Millennium Hall, when open. Regular daily Scottish Citylink buses link Invermoriston with Inverness and Fort William, as well as the Isle of Skye.

STAGE 4B

Fort Augustus to Invermoriston (low-level)

Start	Caledonian Canal Centre, Fort Augustus (NH 379 092)
Finish	Glenmoriston Arms Hotel, Invermoriston (NH 420 168)
Distance	12km (7.5 miles)
Total ascent	300m (985ft)
Time	3hr
Terrain	Forest tracks and paths with some short, steep slopes
Maps	OS Landranger 34, OS Explorer 416S, Harvey Great Glen Way
Refreshments	Invermoriston has a hotel with a bar/restaurant and one other café
Public Transport	Regular daily Scottish Citylink buses link Fort Augustus and Invermoriston with Inverness and Fort William

Before making firm plans to follow the low-level route from Fort Augustus to Invermoriston please note that it might sometimes be closed for timber harvesting. Check in advance on the Great Glen Way website, and if the route is closed switch to the high-level option (Stage 4A). This is a short day, and some walkers might add it to the previous day's walk if they are trying to cover the Great Glen Way in a hurry. Alternatively, the morning could be spent exploring Fort Augustus, or taking a short cruise on Loch Ness.

The low-level route of the Great Glen Way often runs close to Loch Ness, but the forested slopes usually shield it from view, so walkers see less of it than they might imagine. Invermoriston is a tiny village, which can be explored easily in the evening. Alternatively, it is worth looking for fine waterfalls on the lower reaches of the River Moriston. If planning to stay in the village, it is wise to book lodgings in advance, although it is a simple matter to catch a bus elsewhere in search of accommodation.

Leave the Caledonian Canal Centre in **Fort Augustus** by following the busy **A82** in the direction of Inverness. Turn left up a minor road called Bunoich Brae (or more

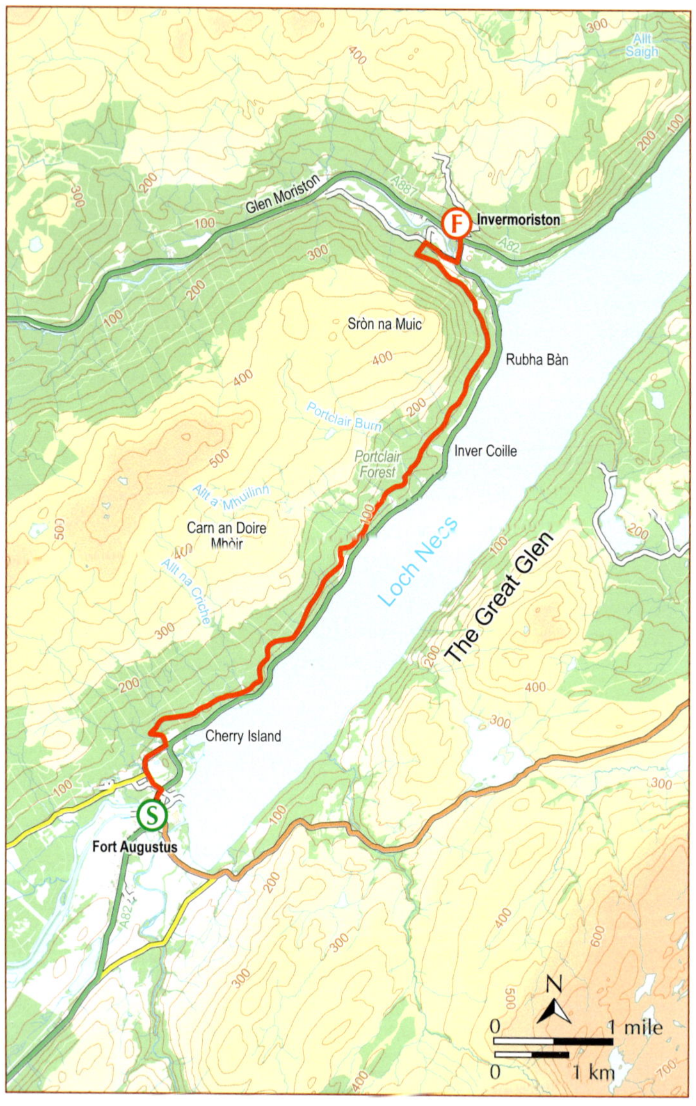
Allt Saigh
Glen Moriston
A887
Invermoriston
A82
Sròn na Muic
Rubha Bàn
Portclair Burn
Portclair Forest
Inver Coille
Allt a' Mhuilinn
Carn an Doire Mhòir
Allt na Criche
Loch Ness
The Great Glen
Cherry Island
Fort Augustus
A82
0
1 mile
0
1 km

The low-level route generally follows easy forest tracks

correctly short-cut up a tarmac path just beforehand). Follow the road uphill, past Morag's Lodge, an independent hostel, keeping straight ahead at a junction. ▸

A left turn at the junction, for Jenkins Park and Auchterawe, leads to the Great Glen Way Rangers' base.

The narrow road passes a few B&Bs and runs down towards the busy main road. Just before the road, at Three Bridges, turn left along a riverside path. Cross a footbridge in a wood, then climb a steep slope covered in tall, stately pines. Turn right along a forest track and follow it gently downhill. There are good views from a noticeboard overlooking the head of **Loch Ness** and **Cherry Island**.

Follow the track downhill to a junction where the high-level and low-level routes part. Turn right; the track descends gently and leads through a gate, almost back onto the main road. Turn left to follow another track away from the road, quickly swinging right to cross the tumbling stream of **Allt na Criche**.

For 1:25K route map see booklet pages 22–26.

The woods are mixed, with some fine oaks and birch, but as the broad track bends and climbs,

Fine waterfalls are seen from the path beside Allt na Criche

avoiding a left turn, there are more conifers. Pass a gate and climb among tall conifers, with lush margins of heather, bilberry, mosses, ferns and wood sorrel. There is a slight dip in the track, then keep straight ahead at a junction to climb gradually among tall trees on the slopes of Druim na Garbh Leachtrach. Walk downhill, then uphill, then enjoy good views over a slope of young trees, across **Loch Ness** to the rugged hill of Beinn a' Bhacaidh. Another gentle rise leads to a stone-slab seat, with splendid views both ways along the length of Loch Ness.

Views are lost on a descent into tall forest, where a concrete bridge spans a waterfall on the **Allt a' Mhuilinn**. There is a gentle ascent with a view across a younger part of the forest, again taking in the hill of Beinn a' Bhacaidh across Loch Ness. Walk gently downhill, losing the views. Cross a concrete bridge over **Portclair Burn**, then cross a dip in the track. ◂ Climb gently to cross another concrete bridge over a small waterfall. There is a good view of Loch Ness on the way downhill, overlooking a clear-felled slope, then views

A campsite at Inver Coille is marked off-route, down to the right.

are lost and the gentle descent becomes steeper. The main track suddenly swings sharp right, so keep straight ahead up another track.

For 1:25K route map see booklet pages 26–32.

The track climbs over a crest and swings left into **Glen Moriston**, and there is another view of Loch Ness after making the turn. Keep right at a junction and almost immediately note the high-level route joining from the left, around 90m (295ft).

Step to the right and follow an old track running just below the forest track, passing big beech trees, birch and alder, rather than conifers. Either track could be used, but whichever is chosen, it is important to watch for a waymarked path dropping suddenly on the right, winding down a clear-felled slope. Turn right along a road and follow it to a junction with the main A82 road. Turn left, but note the ravaged remains of Telford's Bridge spanning the River Moriston, and the splendid Moriston Falls that spill beneath it. The main road runs into the little village of **Invermoriston**. ▸

For information about Invermoriston see Stage 4A.

Telford's Bridge spans the River Moriston and the Falls of Moriston near Invermoriston

STAGE 5A

Invermoriston to Drumnadrochit (high-level)

Start	Glenmoriston Arms Hotel, Invermoriston (NH 420 168)
Finish	Village Green, Drumnadrochit (NH 508 300)
Distance	22.5km (14 miles)
Total ascent	710m (2330ft)
Time	5hr 45min
Terrain	Forest tracks and paths with some short, steep slopes. Moorland road.
Maps	OS Landrangers 26 and 34, OS Explorer 416S, Harvey Great Glen Way
Refreshments	Café at a pottery at Grotaig. Plenty of restaurants, cafés and take-aways around Drumnadrochit
Public Transport	Regular daily Scottish Citylink buses link Invermoriston and Drumnadrochit with Inverness and Fort William

There are two options for linking Invermoriston and Drumnadrochit. The high-level route should be open at all times, but in really bad weather it might be wise to take the low-level option (Stage 5B). Despite height being gained, and the route running just outside the forest, there are no views of Loch Ness at first because the hills of Creag nan Eun and Meall na Sròine are in the way. There is an option to switch to the low-level route by walking down a forest track to Alltsigh, otherwise keep climbing to reach the highest point on the Great Glen Way on the slopes of Creag Dhearg. The high-level and low-level routes are reunited shortly afterwards, and both feature good views of Loch Ness.

Bear in mind that a pottery at Grotaig has a café, but otherwise there are no refreshments until Lewiston and Drumnadrochit are reached at the end of the day.

Leave **Invermoriston** via the A887, signposted for Kyle of Lochalsh and referred to locally as the Skye Road. Turn right at the Clog and Craft Shop, where a milestone warns 'Last Clog Shop before Skye – 52 miles'. A steep and narrow zigzag road climbs past Craik na Dav B&B, up a well-wooded slope bearing sycamore, beech, oak and birch, with a holly understorey at a higher level. Dense conifers once flanked the higher part of the road, but these have been felled. Cross a bridge over a stream and turn right almost immediately to follow a forest track crossing another bridge over the same stream. ▶

Before reaching the road/track junction, a steep and winding gravel path offers a short-cut uphill.

A junction is reached, where the high-level and low-level routes part. Turn left along a path which rises to a junction at the corner of a drystone wall. Turn right and keep climbing, with forest to the right and a field to the left. Old birch trees are dotted around on the slopes outside the forest. Walk down a winding path, with stone

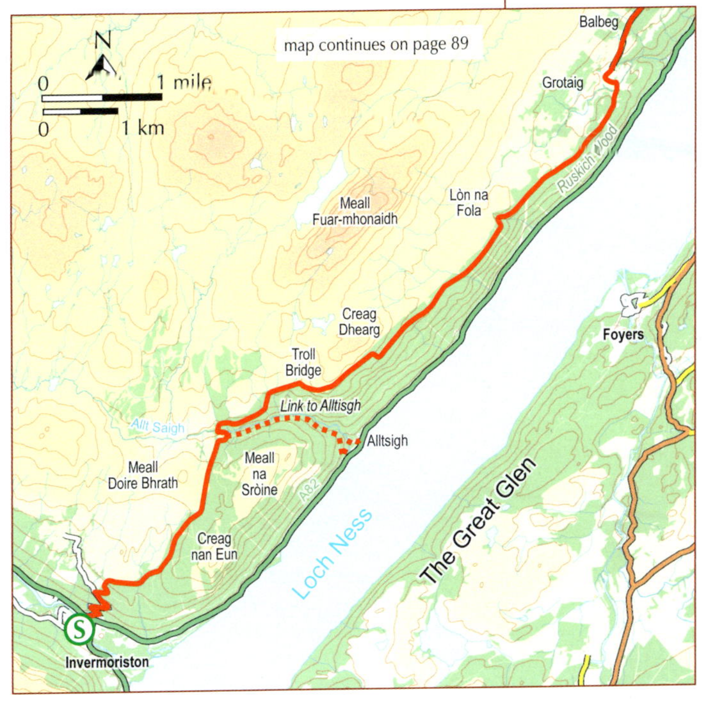

The high-level route crosses the 'Troll Bridge' above a waterfall

Turning right down the track leads, in 2km (1.25 miles), to the low-level route at Alltsigh, close to Lochside Hostel and bus services.

steps where it gets steeper, and cross a footbridge over a stream.

The path climbs and joins a track in a forest that has been partly clear-felled. Turn left to follow the track to a turning space, then continue along a path, noting a curious sculpture on the left, The Viewcatcher, where tree branches have been woven into a circle, mounted on a stone plinth. Follow the path past the little hill of **Meall Doire Bhrath**, around 330m (1080ft), and pass a couple of stone slabs that flank the path like old gateposts. The path descends to a track, and a left turn quickly leads across a concrete bridge spanning **Allt Saigh**. ◀

Follow the track onwards through the forest until it ends, then walk up a winding path that soon runs just outside the forest, beside a tall deer fence. Cross two footbridges; the second one being the rustic **Troll Bridge**, perched above a waterfall. The path climbs and winds further up a steep slope, featuring a few stone steps at one point. Pass a stone-built windbreak shelter, where there is a fine view of Loch Ness. The highest point on the Great Glen Way comes soon afterwards, around 415m (1360ft) on the rugged slopes of **Creag Dhearg**.

A whitewashed pepperpot lighthouse marks where the Caledonian Canal joins Loch Lochy near Gairlochy

THE GREAT GLEN WAY

The Great Glen Way is one of Scotland's Great Trails and follows the course of the Caledonian Canal through the Highlands from Fort William to Inverness over up to 79 miles (124km). The waymarked trail includes easy, level stretches, undulating forest tracks, lakeside paths and old drove and military roads as well as high-level alternatives for those looking for a greater challenge. Typically taking a week, it is an ideal introduction to long-distance walking.

Contents and using this guide

This booklet of Ordnance Survey 1:25,000 Explorer® maps has been designed for convenient use on the trail and includes:

- a key to map pages (pages 2–3) showing where to find the maps for each stage.
- the full and up-to-date line of the trail.
- an extract from the OS Explorer map legend (pages 42–44).

The companion guidebook – *The Great Glen Way* – describes the full route in both directions with lots of other practical and historical information.

Cicerone's EU representative for GPSR compliance is Easy Access System Europe, Mustamäe tee 50, 10621 Tallinn, Estonia. Email gpsr.requests@easproject.com.

Second edition 2025
ISBN: 978 1 78631 142 9
First edition 2016

Printed in China on responsibly sourced paper on behalf of Latitude Press Ltd.

FSC www.fsc.org MIX Paper | Supporting responsible forestry FSC® C010256

22–26
THE
Loch Garry
18–20
16–18
Invergarry
Ben Tee
10–16
17–22
River Spey
Carn Dearg
Achnacarry
Loch Arkaig
Loch Lochy
Loch Laggan
6–10
Gairlochy
Glen Spean
Loch Treig
N
Fort William
Ben Nevis
0 5 miles
0 5 10 km
to Glasgow

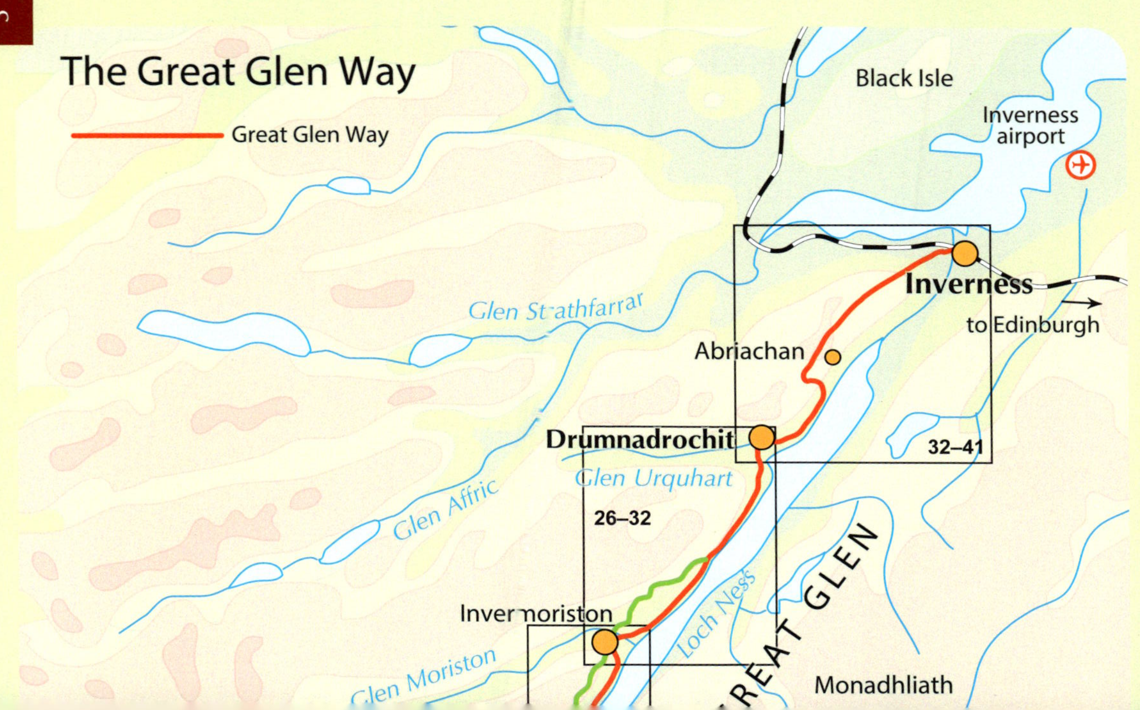
The Great Glen Way
Great Glen Way
Black Isle
Inverness airport
Inverness
to Edinburgh
Abriachan
Drumnadrochit
32–41
Glen Strathfarrar
Glen Urquhart
26–32
Glen Affric
Invermoriston
Loch Ness
GREAT GLEN
Glen Moriston
Monadhliath

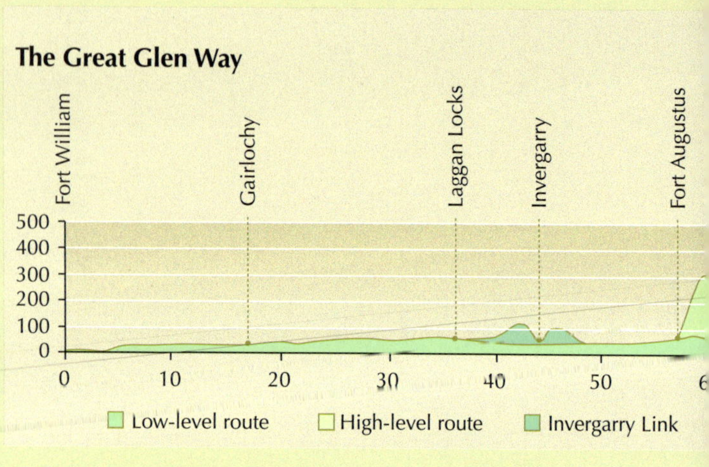

THE GREAT GLEN WAY

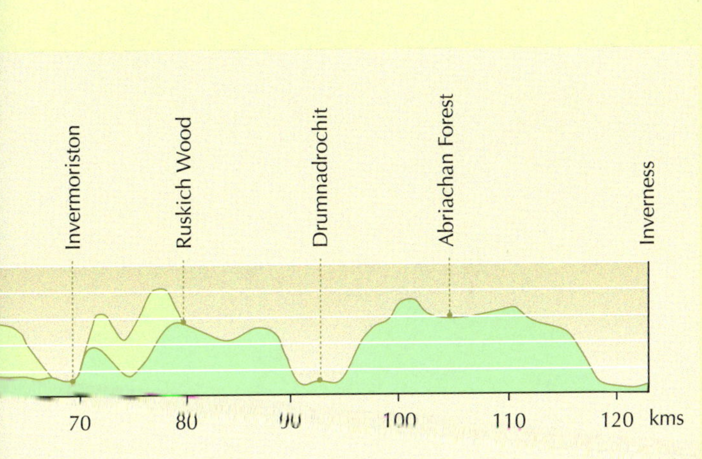
Invermoriston
Ruskich Wood
Drumnadrochit
Abriachan Forest
Inverness
70
80
90
100
110
120
kms

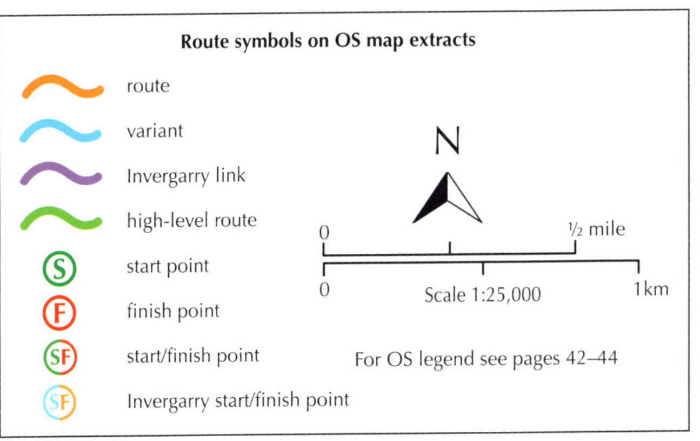
Route symbols on OS map extracts
route
variant
Invergarry link
high-level route
S
start point
F
finish point
SF
start/finish point
SF
Invergarry start/finish point
N
0
½ mile
0
1km
Scale 1:25,000
For OS legend see pages 42–44

Fort William to Gairlochy

Start: Railway station, Fort William

Finish: Gairlochy Bottom Lock

Distance: 17km (10.5 miles)

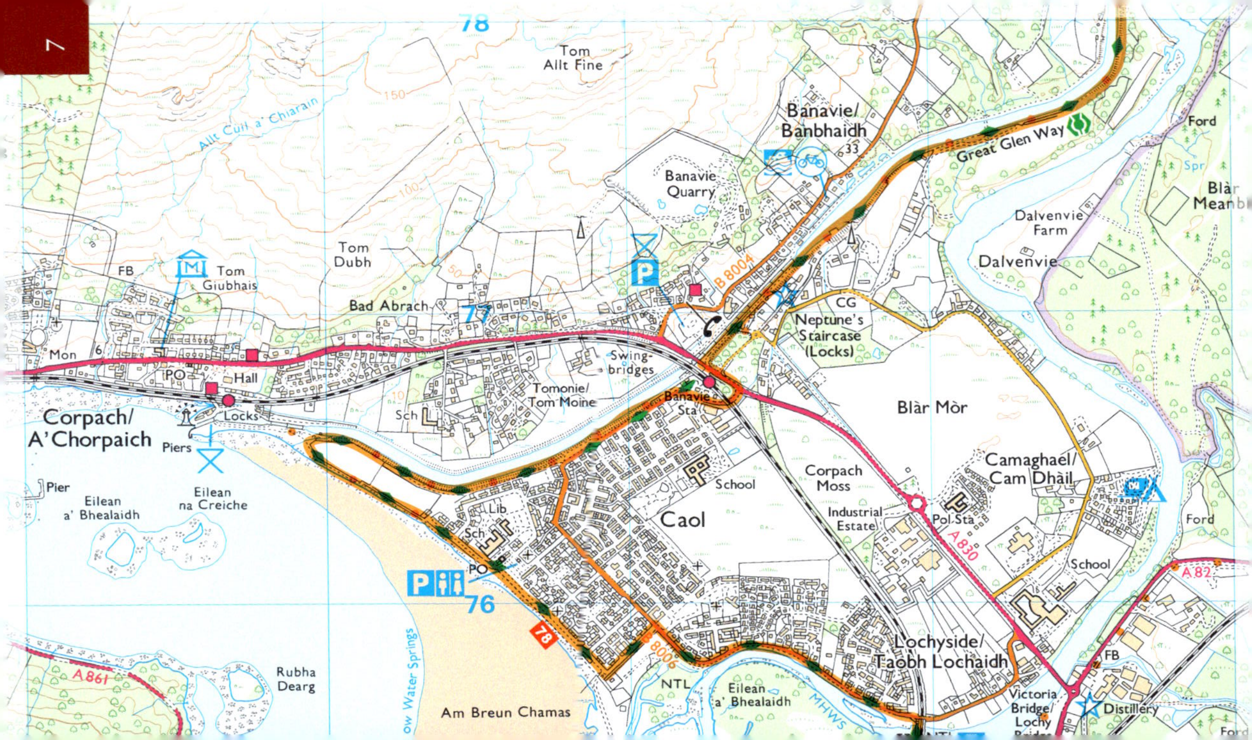

7
78
Tom Allt Fine
Allt Cùil a' Chiarain
Banavie/ Banbhaidh
Great Glen Way
Ford
Spr
Banavie Quarry
Blàr Meanb
Dalvenvie Farm
Dalvenvie
Tom Dubh
FB
Tom Giubhais
B 8004
Bad Abrach
77
CG
Neptune's Staircase (Locks)
Mon
PO
Hall
Swing-bridges
Tomonie/ Tom Mòine
Banavie Sta
Blàr Mòr
Sch
Corpach/ A'Chorpaich
Locks
Piers
Pier
Eilean a' Bhealaidh
Eilean na Creiche
Corpach Moss
Industrial Estate
Camaghael/ Cam Dhàil
School
Lib
Caol
Pol Sta
A 830
Ford
School
A 82
PO
76
78
B 8006
Lochyside/ Taobh Lochaidh
FB
A 861
Rubha Dearg
ow Water Springs
Am Breun Chamas
NTL
Eilean a' Bhealaidh
MHWS
Victoria Bridge/ Lochy
Distillery

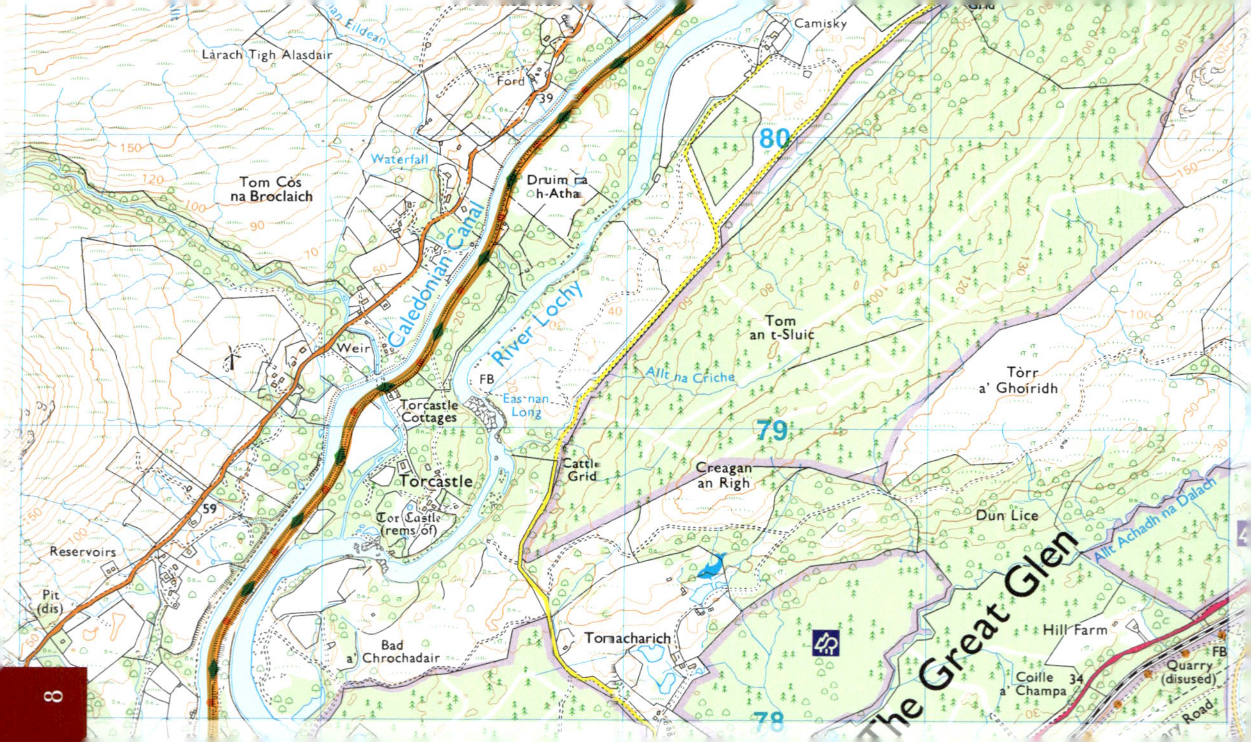
Làrach Tigh Alasdair
Camisky
Ford
39
Waterfall
Tom Còs na Broclaich
Druim na h-Atha
80
Caledonian Canal
River Lochy
Tom an t-Sluic
Weir
FB
Allt na Crìche
Tòrr a' Ghoiridh
Torcastle Cottages
Eas nan Long
79
Cattle Grid
Creagan an Righ
Torcastle
59
Tor Castle (rems of)
Dun Lice
Allt Achadh na Dalach
Reservoirs
The Great Glen
Pit (dis)
Hill Farm
Bad a' Chrochadair
Tomacharich
FB
Quarry (disused)
Coille a' Champa
34
78
Road

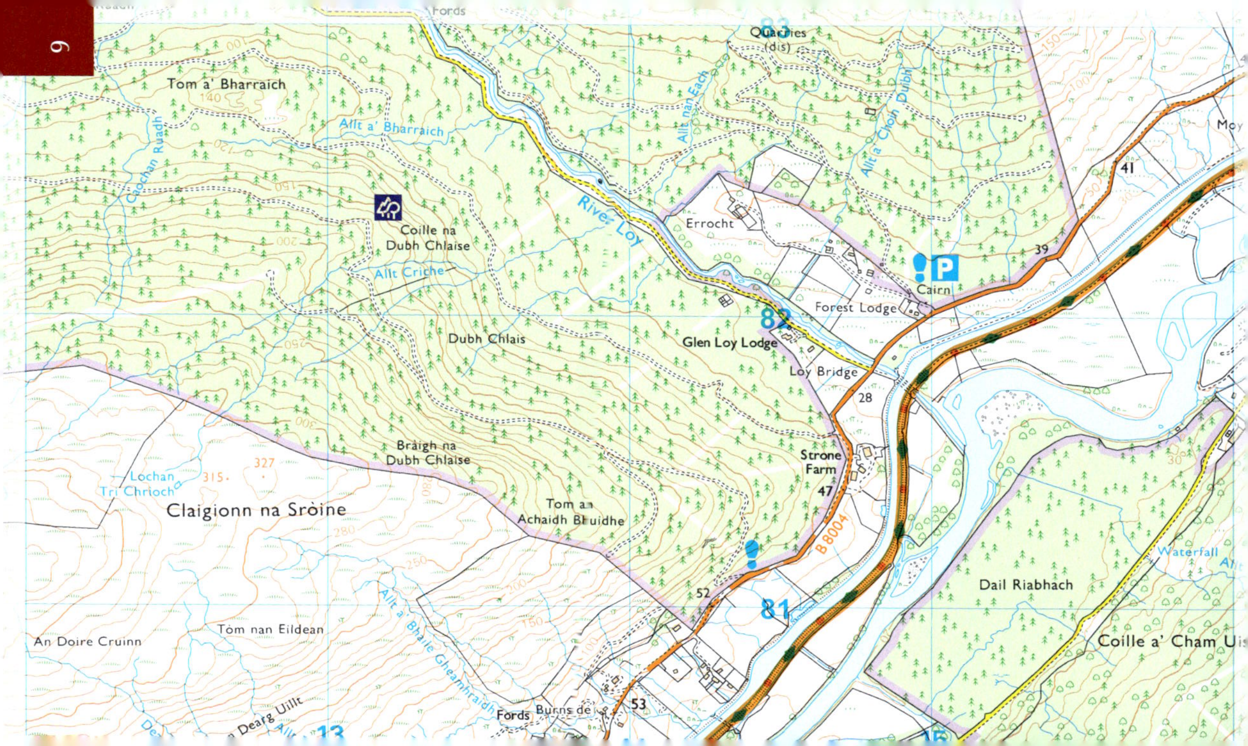

9
Tom a' Bharraich
Allt a' Bharraich
Caochan Ruadh
Coille na
Dubh Chlaise
Allt Criche
Dubh Chlais
River Loy
Quarries
(dis)
Allt nan Each
Allt a' Choin Dubh
Moy
Errocht
Cairn
Forest Lodge
Glen Loy Lodge
Loy Bridge
Strone
Farm
Bràigh na
Dubh Chlaise
Lochan
Tri Chrìoch
Claigionn na Sròine
Tom an
Achaidh Bhuidhe
B 8004
Waterfall
Dail Riabhach
Coille a' Cham Uis
An Doire Cruinn
Tom nan Eildean
Allt a' Bhaile Gheamhraidh
Fords
Burns de
Dearg Uillt

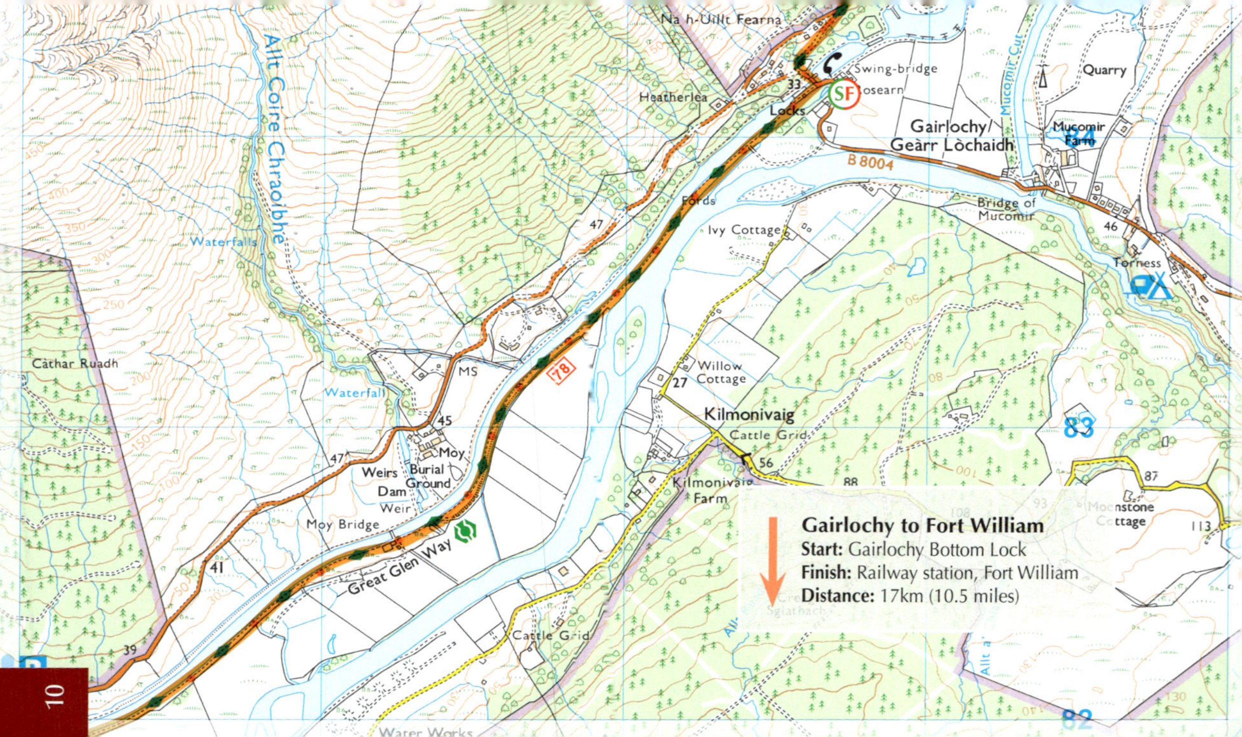

Gairlochy to Fort William
Start: Gairlochy Bottom Lock
Finish: Railway station, Fort William
Distance: 17km (10.5 miles)
10
Allt Coire Chraoibhe
Na h-Uillt Fearna
Swing-bridge
Heatherlea
Locks
Gairlochy/
Geàrr Lòchaidh
B 8004
Mucomir Cut
Quarry
Mucomir Farm
Bridge of Mucomir
Torness
Fords
Ivy Cottage
Waterfalls
Cathar Ruadh
Waterfall
MS
Willow Cottage
Kilmonivaig
Cattle Grid
Kilmonivaig Farm
Moy
Weirs
Burial Ground
Dam
Weir
Moy Bridge
Great Glen Way
Moonstone Cottage
Water Works

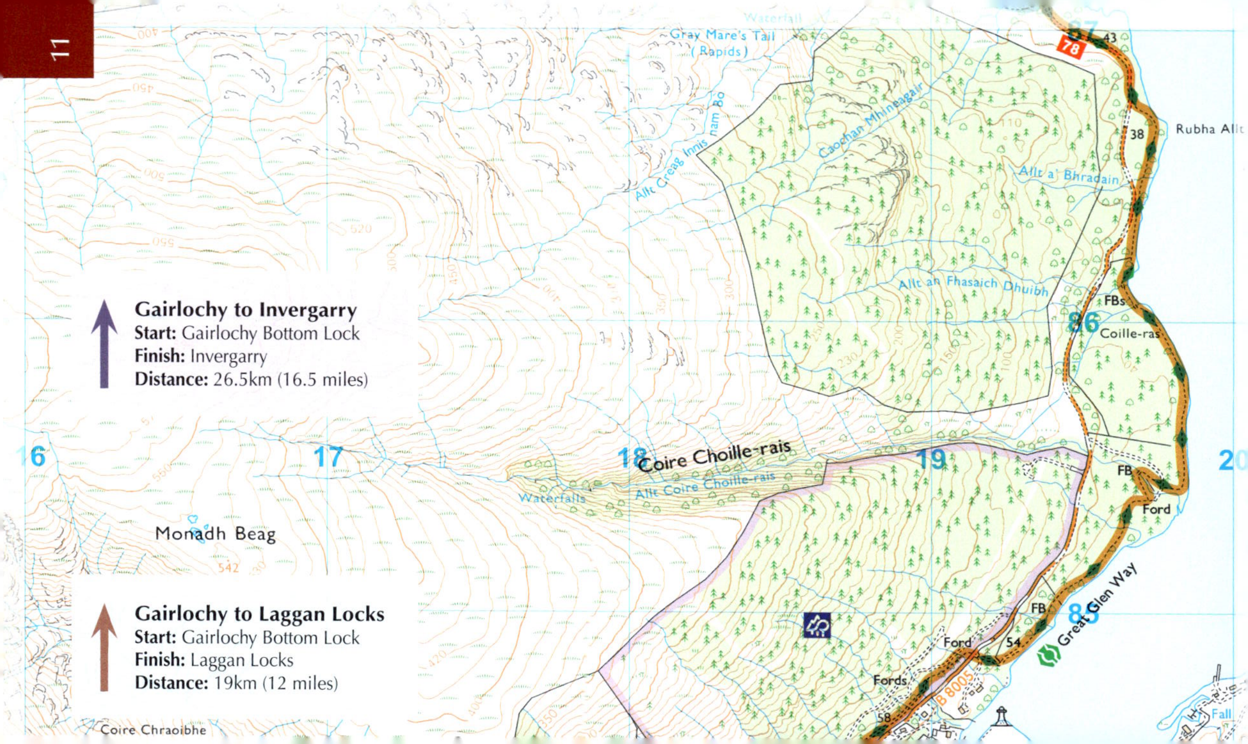

11
Gairlochy to Invergarry
Start: Gairlochy Bottom Lock
Finish: Invergarry
Distance: 26.5km (16.5 miles)
Gairlochy to Laggan Locks
Start: Gairlochy Bottom Lock
Finish: Laggan Locks
Distance: 19km (12 miles)
Waterfall
Gray Mare's Tail
(Rapids)
Allt Creag Innis nam Bo
Caochan Mhineagair
Rubha Allt
Allt a' Bhradain
Allt an Fhasaich Dhuibh
FBs
Coille-ras
Coire Choille-rais
Allt Coire Choille-rais
Waterfalls
Monadh Beag
542
FB
Ford
Great Glen Way
FB
Ford
54
Fords
B 8005
58
Coire Chraoibhe
Fall
78
43
38

Creag D
Gleannan Dubh
Allt na Caillich
Gleann Cia-aig
Waterfall
Tom an Fhithich
Allt Tom an Fhithich
Coille Achadh nan Sabhal
Torr a' Chronain
Eas Chia-aig (Waterfalls)
CG
B 8005
Mile Dorcha
FB
Meml
Creag an t-Saighdeir
Torr a' Mhuilt
Weir
River Arkaig
Achnacarry House (remains of)
FB
Achnacarry
Beech Cottage
Bunarkaig
Torr an Rathaid
Creag Innis nam Bò
Waterfall
Gray Mare's Tail (Rapids)
78
Rubha Allt a' Bhradain
Caochan Mhineagair
Allt Creag Innis nam Bò
Allt a' Bhradain
Allt an Fhasaich Dhuibh
FBs
33
32
43
38

Continuation of main route
Great Glen Way
Glen Way
Clunes Forest
Allt Glas
Clunes
Ford
Goirtean nan Craobh
Blàr an Lochain
Torr a'Chromain
Milestone Hill
Cladh Tom Mhòir
Innis nan Cnàmh
Innis nam Bòrd
Obelisk
Allt Dubh
Allt Criche
Carn a' Ghrianain
Lower Glenfintaig Farm
Glenfintaig House
Slipway
Druim Liath
Dun (rems of)
Waterfalls
Weir
Dochanassie
90
89
88
87

Sròn Bhreac
Dubha
Ford
Glas-Dhoire Mòr
88
64
75
Loch Loc
Jetties
Letterfinlay
Letterfinlay Lodge Hotel
FB
53
Jetty
FBs
Alltruadh
94
Innis Mhic Gille Ruaidh
Coill Innis Mhic Gille Ruaidh
135
Allt na Sealbhaig
Allt na Leitire
Druim Ghlaoidh
537
Tom Eachrain
MS
Weir
22
23
24
25
26
91
90
89

Fords
Fords
Cam Bhealach
Allt Glas-Dhoire
Ford
Fords
Waterfall
Great Glen Way
Cam Choirein
839
Meall Dubh
Glas-dhoire
Glas-Dhoire Beag
Coire Leacachain
na Teanga
Dearg Allt
Allt Glas-Dhoire Mòr
Ford
Coire Lochain
P
94
93
92

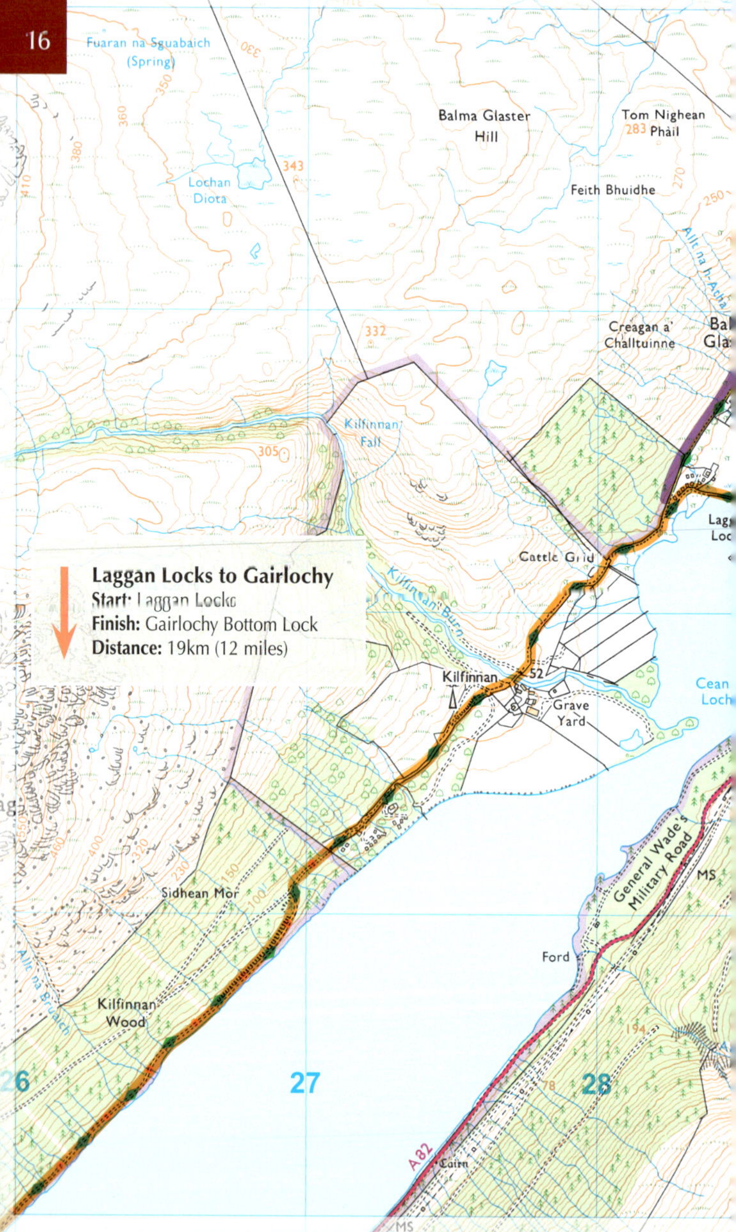

Laggan Locks to Gairlochy

Start: Laggan Locks
Finish: Gairlochy Bottom Lock
Distance: 19km (12 miles)

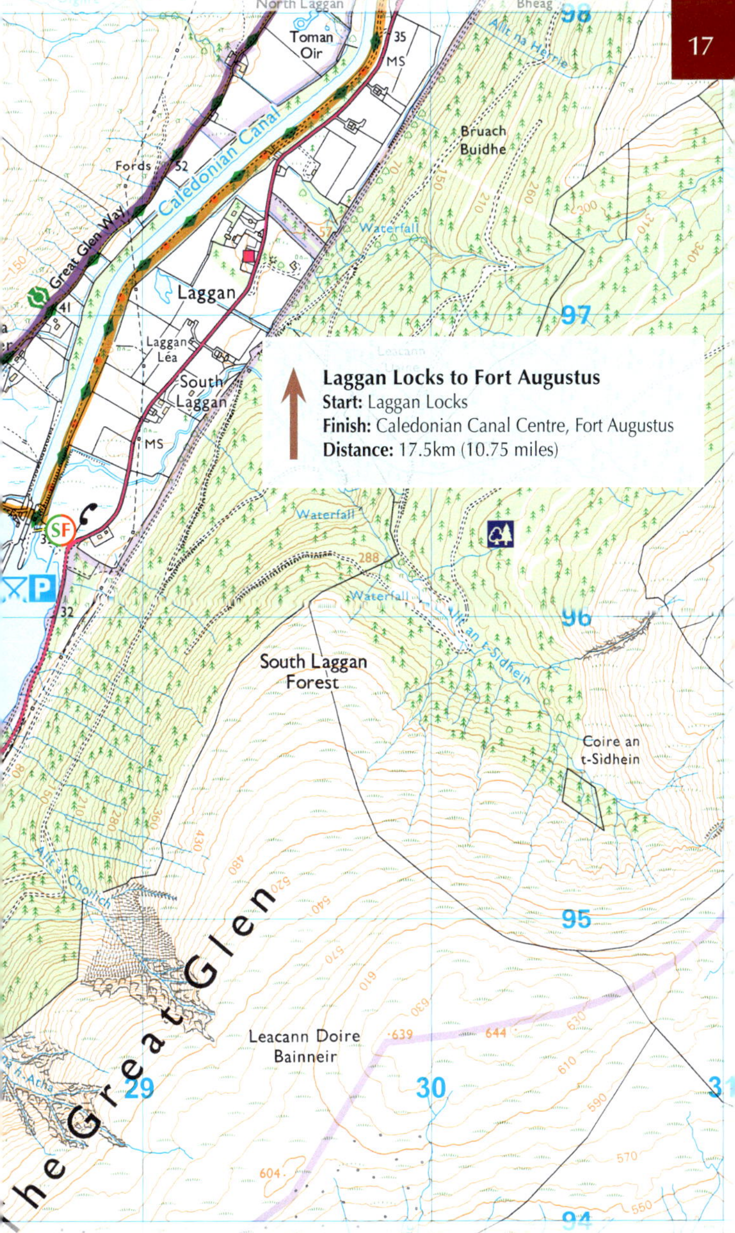

Laggan Locks to Fort Augustus

Start: Laggan Locks
Finish: Caledonian Canal Centre, Fort Augustus
Distance: 17.5km (10.75 miles)

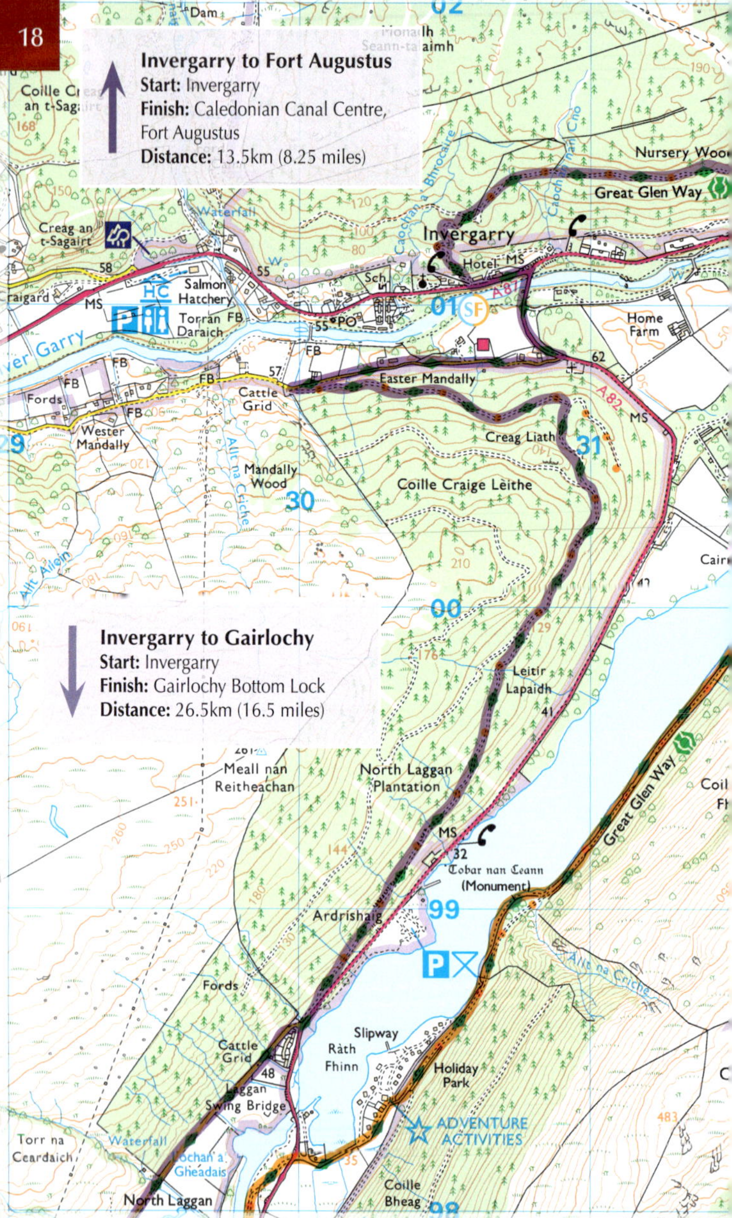

Invergarry to Fort Augustus
Start: Invergarry
Finish: Caledonian Canal Centre, Fort Augustus
Distance: 13.5km (8.25 miles)
Invergarry to Gairlochy
Start: Invergarry
Finish: Gairlochy Bottom Lock
Distance: 26.5km (16.5 miles)
Invergarry
Great Glen Way
Nursery Wood
Creag an t-Sagairt
Salmon Hatchery
Torran Daraich
Hotel
Home Farm
Easter Mandally
Wester Mandally
Cattle Grid
Fords
Creag Liath
Coille Craige Lèithe
Mandally Wood
Allt na Criche
Allt Ailein
Leitir Lapaidh
Meall nan Reitheachan
North Laggan Plantation
Tobar nan Ceann (Monument)
Ardrishaig
Slipway
Ràth Fhinn
Holiday Park
Adventure Activities
Laggan Swing Bridge
Torr na Ceardaich
Waterfall
Lochan a' Gheadais
North Laggan
Coille Bheag

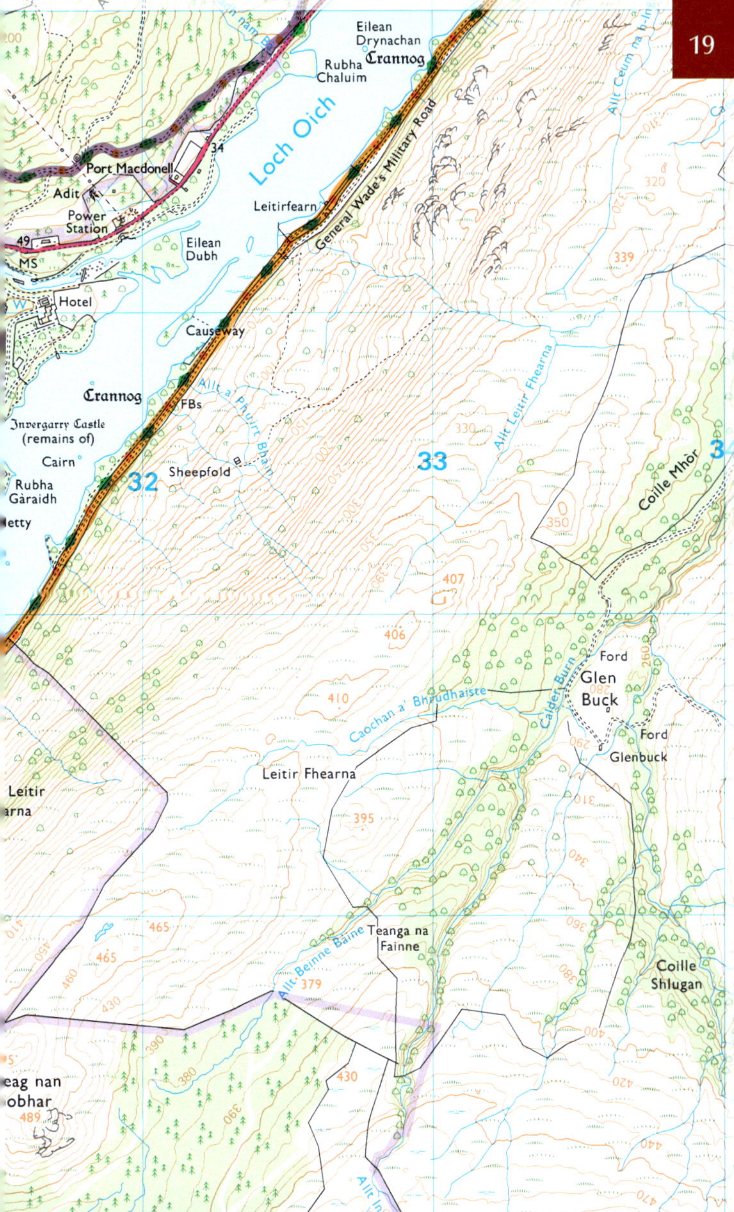
Loch Oich
Eilean Drynachan
Crannog
Rubha Chaluim
General Wade's Military Road
Port Macdonell
Adit
Power Station
Leitirfearn
Eilean Dubh
MS
Hotel
Causeway
Crannog
FBs
Allt a' Phuirt Bhàin
Invergarry Castle (remains of)
Cairn
Sheepfold
Rubha Gàraidh
32
33
Allt Leitir Fhearna
Coille Mhòr
Allt Ceum na h-Inghin
Ford
Glen Buck
Calder Burn
Caochan a' Bhrudhaiste
Ford
Glenbuck
Leitir Fhearna
Leitir Fearna
Teanga na Fainne
Allt Beinne Baine
Coille Shlugan
Allt Innis
407
406
410
395
465
379
430
489
339
350
330
320

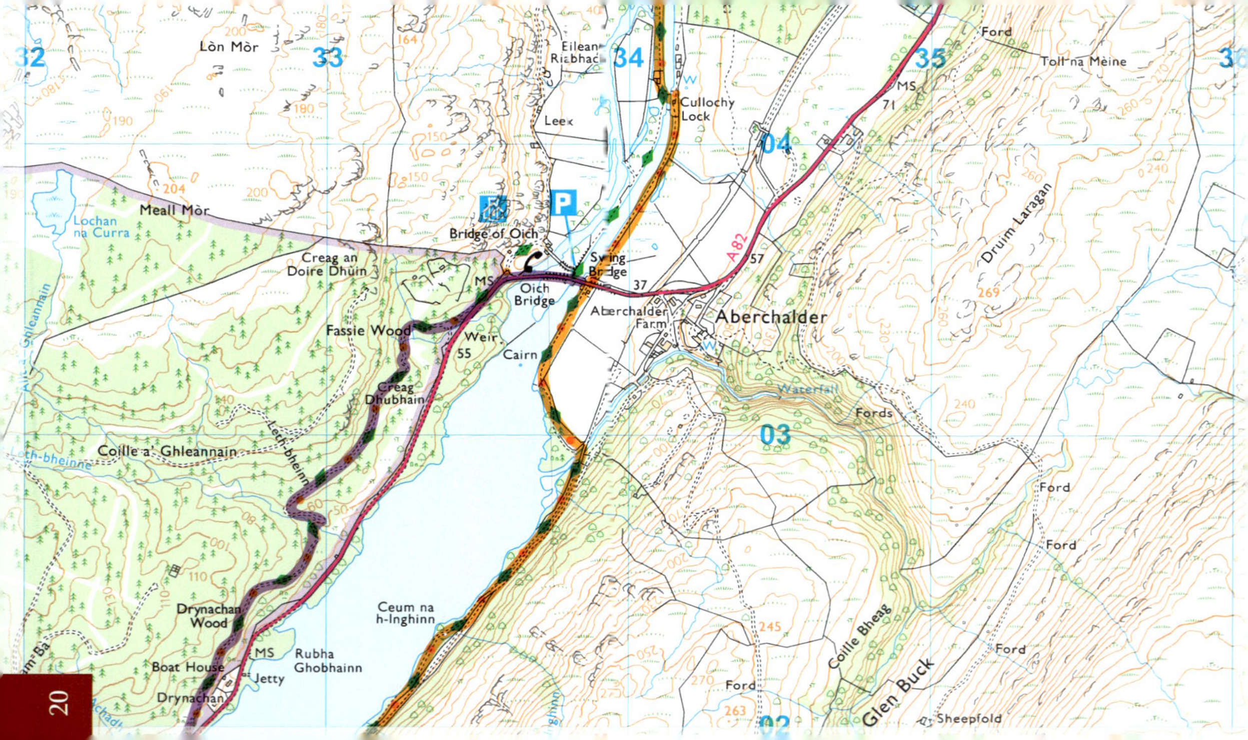

Lòn Mòr
Eilean Riabhach
Ford
Toll na Mèine
Cullochy Lock
Leek
Meall Mòr
Lochan na Curra
Bridge of Oich
Creag an Doire Dhùin
MS
Swing Bridge
37
57
A 82
Druim Laragan
Oich Bridge
Aberchalder Farm
Aberchalder
Fassie Wood
Weir
55
Cairn
Creag Dhubhain
Waterfall
Fords
Coille a' Ghleannain
Leth-bheinn
Drynachan Wood
Ceum na h-Inghinn
Boat House
Rubha Ghobhainn
Jetty
Drynachan
Coille Bheag
Glen Buck
Sheepfold
71
32
33
34
35
03
04

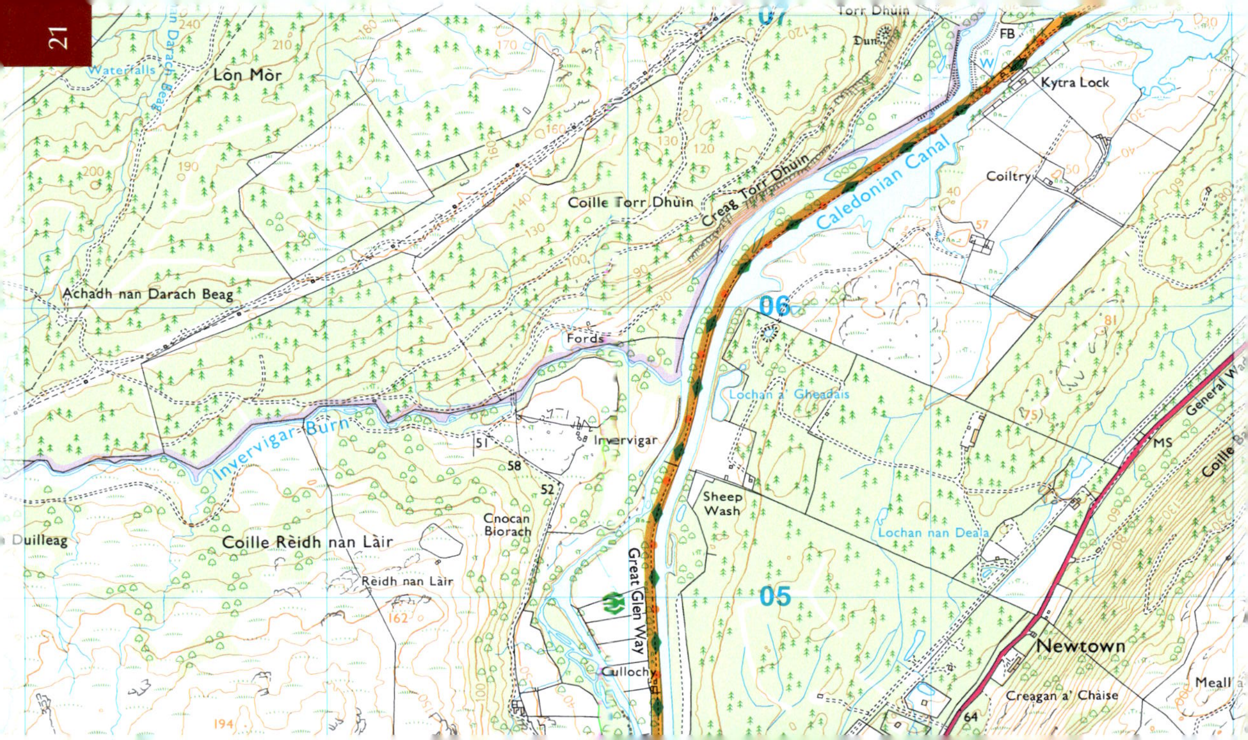

Waterfalls
Lòn Mòr
Achadh nan Darach Beag
Coille Torr Dhùin
Creag Torr Dhùin
Torr Dhùin
Dun
FB
Kytra Lock
Caledonian Canal
Coiltry
Fords
Lochan a' Gheadais
Invervigar Burn
Invervigar
General Wade
MS
Sheep Wash
Cnocan Biorach
Duilleag
Coille Rèidh nan Làir
Reidh nan Làir
Lochan nan Deala
Great Glen Way
Cullochy
Newtown
Creagan a' Chàise
Meall
05
06

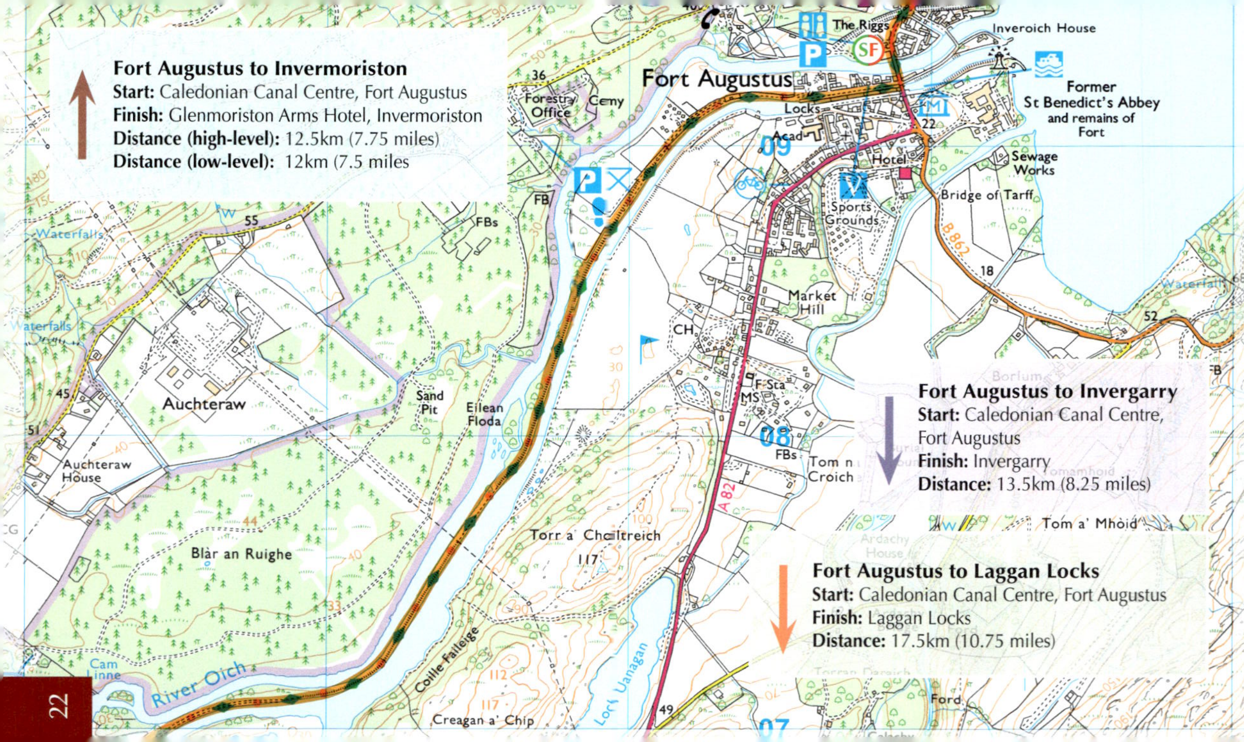
Fort Augustus to Invermoriston
Start: Caledonian Canal Centre, Fort Augustus
Finish: Glenmoriston Arms Hotel, Invermoriston
Distance (high-level): 12.5km (7.75 miles)
Distance (low-level): 12km (7.5 miles
Fort Augustus to Invergarry
Start: Caledonian Canal Centre, Fort Augustus
Finish: Invergarry
Distance: 13.5km (8.25 miles)
Fort Augustus to Laggan Locks
Start: Caledonian Canal Centre, Fort Augustus
Finish: Laggan Locks
Distance: 17.5km (10.75 miles)
Fort Augustus
The Riggs
Inveroich House
Former St Benedict's Abbey and remains of Fort
Locks
Acad
Hotel
Sewage Works
Bridge of Tarff
Sports Grounds
Market Hill
Forestry Office
Cemy
FB
FBs
Waterfalls
Auchteraw
Auchteraw House
Sand Pit
Eilean Floda
CH
F Sta
MS
Tom n Croich
Torr a' Chaltreich
Blàr an Ruighe
Coille Falleige
Creagan a' Chip
Loch Uanagan
River Oich
Cam Linne
Tom a' Mhòid
Ford
A82
B862

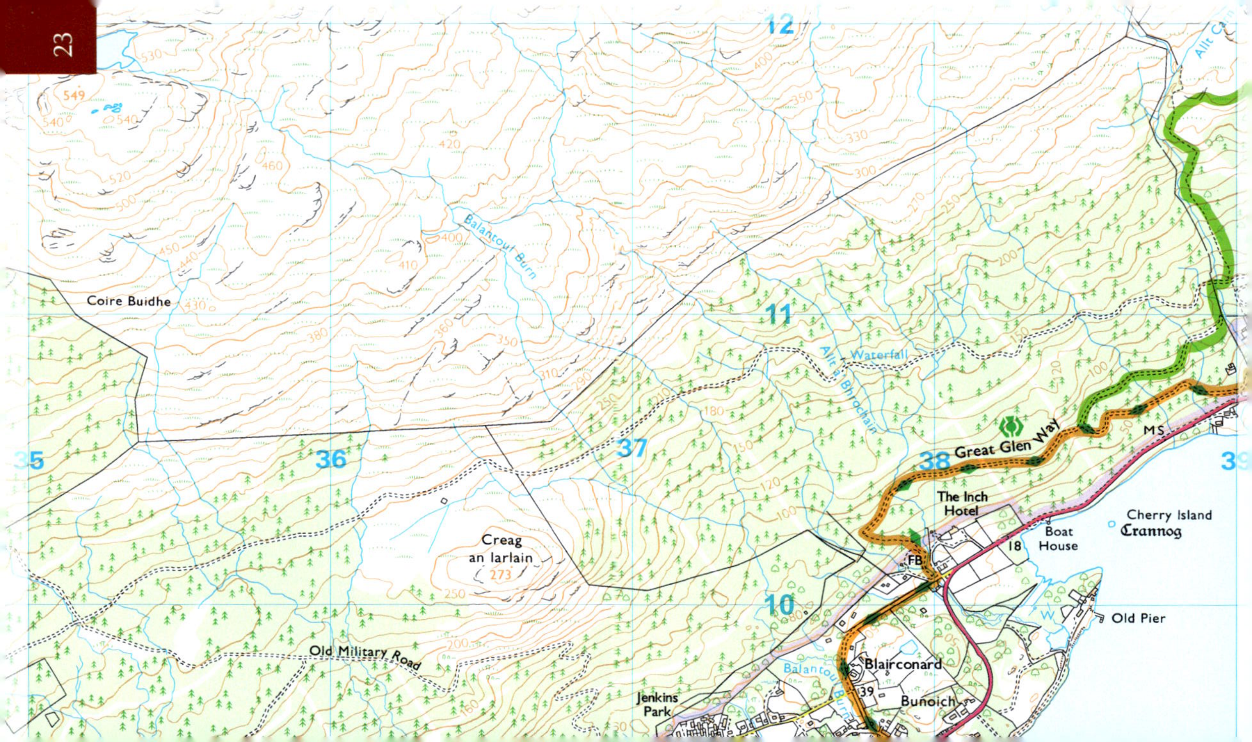
Coire Buidhe
Balantoul Burn
Allt a' Bhrochain
Waterfall
Great Glen Way
Creag an Iarlain
273
549
The Inch Hotel
Cherry Island
Crannog
Boat House
Old Pier
FB
MS
Old Military Road
Jenkins Park
Balantoul Burn
Blairconard
Bunoich

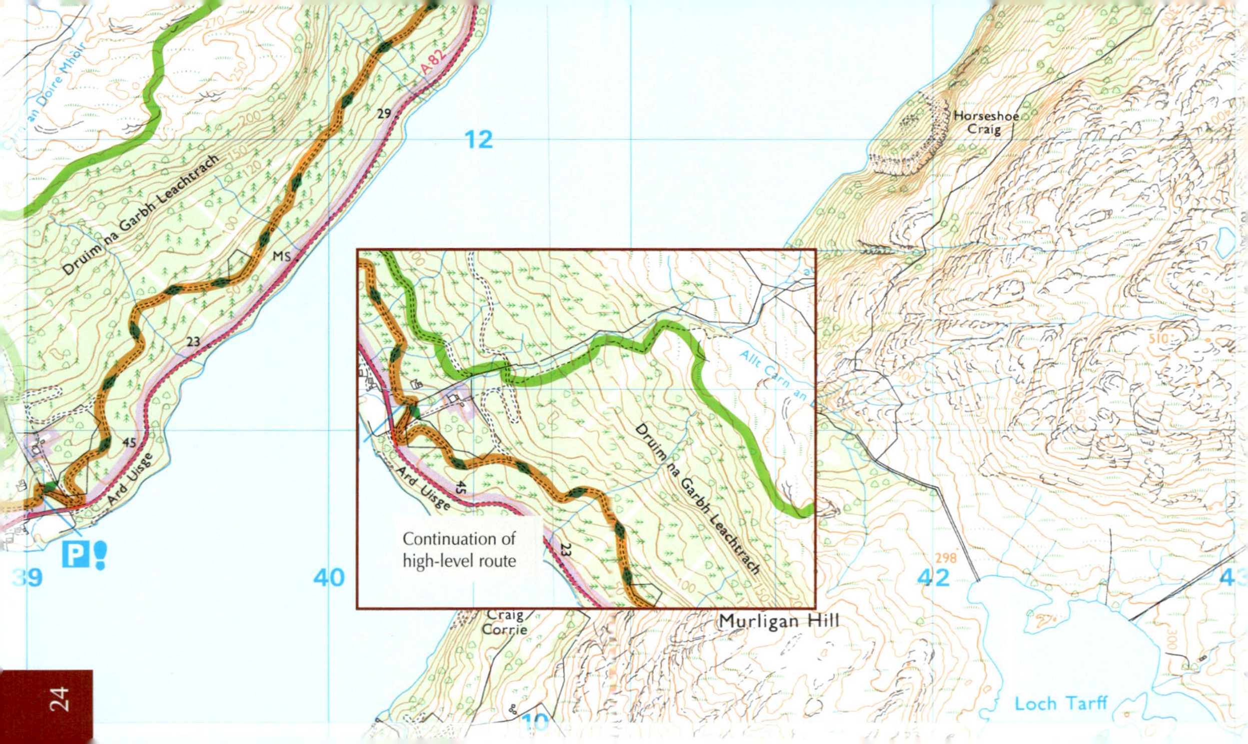
Carn an Doire Mhòir
Druim na Garbh Leachtrach
A82
Ard Uisge
Horseshoe Craig
Continuation of high-level route
Allt Carn an
Craig Corrie
Murligan Hill
Loch Tarff
12
39
40
42
43
10

25
Portclair Forest
Portclair Burn
Loch a' Mhuilinn
Innerack Burn
Allt a' Mhuilinn
Carn an Doire Mhòir
Waterfall
Wester Portclair
Easter Portclair
Inver Coille Campsite
MS
Boat House
Tigh-na-roinn
Jetty
MS
13
14
15
19
20
21
28

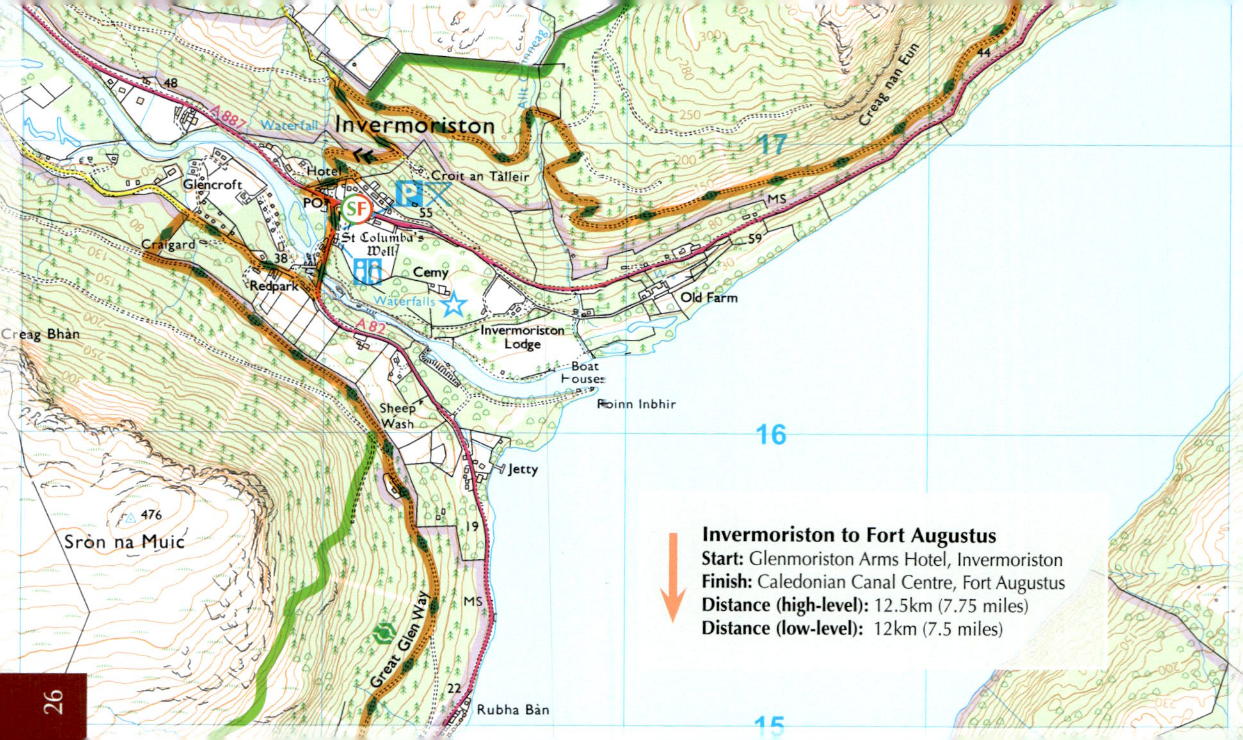

Invermoriston to Fort Augustus
Start: Glenmoriston Arms Hotel, Invermoriston
Finish: Caledonian Canal Centre, Fort Augustus
Distance (high-level): 12.5km (7.75 miles)
Distance (low-level): 12km (7.5 miles)

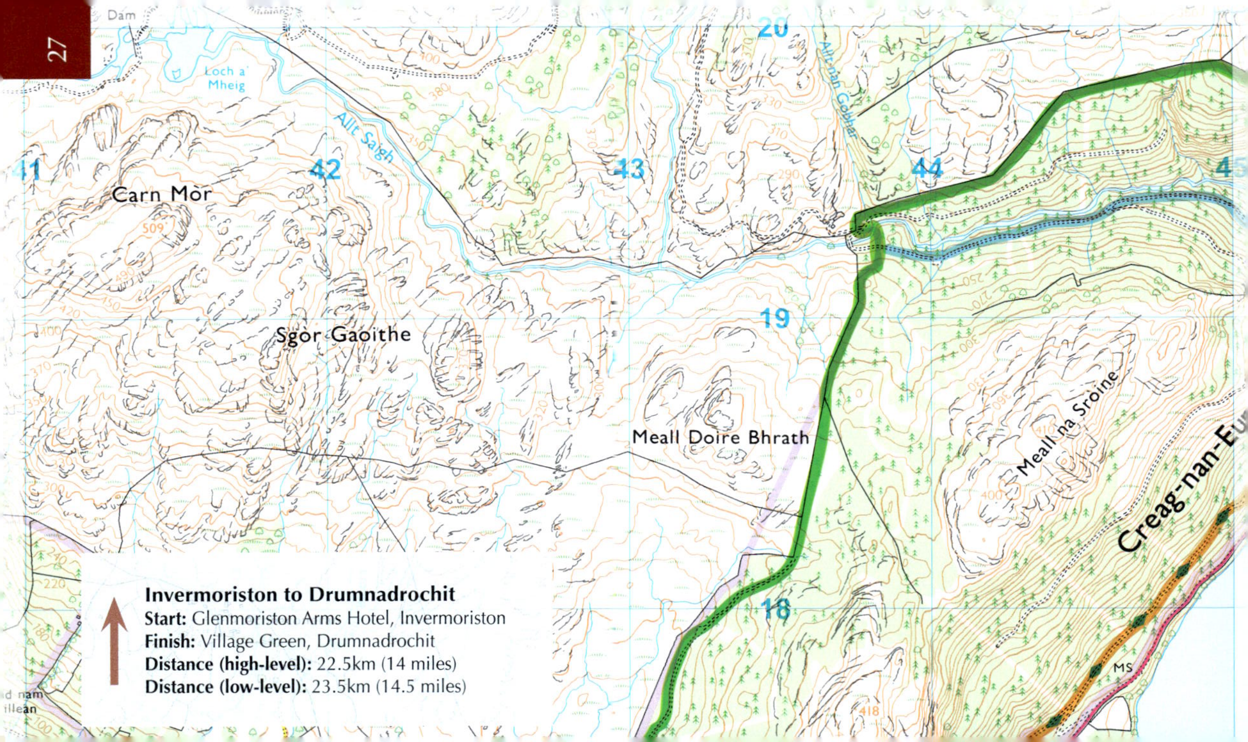

Invermoriston to Drumnadrochit
Start: Glenmoriston Arms Hotel, Invermoriston
Finish: Village Green, Drumnadrochit
Distance (high-level): 22.5km (14 miles)
Distance (low-level): 23.5km (14.5 miles)

Eun Forest
Great Glen Way
Alltsigh
Glen
Allt a' Mhinn
Dearg Lochain
Carn Dearg
Bonagour's Cave
20
19
18

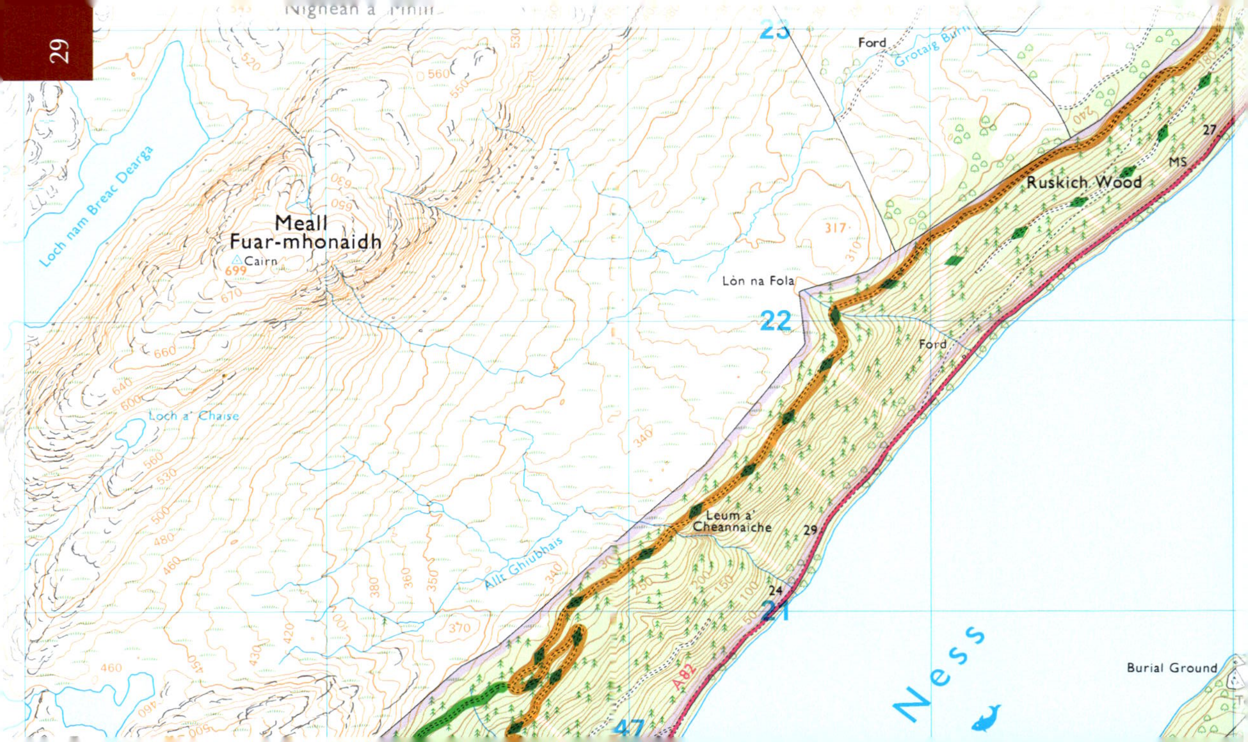
Loch nam Breac Dearga
Meall
Fuar-mhonaidh
Cairn
699
Loch a' Chaise
Allt Ghiubhais
Ford
Grotaig Burn
Ruskich Wood
MS
Lòn na Fola
Ford
Leum a'
Cheannaiche
A82
Ness
Burial Ground

Old School House
Bunloit Farm
Ancarraig Lodges
Burloit
Allt Seileach
Inchconachar
Balbeg
Lag ant-Seapail
Grotaig
POTTERY
Dùn Scriben fort
Inchtellach House
Inverfarigaig
Farigaig
MS
25
24
23

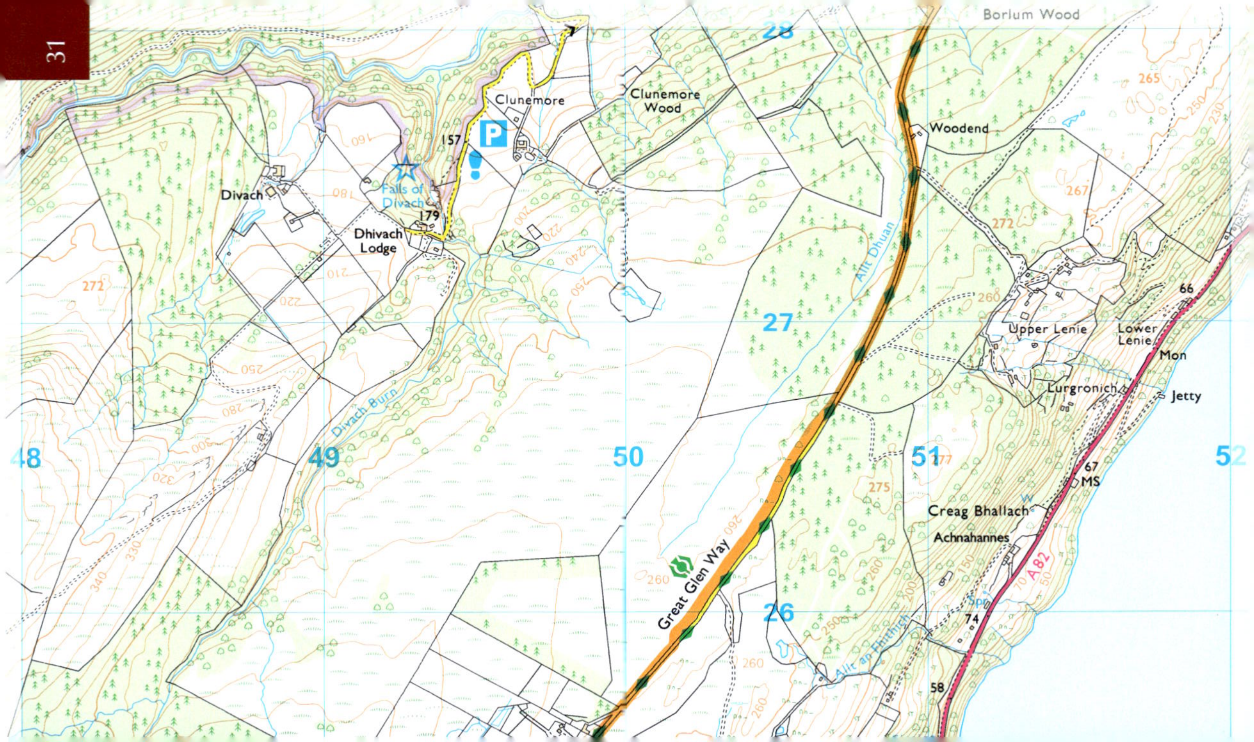
Borlum Wood
Clunemore
Clunemore Wood
Woodend
Divach
Falls of Divach
Dhivach Lodge
Divach Burn
Allt Dhuan
Great Glen Way
Upper Lenie
Lower Lenie
Mon
Lurgronich
Jetty
MS
Creag Bhallach
Achnahannes
A82
Allt an Fhithich
48
49
50
51
52
26
27
28

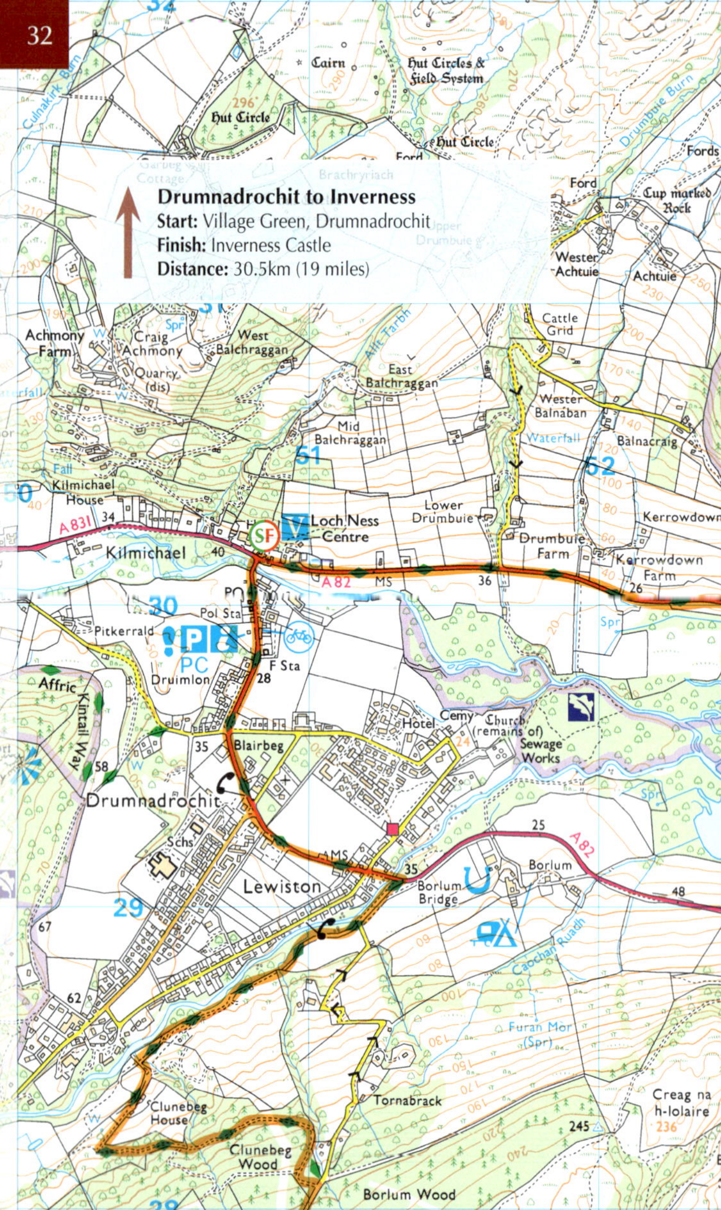
Drumnadrochit to Inverness
Start: Village Green, Drumnadrochit
Finish: Inverness Castle
Distance: 30.5km (19 miles)
Cairn
Hut Circles & Field System
Hut Circle
Hut Circle
Culnakirk Burn
Drumbuie Burn
Ford
Fords
Ford
Cup marked Rock
Wester Achtuie
Achtuie
Cattle Grid
Achmony Farm
Craig Achmony
Quarry (dis)
West Balchraggan
Allt Tarbh
East Balchraggan
Mid Balchraggan
Wester Balnaban
Balnacraig
Waterfall
Kilmichael House
Kilmichael
A831
Loch Ness Centre
Lower Drumbuie
Drumbuie Farm
Kerrowdown
Kerrowdown Farm
A82
MS
Pitkerrald
Pol Sta
F Sta
PC
Druimlon
Affric Kintail Way
Blairbeg
Hotel
Cemy
Church (remains of)
Sewage Works
Drumnadrochit
Schs
Lewiston
AMS
Borlum Bridge
Borlum
A82
Caochan Ruadh
Furan Mor (Spr)
Tornabrack
Clunebeg House
Clunebeg Wood
Borlum Wood
Creag na h-Iolaire

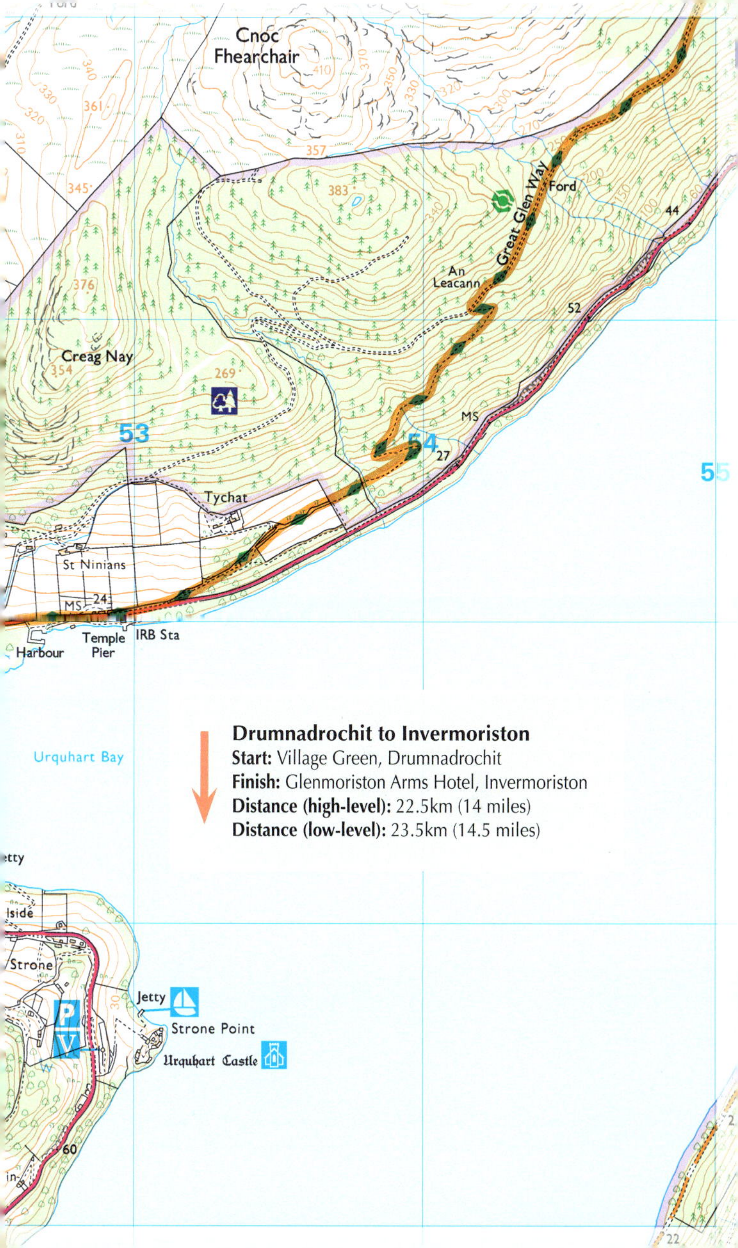

Drumnadrochit to Invermoriston

Start: Village Green, Drumnadrochit

Finish: Glenmoriston Arms Hotel, Invermoriston

Distance (high-level): 22.5km (14 miles)

Distance (low-level): 23.5km (14.5 miles)

Leitire
a' Bhathaich
Achpopuli
Allt Lòn
Spr
Allt Lòn a' Chreagain
Creag Bhàn
Caochan a' Challa
Benlie
Allt Bheinnellidh
Cnoc Bheinnellidh
Hut Circles & Field System
Waterfall
Allt Coire Shalachaidh
Ford
Cnoc an t-Saraidh
337
Coire Shalachaidh
Hut Circle
Creag an Tom Bhealaidh
Clach-Mohr
Hotel
MS
Brachla Harbour
Brachla
Corryfoyness
Fords
Torran Binneach
Allt Coire Foithaneas
Coire Foithaneas
Meall na h-Eilrig
465
Cairn
Creag Mhic Dhomhnuill Oig
Creag nan Cadhag
Cordachan
A82
Cnoc

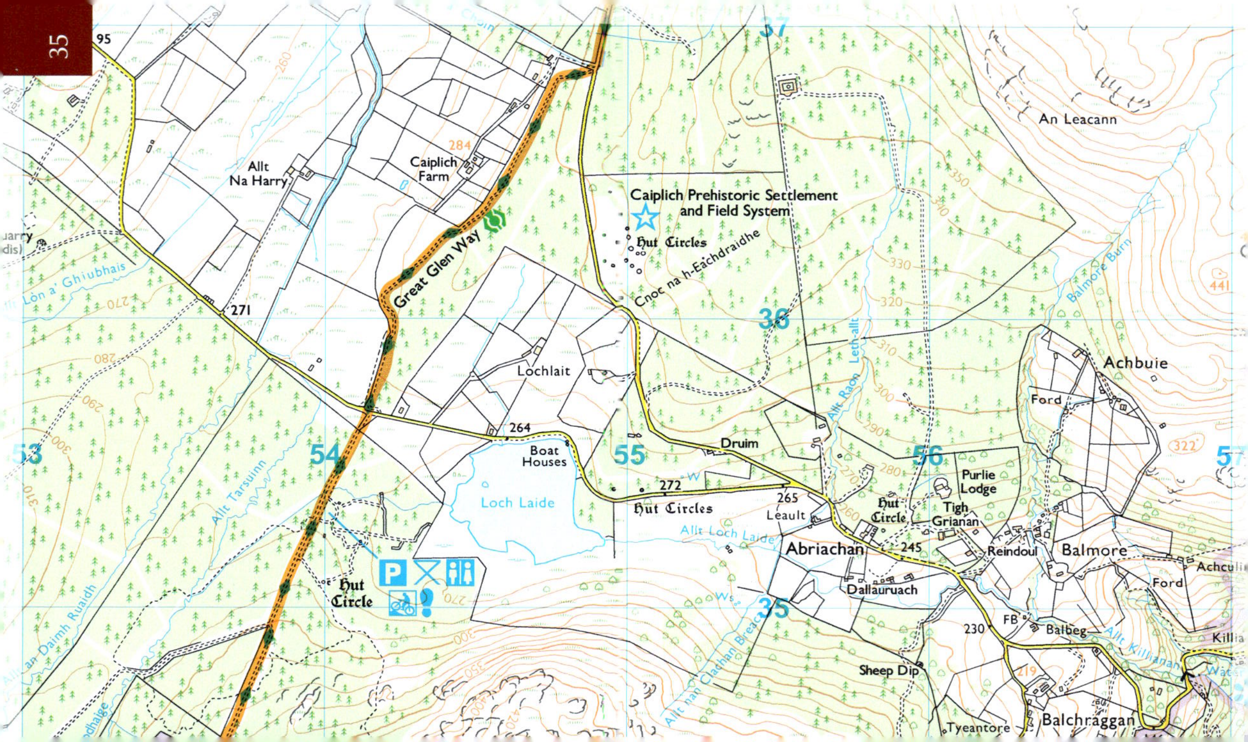
Allt Na Harry
Caiplich Farm
Great Glen Way
Caiplich Prehistoric Settlement and Field System
Hut Circles
Cnoc na h-Eachdraidhe
An Leacann
Allt Lòn a' Ghiubhais
Balmore Burn
Lochlait
Achbuie
Ford
Boat Houses
Loch Laide
Druim
Allt Raon
Leth-allt
Allt Tarsuinn
Hut Circles
Leault
Purlie Lodge
Hut Circle
Tigh Grianan
Allt Loch Laide
Abriachan
Reindoul
Balmore
Achculi
Hut Circle
Dallauruach
Allt an Daimh Ruaidh
FB
Balbeg
Allt Killianan
Sheep Dip
Allt nan Clachan Breaca
Tyeantore
Balchraggan
95
271
264
272
265
245
230
219
284
322
441

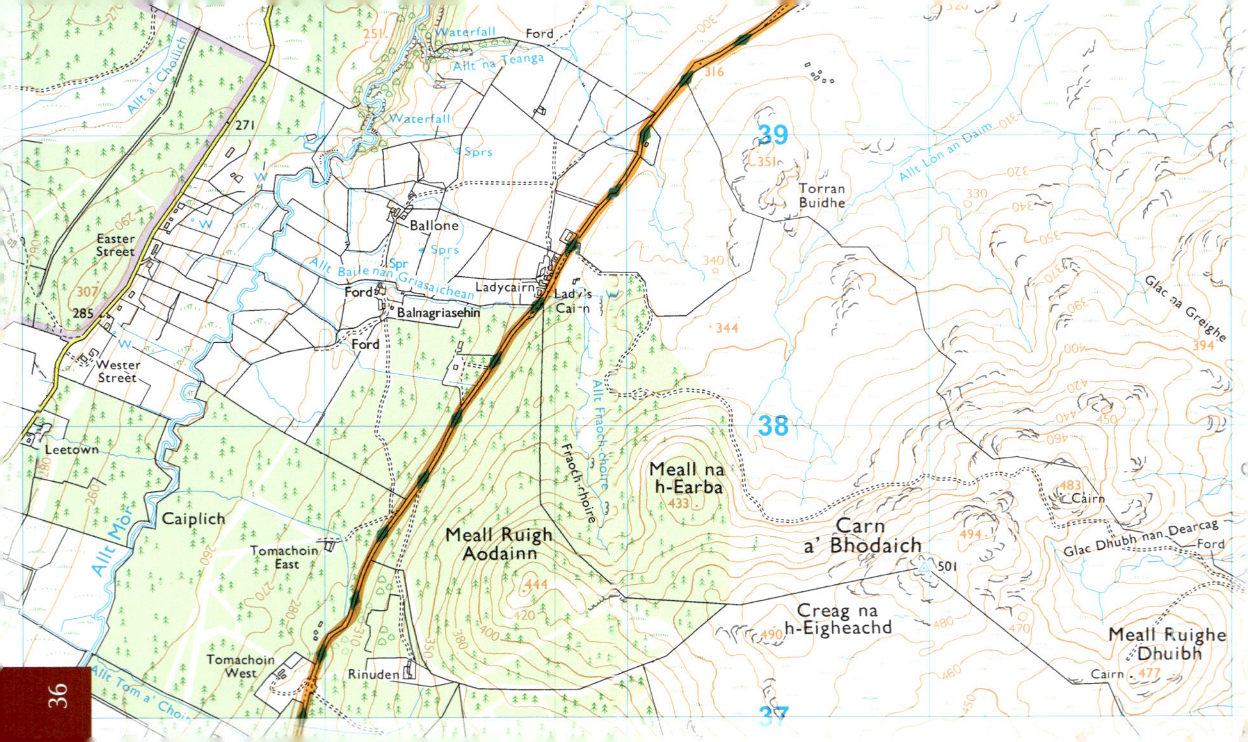
Allt a' Choilich
271
Waterfall
Ford
Allt na Teanga
316
Waterfall
Sprs
39
351
Allt Lòn an Daim
Torran Buidhe
Easter Street
Ballone
Sprs
Spr
Allt Baile nan Griasaichean
Ford
Ladycairn
Lady's Cairn
307
285
Balnagriasehin
344
Glac na Greighe
394
Ford
Wester Street
Allt Fraoch-choire
Fraoch-choire
38
Leetown
Meall na h-Earba
433
483
Cairn
Caiplich
Allt Mòr
Meall Ruigh Aodainn
Carn a' Bhodaich
494
Glac Dhubh nan Dearcag
Ford
Tomachoin East
501
444
Creag na h-Eigheachd
490
Meall Ruighe Dhuibh
Tomachoin West
Rinuden
Cairn
477
Allt Tom a' Choir
37

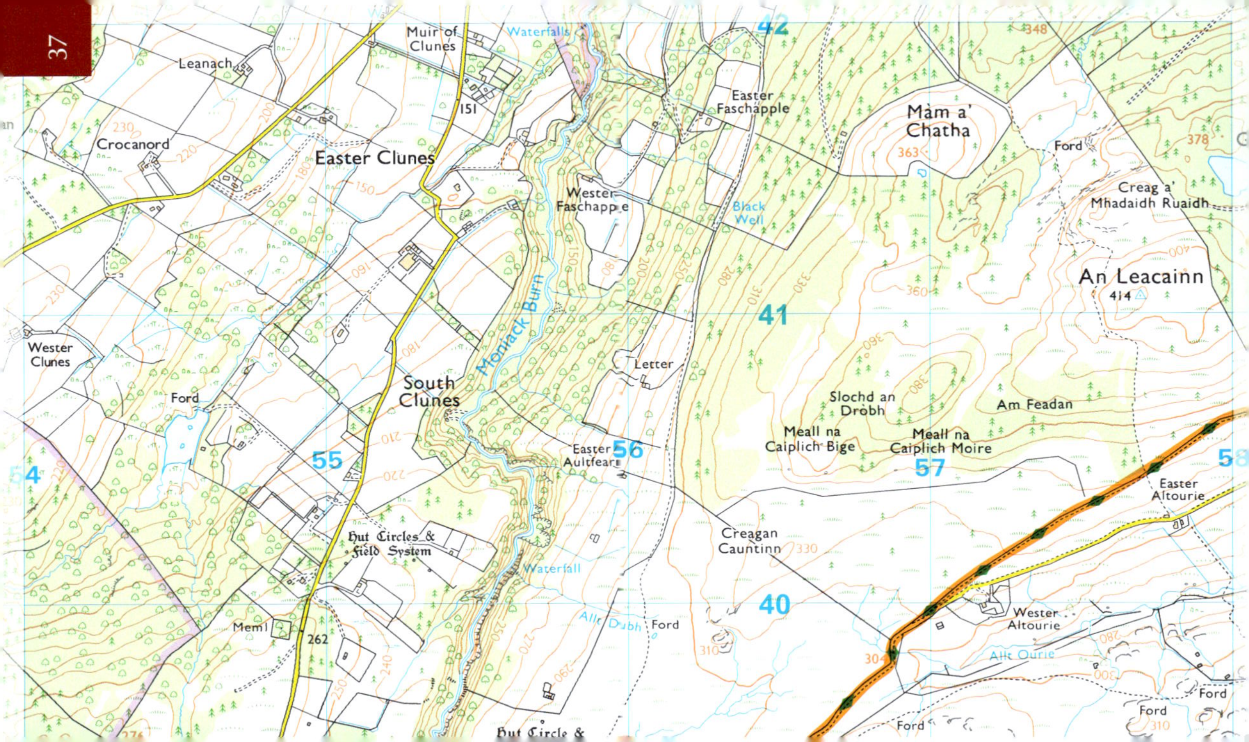
Leanach
Muir of Clunes
Waterfalls
151
Crocanord
Easter Clunes
Easter Faschapple
Màm a' Chatha
363
Ford
378
348
Creag a' Mhadaidh Ruaidh
Wester Faschapple
Black Well
An Leacainn
414
Moniack Burn
Wester Clunes
Ford
South Clunes
Letter
Slochd an Drobh
Am Feadan
Meall na Caiplich Bige
Meall na Caiplich Moire
Easter Aultfearn
Easter Altourie
Creagan Cauntinn
Hut Circles & Field System
Waterfall
Allt Dubh
Ford
Meml
262
304
Wester Altourie
Allt Ourie
Ford
Ford
Ford
Hut Circle &

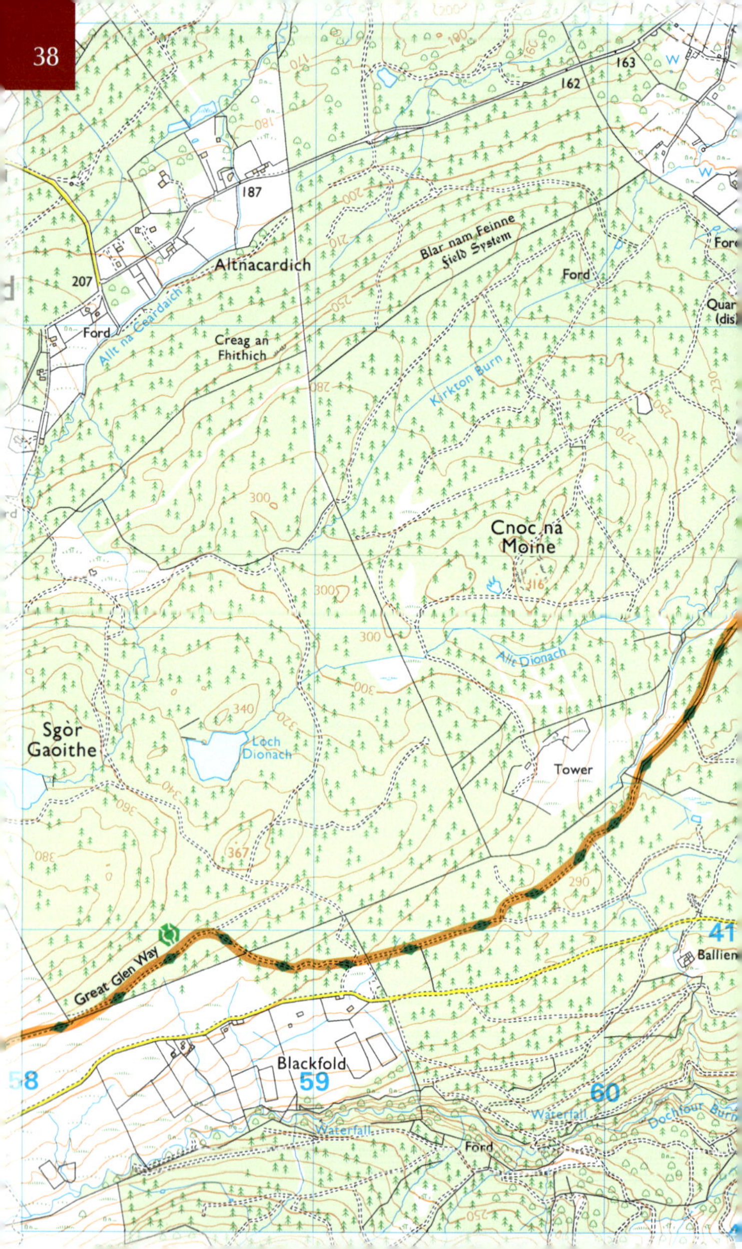

Altnacardich
Blar nam Feinne
Field System
Ford
Allt na Ceardaich
Creag an
Fhithich
Kirkton Burn
Cnoc na
Moine
Allt Dionach
Sgòr
Gaoithe
Loch
Dionach
Tower
Great Glen Way
Ballien
Blackfold
Waterfall
Ford
Dochfour Burn
58
59
60
41

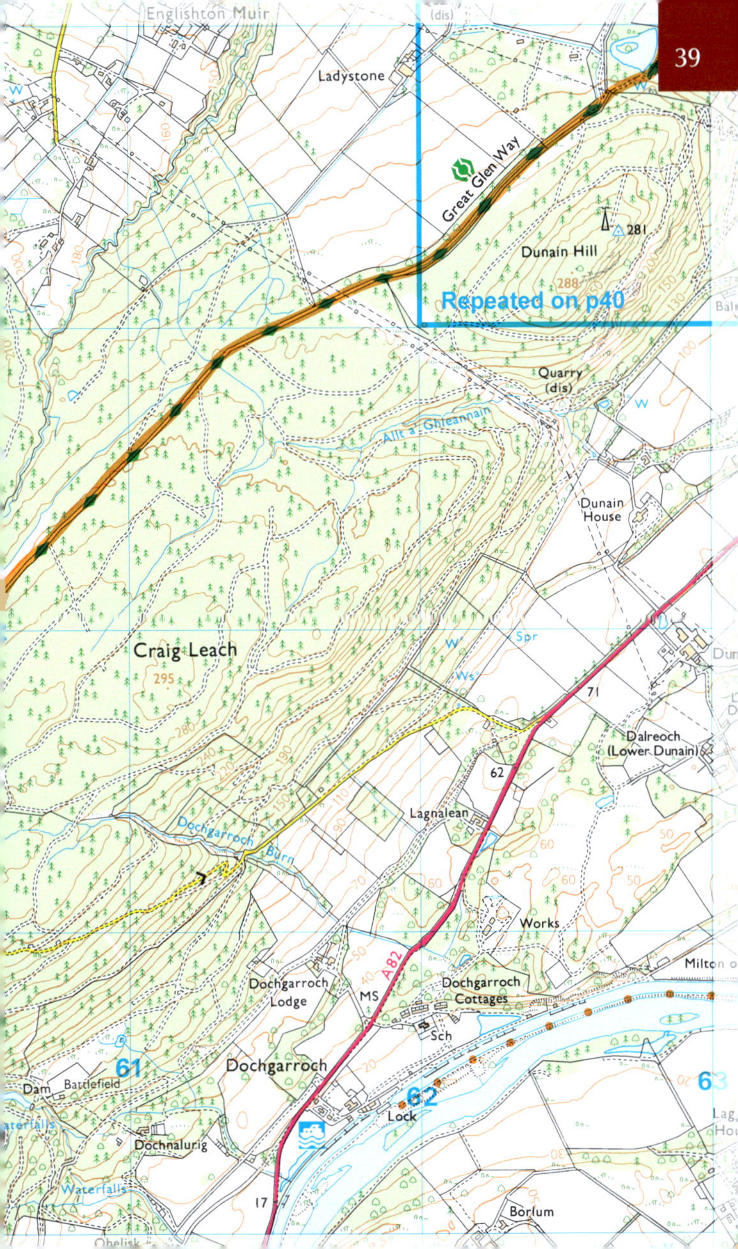
Englishton Muir
Ladystone
Great Glen Way
Dunain Hill
281
288
Repeated on p40
Quarry (dis)
Allt a' Ghleannain
Dunain House
Craig Leach
295
Spr
71
Dalreoch (Lower Dunain)
62
Lagnalean
Dochgarroch Burn
Works
Dochgarroch Lodge
A82
MS
Dochgarroch Cottages
Sch
Dochgarroch
Lock
Dam
Battlefield
Waterfalls
Dochnalurig
Borlum
Milton

Mean Low Water Springs
Mean High Water Springs
Bunchrew House
(Hotel)
Mains of
Bunchrew
Cnoc
Cottage
Bruichnain
Blackpark
Craigphadrig Forest
Craig Phadrig
Fort
Cistern
Ford
Scorguie
Clachn
Allt na h-Athe
Antfill Burn
Birchwood
Leachkin
Hospl
Chambered Cairn
(rems of)
Quarry
(dis)
Resr
Great Glen Way
Dunain Hill
Ruighard
Kilvean
Cemy
Balnacraig
Fort
Repeated from p39

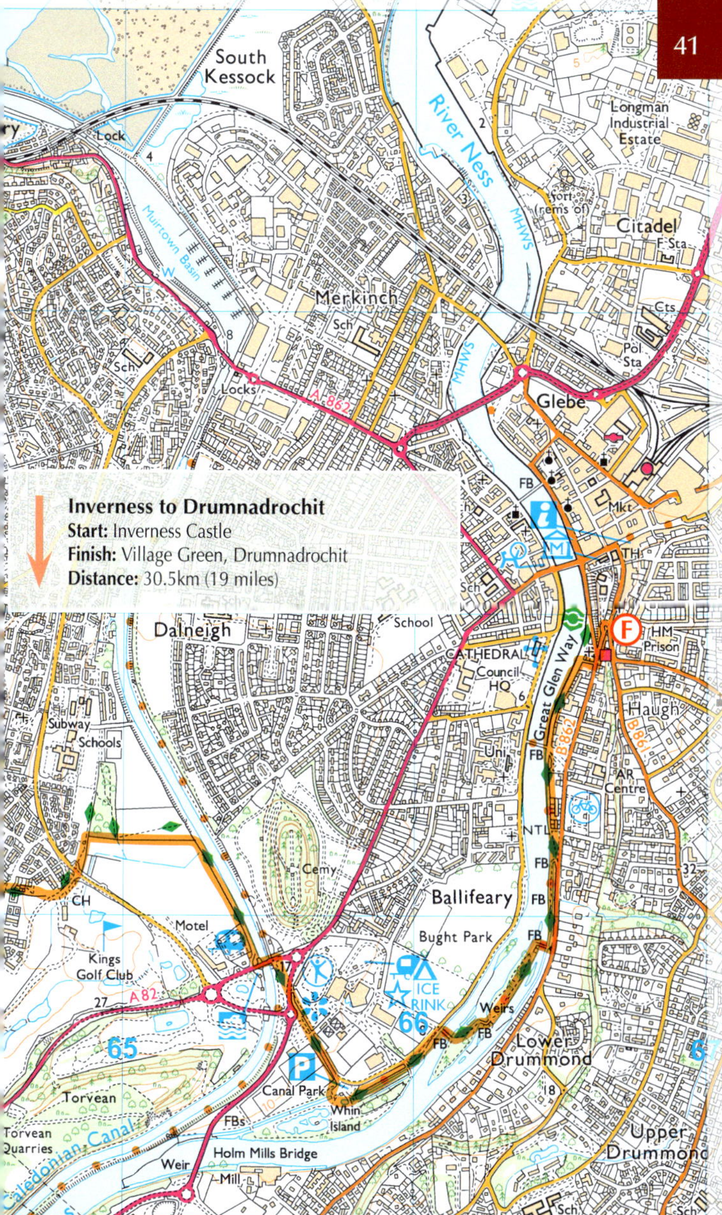
South Kessock
River Ness
Longman Industrial Estate
Lock
Muirtown Basin
Fort (rems of)
Citadel
Merkinch
Glebe
Locks
A 862
MHWS
Inverness to Drumnadrochit
Start: Inverness Castle
Finish: Village Green, Drumnadrochit
Distance: 30.5km (19 miles)
Dalneigh
School
HM Prison
CATHEDRAL
Council HQ
Great Glen Way
Haugh
B862
B861
Subway
Schools
Uni
AR Centre
Cemy
Ballifeary
Bught Park
Motel
Kings Golf Club
A82
ICE RINK
Weirs
Lower Drummond
Canal Park
Whin Island
Torvean
Torvean Quarries
Caledonian Canal
Holm Mills Bridge
Weir
Mill
Upper Drummond

LEGEND OF SYMBOLS USED ON ORDNANCE SURVEY® 1:25,000 (EXPLORER) MAPPING

ROADS AND PATHS **Not necessarily rights of way**

M1 or A6(M)	Motorway	S Service Area	7 Junction Number
A 35	Dual carriageway	S Service Area	T1 Toll road junction
A30	Main road		
B 3074	Secondary road		
	Narrow road with passing places		
	Road under construction		
	Road generally more than 4 m wide		
	Road generally less than 4 m wide		
	Other road, drive or track, fenced and unfenced		
	Gradient: steeper than 20% (1 in 5); 14% (1 in 7) to 20% (1 in 5)		
Ferry	Ferry; Ferry P – passenger only		
	Path		

RAILWAYS

Multiple track } standard
Single track } gauge

Narrow gauge or Light rapid transit system (LRTS) and station

Road over; road under; level crossing

Cutting; tunnel; embankment

Station, open to passengers; siding

PUBLIC RIGHTS OF WAY

Footpath

Bridleway

Byway open to all traffic

Restricted byway

The representation on this map of any other road, track or path is no evidence of the existence of a right of way

ARCHAEOLOGICAL AND HISTORICAL INFORMATION

Symbol	Description	Symbol	Description	Symbol	Description
⚲	Site of antiquity	VILLA	Roman	☆	Visible earthwork
⚔ 1066	Site of battle (with date)	Castle	Non-Roman		

Information provided by English Heritage for England and the Royal Commissions on the Ancient and Historical Monuments for Scotland and Wales

OTHER PUBLIC ACCESS

• • •	Other routes with public access	The exact nature of the rights on these routes and the existence of any restrictions may be checked with the local highway authority. Alignments are based on the best information available
◆ ◆ ◆	Recreational route	
◆ ◆ ◆	National Trail	Long Distance Route
- - - - -	Permissive footpath	Footpaths and bridleways along which landowners have permitted public use but which are not rights of way. The agreement may be withdrawn
— — —	Permissive bridleway	
• • •	Traffic-free cycle route	
1 1	National cycle network	route number – traffic free; on road

ACCESS LAND

Firing and test ranges in the area. Danger! Observe warning notices

Access permitted within managed controls, for example, local byelaws. Visit **www.access.mod.uk** for information

Scotland

National Trust for Scotland, always open

National Trust for Scotland, limited access – observe local signs

Forestry Commission Land

Woodland Trust Land

In Scotland, everyone has access rights in law* over most land and inland water, provided access is exercised responsibly. **This includes walking, cycling, horse-riding and water access, for recreational and educational purposes, and for crossing land or water**. Access rights do not apply to motorised activities, hunting, shooting or fishing, nor if your dog is not under proper control. The **Scottish Outdoor Access Code** is the reference point for responsible behaviour, and can be obtained at **www.outdooraccess-scotland.com** or by phoning your local Scottish Natural Heritage office.

* Land Reform (Scotland) Act 2003

BOUNDARIES

— + — +	National
— · — · —	County (England)
— — — —	Unitary Authority (UA), Metropolitan District (Met Dist), London Borough (LB) or District (Scotland & Wales are solely Unitary Authorities)
· · · · · · ·	Civil Parish (CP) (England) or Community (C) (Wales)
▬ ▬	National Park boundary

VEGETATION

Limits of vegetation are defined by positioning of symbols

- Coniferous trees
- Non-coniferous trees
- Coppice
- Orchard
- Scrub
- Bracken, heath or rough grassland
- Marsh, reeds or saltings

HEIGHTS AND NATURAL FEATURES

52 · Ground survey height
284 · Air survey height

Surface heights are to the nearest metre above mean sea level. Where two heights are shown, the first height is to the base of the triangulation pillar and the second (in brackets) to the highest natural point of the hill

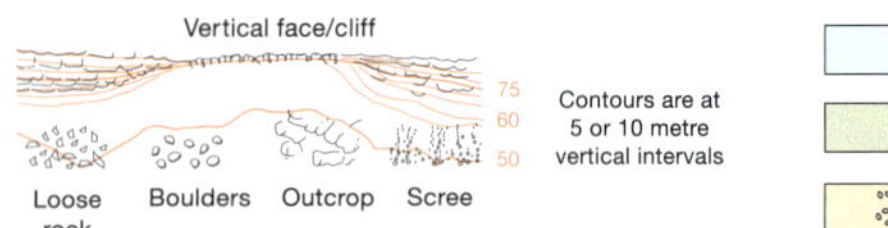

Contours are at 5 or 10 metre vertical intervals

Water

Mud

Sand; sand and shingle

SELECTED TOURIST AND LEISURE INFORMATION

- Building of historic interest
- Cadw
- Heritage centre
- Camp site
- Caravan site
- Camping and caravan site
- Castle / fort
- Cathedral / Abbey
- Craft centre
- Country park
- Cycle trail
- Mountain bike trail
- Cycle hire
- English Heritage
- Fishing
- Forestry Commission Visitor centre
- Garden / arboretum
- Golf course or links
- Historic Scotland
- Information centre, all year
- Information centre, seasonal
- Horse riding
- Museum
- National Park Visitor Centre (park logo) e.g. Yorkshire Dales

- Nature reserve
- National Trust
- Other tourist feature
- P Parking
- P&R Park and ride, all year
- P&R Park and ride, seasonal
- Picnic site
- Preserved railway
- PC Public Convenience
- Public house/s
- Recreation / leisure / sports centre
- Roman site (Hadrian's Wall only)
- Slipway
- Telephone, emergency
- Telephone, public
- Telephone, roadside assistance
- Theme / pleasure park
- Viewpoint
- Visitor centre
- Walks / trails
- World Heritage site / area
- Water activites
- Boat trips
- Boat hire

(For complete legend and symbols, see any OS Explorer map.)

The Great Glen Way

This map booklet accompanies the latest edition of Paddy Dillon's guidebook to walking the Great Glen Way. The route, including the Invergarry Link and high-level and low-level options between Fort Augustus and Drumnadrochit, is described in full from south to north and from north to south. The guidebook features annotated 1:100,000 mapping alongside detailed step-by-step route descriptions and full planning information.

Main photo: *A stack of five locks are passed as the Caledonian Canal enters Fort Augustus.*

Winter view across Loch Lochy from Bunarkaig (Stage 2, S–N; Stage 5, N–S)

The path continues easily, traversing the slopes then drifting into the forest. Follow it downhill, occasionally using stone steps, to reach a junction with a forest track near another stone-built windbreak. Again, there is a fine view of Loch Ness. Turn left along the track, where the slopes have been clear-felled and replanted, leaving occasional sparse Scots pines standing tall, with abundant rosebay willowherb. Looking far across Loch Ness, the remote Monadh Liath range rolls southwards into the distance.

A track junction is reached where the low-level route climbs to re-join the high-level route. Keep left to continue, later crossing a bridge over a waterfall. Follow the track until it ends beyond **Lòn na Fola**, in the forest above **Ruskich Wood**. Continue along a clear undulating path, noting how the forest edges are often softened by birch. The path generally heads downhill, with only occasional views of Loch Ness.

The path becomes convoluted and passes through gates while running parallel to a track below a fort on the little hill of Dùn Scriben. Emerge from the forest into a field, passing through patchy woodlands before crossing a concrete bridge over Grotaig Burn. Walk up to a road, where the route turns right and passes a small car park. ▸

Turning left leads, in less than 200 metres, to the Loch Ness Clay Works pottery and Walker's Café at Grotaig.

Snow on a roadside path above Ancarraig, with a view of Meall Fuar-mhonaidh

Follow a path running parallel to the minor road around **Balbeg**. There are occasional glimpses of Loch Ness while passing isolated houses and farms. Look back to see the humped hills of Meall Fuar-mhonaidh and Creag Dhearg. After the roadside path ends, follow the road past the Ancarraig lodges access, then gorse grows on either side as the road rises up a boggy moorland slope. Later, a swathe of rough grassland lies to the right, while improved pasture lies to the left. The road undulates over 250m (820ft) on a heather moorland, and there is another path running parallel. Follow the road as it runs into a forest and heads gently downhill, then after passing a house at **Woodend**, it falls more steeply.

Turn left as signposted for the Great Glen Way. Go through a gate and walk down a forest track to another gate. Turn right down a broad forest path, which soon turns left. There is a brief glimpse of Drumnadrochit before the path enters a dense part of the forest, later crossing a footbridge to go through a gate. There are further views of the village as the path runs down across a bracken-clad slope dotted with fine oaks. Swing right to reach Clunebeg Lodge B&B. Follow the access track downhill from Clunebeg House, admiring tall beech and oaks alongside.

Walkers who wish to reach the campsite at Borlum, or the celebrated ruins of Urquhart Castle, should turn right and follow the path running parallel to the main road.

The track levels out beside the bouldery River Coiltie. Houses seen on the far side are part of the village of Lewiston. A variety of densely packed trees usually screen the river from view as the track runs to join a minor road at a sign for the Clunebeg Estate. Follow the road straight ahead to reach a picnic area at a junction with the busy A82 road. ◂

Urquhart Castle is 2km (1.25 miles) off-route, or 3.25km (2 miles) from Drumnadrochit, perched on Strone Point overlooking Loch Ness. It can be reached safely on foot as there is a path beside the busy A82 road, and Scottish Citylink buses serve both Drumnadrochit and the castle. The situation is splendid and it is a renowned place for those keeping a lookout for the Loch Ness 'monster'! Once one of the largest castles in Scotland, Urquhart Castle's sprawling ruins take time to explore. A visitor centre offers a thorough grounding in its construction and history, plus a café. Urquhart Castle is open all year and there is an entrance charge (tel 01456 450551). For more information see Stage 5B.

Turn left to follow the A82 road across the River Coiltie to pass through **Lewiston**. The road passes a café, roundabout, pharmacy/post office and Co-op, where there is an ATM, to reach the nearby village of **Drumnadrochit**, which has a greater range of services.

Drumnadrochit (Gaelic – *Druim na Drochaid*) is a busy little village with plenty to catch the attention of passing tourists. Two attractions vying for attention are Nessieland, beside the Loch Ness Lodge Hotel, open all year (tel 01456 450342,

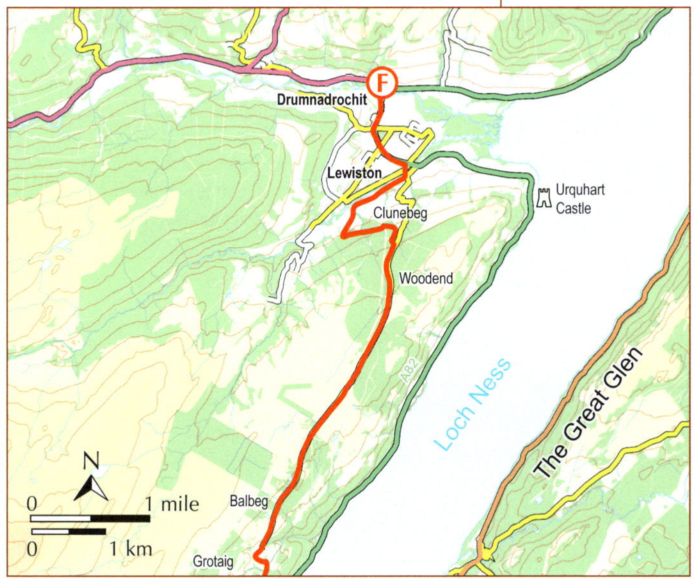

Drumnadrochit appears surrounded by woodland in this distant view

nessieland.co.uk), and the Loch Ness Centre & Exhibition at the Drumnadrochit Hotel, open all year (tel 01456 450573, **lochness.com**). There are entrance charges to both places. Whatever you want to know about Loch Ness and its 'monster', this is the place to take on board all the opinions, then you can make up your own mind. If nothing more than a 'Nessie' souvenir is required, a handful of gift shops around the village deal in the widest selection of products.

There is accommodation to suit every pocket, from hotels to guest houses and B&Bs, with an independent hostel in Lewiston and a campsite further along the road at Borlum. Most facilities are clustered round the village green at Drumnadrochit. There are toilets, bars, restaurants, cafés and take-aways. There are souvenir and gift shops. Regular daily Scottish Citylink buses link Drumnadrochit with Inverness and Fort William. Cruises on Loch Ness are also available (www.lochness-cruises.com).

STAGE 5B

Invermoriston to Drumnadrochit (low-level)

For 1:25K route map see booklet pages 26–32.

Start	Glenmoriston Arms Hotel, Invermoriston (NH 420 168)
Finish	Village Green, Drumnadrochit (NH 508 300)
Distance	23.5km (14.5 miles)
Total ascent	600m (1970ft)
Time	5hr 30min
Terrain	Forest tracks and paths, only occasionally steep. Moorland road.
Maps	OS Landrangers 26 and 34, OS Explorer 416S, Harvey Great Glen Way
Refreshments	Café at a pottery at Grotaig. Plenty of restaurants, cafés and take-aways around Drumnadrochit
Public Transport	Regular daily Scottish Citylink buses link Invermoriston and Drumnadrochit with Inverness and Fort William, and these services can also be accessed at the Lochside Hostel at Alltsigh

Before making firm plans to follow the low-level route from Invermoriston to Drumnadrochit please note that it might sometimes be closed for timber harvesting. Check in advance on the Great Glen Way website, and if the route is closed switch to the high-level option (Stage 4A). This low-level route is easier, but it is also slightly longer. Most of the day's walk is spent close to Loch Ness, but the slopes are densely forested and there are only occasional views. This will change as more and more areas are clear-felled. As the route climbs higher, it re-joins the high-level route and continues to Grotaig, where Loch Ness passes from view. Walkers continue beside or along a road most of the way to Lewiston and Drumnadrochit.

Two attractions feature at the end of the day, where rival exhibitions are devoted to Loch Ness and its 'monster'. Be sure to arrive in good time if intending to visit either or both of these places, as they are packed with plenty of interest.

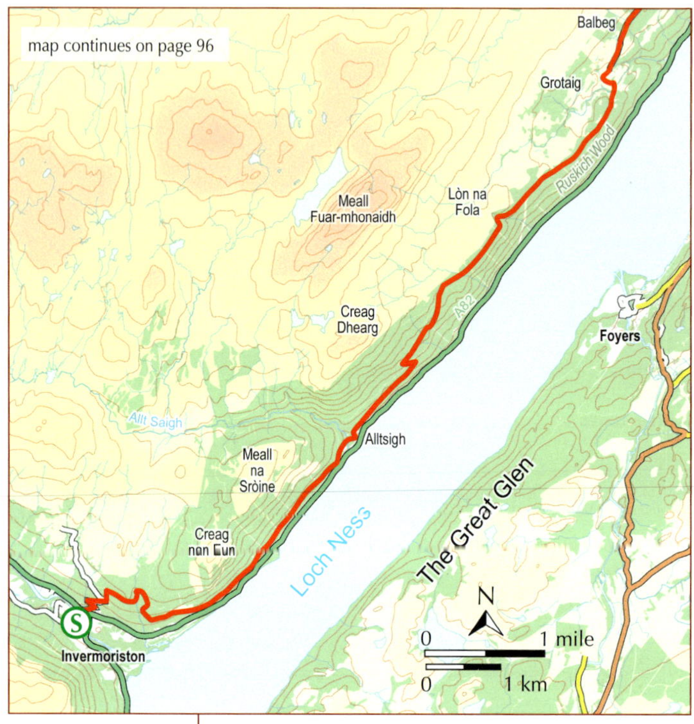

Before reaching the road/track junction, a steep and winding gravel path offers a short-cut uphill.

Leave **Invermoriston** via the A887, signposted for Kyle of Lochalsh, referred to locally as the Skye Road. Turn right at the Clog and Craft Shop, where a milestone warns 'Last Clog Shop before Skye – 52 miles'. A steep and narrow zigzag road climbs past Craik na Dav B&B, up a well-wooded slope bearing sycamore, beech, oak and birch, with a holly understorey at a higher level. Dense conifers once flanked the higher part of the road, but these have been felled. Cross a bridge over a stream and turn right almost immediately to follow a forest track crossing another bridge over the same stream. ◂

A junction is reached, where the low-level and high-level routes part. Keep straight ahead along the track to cross a crest, where a thinner part of the plantation reveals some of the former heather cover and low rocky outcrops.

The track swings left, then right, to cross a concrete bridge over a stream. Follow the track through a tall gateway, then turn right downhill from a junction. Turn right at another junction as marked, but also consider turning left as signposted for a nearby viewpoint. This short detour reveals a narrow path winding up a slope covered in ling and bell heather to reach the crude 'Stone Seat', where there is a fine view over **Loch Ness**. The village of Invermoriston, despite being close at hand, is completely hidden from view. Retrace your steps to the junction.

Walk down a narrow and bendy forest path as marked, landing on a forest track below. Turn left and follow the track gently downhill, with only occasional glimpses of Loch Ness. A post draws attention to the 'Stone Cave', said to have been built to offer shelter to a washerwoman on her frequent journeys between Alltsigh and Invermoriston. It still offers splendid shelter. Later, there is a slight climb to a bend where there is a good

The Stone Cave is on the low-level route between Invermoriston and Alltsigh

viewpoint revealing the length of Loch Ness, but also turn around and admire the fine variety of trees stacked against the cliffs of **Creag nan Eun**.

Continue down the track, passing a rugged slope of gorse bushes where no forest trees were ever planted, losing views of the loch. Keep straight ahead at a track junction beside a rock cutting, climbing gently for a while. ◂ Walk gently downhill, uphill, then downhill along a track fringed with broom. Drop more steeply from a junction of tracks and cross a concrete bridge over a rocky gorge at **Alltsigh**. There is a waterfall in the gorge, as well as a variety of trees, while a diligent search reveals an old packhorse bridge.

It is possible to turn left at the junction, walk up the track, and link with the high-level route.

For Alltsigh a marker post simply states 'Hostel' and points down a track and through a gate. The track passes a white house and quickly reaches the busy A82 road beside Loch Ness. Turn right to reach the Lochside Hostel and a bus stop. The hostel occupies a site offering splendid views across the loch.

A view of Loch Ness and Beinn a' Bhacaidh from a point near Alltsigh and the Lochside Hostel

Those who don't need to detour to Alltsigh can simply walk straight up a forest track as marked, climbing among tall conifers with no views. Later, there are good views back through the Great Glen. The track bends sharp left and sharp right as it climbs, with views through the glen becoming even more extensive, as well as taking in the village of Foyers across the loch.

The track bends quickly left and right to climb further, then there is another sharp left and sharp right turn, where views through the Great Glen stretch far beyond Fort Augustus to reveal a glimpse of distant Loch Oich. Looking far across Loch Ness, the remote Monadh Liath range rolls southwards into the distance. Clear-felled slopes are profusely covered in rosebay willowherb, with a few Scots pines standing tall.

The high-level route joins from the left, but continue walking straight ahead, later crossing a bridge over a waterfall. Follow the track until it ends beyond **Lòn na Fola**, in the forest above **Ruskich Wood**. Continue along an undulating path, noting how the forest edges are often softened by birch. The path generally heads downhill, with only occasional views of Loch Ness.

The path becomes convoluted and passes through gates while running parallel to a track below a fort on the little hill of Dùn Scriben. Emerge from the forest into a field, passing through patchy woodlands before crossing a concrete bridge over Grotaig Burn. Walk up to a road, where the route turns right and passes a small car park. ▸

Turning left leads, in less than 200 metres, to the Loch Ness Clay Works pottery and Walker's Café at Grotaig.

Follow a path running parallel to the minor road around **Balbeg**. There are occasional glimpses of Loch Ness while passing isolated houses and farms. Look back to see the humped hills of Meall Fuar-mhonaidh and Creag Dhearg. After the roadside path ends, follow the road past the Ancarraig Lodges access, then gorse grows on either side as the road rises up a boggy moorland slope. Later, a swathe of rough grassland lies to the right, while improved pasture lies to the left. The road undulates over 250m (820ft) on a heather moorland, and there is another path running parallel. Follow the road as

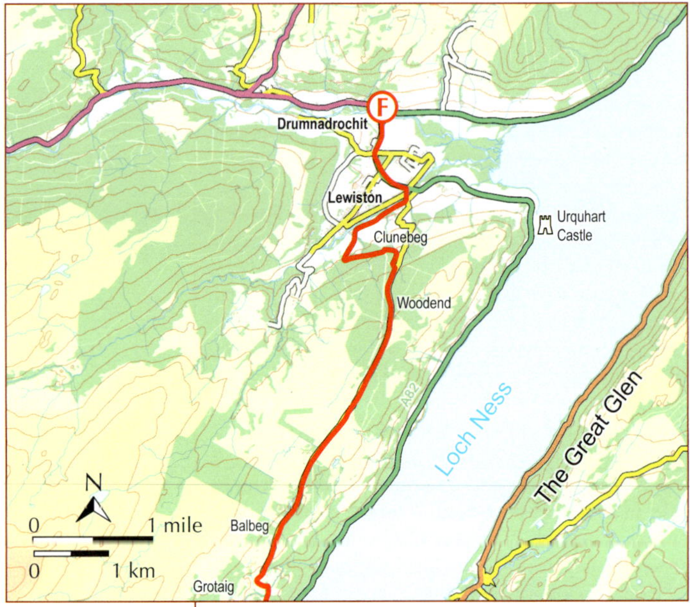

it runs into a forest and heads gently downhill, then after passing a house at **Woodend**, it falls more steeply.

Turn left as signposted for the Great Glen Way. Go through a gate and walk down a forest track to another gate. Turn right down a broad forest path, which soon turns left. There is a brief glimpse of Drumnadrochit before the path enters a dense part of the forest, later crossing a footbridge to go through a gate. There are further views of the village as the path runs down across a bracken-clad slope dotted with fine oaks. Swing right to reach Clunebeg Lodge B&B. Follow the access track downhill from Clunebeg House, admiring tall beech and oaks alongside.

The track levels out beside the bouldery River Coiltie. Houses seen on the far side are part of the village of Lewiston. A variety of densely packed trees usually screen the river from view as the track runs to join a minor road at a big sign for the Clunebeg Estate. Follow the road straight ahead to reach a picnic area at a junction with the busy A82 road. ▶

Walkers who wish to reach the campsite at Borlum, or the celebrated ruins of Urquhart Castle, should turn right and follow the path running parallel to the main road.

Turn left to follow the A82 road across the River Coiltie to reach **Lewiston**. The road passes a café, roundabout, take-away and Co-op supermarket, where there is an ATM, to reach the nearby village of **Drumnadrochit**, which has a greater range of services. For information about Drumnadrochit see Stage 5A.

URQUHART CASTLE

Urquhart Castle is 2km (1.25 miles) off-route, or 3.25km (2 miles) from Drumnadrochit, perched on Strone Point overlooking Loch Ness. It can be reached safely on foot as there is a path beside the busy A82 road, and Scottish Citylink buses serve both Drumnadrochit and the castle. Once one of the largest castles in Scotland, Urquhart Castle's sprawling ruins take time to explore. A visitor centre offers a thorough grounding in its construction and history, plus a café. Urquhart Castle is open all year and there is an entrance charge (tel 01456 450551).

The tower house at Urquhart Castle is a popular place for visitors to keep a lookout for the Loch Ness 'monster'

A Bronze Age promontory fort once stood on Strone Point, and there were other defensive structures on the site before Urquhart Castle was built in the 13th century. Its history is one of intense conflict, in which English and Scots alternately occupied it, with William Wallace and Robert the Bruce each holding the property for a time. Buchan, son of Robert II, held the castle from 1390, ruling with brutal force, and frequently robbing churches. In the 15th and 16th centuries the MacDonalds launched raids on the castle, which was later held by the Grants. The bulk of the damage to the castle was done with explosives in 1692, which prevented it becoming a Jacobite stronghold in subsequent years.Visitors cross a wooden gangway across a defensive ditch, and pass through a gatehouse. However, in the past, most people approaching the castle would have done so through a watergate from Loch Ness. The centrepiece of Urquhart Castle is a stout and impressive tower house, but be sure to take note of the complex arrangement of the ruined defensive walls that surround the site. The best vantage point is of course from the top of the tower house.

Walkers who can't spare the time to detour to the castle can console themselves by studying an interesting floral model of the castle in the middle of the village green in Drumnadrochit.

A floral model of Urquhart Castle in the middle of Drumnadrochit

STAGE 6

Drumnadrochit to Inverness

Start	Village Green, Drumnadrochit (NH 508 300)
Finish	Inverness Castle (NH 666 451)
Distance	30.5km (19 miles)
Total ascent	500m (1640ft)
Time	8hr
Terrain	Road, forest and moorland tracks, then urban pathways through green spaces to the finish
Maps	OS Landranger 26, OS Explorer 416N, Harvey Great Glen Way
Refreshments	Basic campsite café near Abriachan. Plenty of choice in Inverness.
Public Transport	Regular daily Scottish Citylink buses link Drumnadrochit with Inverness and Fort William. Approaching Inverness, there are several points where local city bus services can be accessed. Long-distance bus and rail services are available, and there is an airport nearby.

This is the longest day's walk on the Great Glen Way, and a high point is crossed around 380m (1245ft) in the Abriachan Forest. The forest is managed by the local community, who have cleared, marked and signposted a network of trails. The area is proving popular with visitors and school parties. This is a long stage and the only place it can be broken easily is at an eco-campsite near Abriachan. The route is rather distant from the Great Glen and follows the course of an old drove road, which passes through an interesting remnant Scots pine forest. By the time the route descends back into the glen, it is on the outskirts of Inverness. Take care over route-finding through the suburbs, where one green space after another is linked to provide a route into the very heart of the city.

Once the finish is reached at Inverness Castle, there is a chance to look back along the route through the Great Glen and reflect on your journey across Scotland.

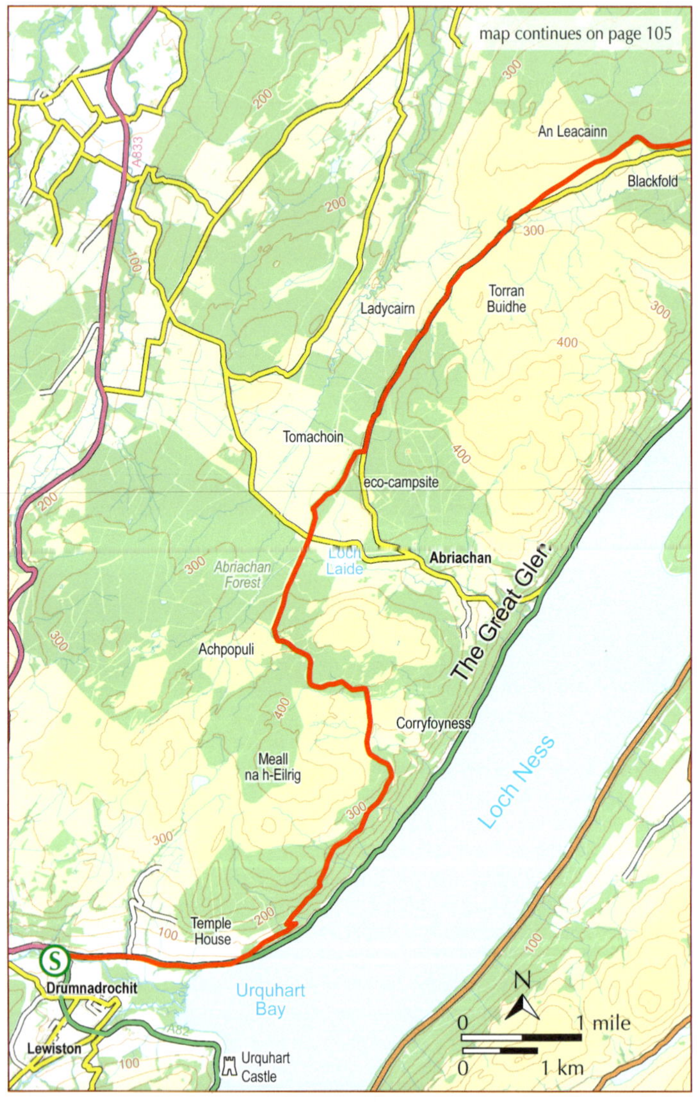
map continues on page 105
An Leacainn
Blackfold
Torran Buidhe
Ladycairn
Tomachoin
eco-campsite
Abriachan
Loch Laide
Abriachan Forest
Achpopuli
The Great Glen
Corryfoyness
Meall na h-Eilrig
Loch Ness
Temple House
Drumnadrochit
Urquhart Bay
Lewiston
Urquhart Castle
A833
A82
N
0 1 mile
0 1 km

Leave **Drumnadrochit** by following the main A82 in the direction of Inverness. Stay on the pavement on the left-hand side throughout, passing a handful of B&B places. There is access on the other side of the road for **Urquhart Bay** Harbour, for cruises on Loch Ness.

> **John Cobb** broke land and water speed records. In 1947 his land speed record stood a little short of 400mph (645kph). On 29 September 1952 he achieved a speed of 206mph (331kph) on Loch Ness, from Urquhart Bay. Unfortunately, his craft *Crusader* disintegrated and sank, taking Cobb's life, and the engine wasn't recovered for 50 years.

Turn left up the access road for **Temple House**, then quickly turn left again, up through a gate, to follow a path beside a tall fence to pass the house. There is a brief glimpse of Urquhart Castle across Urquhart Bay on Loch Ness. The path runs parallel to the road, then climbs through small gates and crosses a narrow access road that leads up to Tychat. Continue through woods,

Urquhart Bay Harbour can be visited on Loch Ness near Drumnadrochit

For 1:25K route map see booklet pages 32–41.

climbing through more small gates, then follow a path across a grassy slope overlooking a stretch of Loch Ness, again with a view of **Urquhart Castle**.

A gate leads into dense forest, but the path is clear and obvious. There is a brief glimpse of **Loch Ness** just before a footbridge, then the path climbs gradually. Little light reaches the forest floor, so only moss and wood sorrel grow alongside the path. When the path turns sharply left and right, it climbs through a more open area of grass and bracken, with several birch trees. The path runs more or less level for a while, then climbs, before descending to cross stepping stones over a small burn. A short ascent leads onto a forest track.

Follow the track onwards, undulating at first, then climbing gradually up a clear-felled slope. There are views over Loch Ness, but they aren't particularly good, and at a higher level the track drifts well away from the loch. Go through a tall gate, out of the forest, onto hummocky moorland with a view of isolated buildings at **Corryfoyness**, which was once a farm. There are boggy hollows spiked with rushes, as well as heathery humps, and scattered birch trees. The track meanders and climbs gradually to a gateway into another forest.

Signs inform visitors that this is managed by the Abriachan Forest Trust, where signposts indicate the Abriachan Forest Walks. The Great Glen Way is waymarked as usual, but signposts also point back to Drumnadrochit and ahead to Inverness. The track meanders and reaches a high point around 380m (1245ft). ◂ There is a fairly steep descent to a building near **Achpopuli**, then the track swings right and leads straight down along a broad forest ride. The is part of an old drove road, and towards the end there is access on the right to a car park and a grass-roofed toilet block, along with plenty of information about the Abriachan Forest Walks.

This was the highest point on the Great Glen Way until new high-level options were opened in 2014.

Abriachan is only a small community of around 120 people, yet in the mid-1990s they managed to raise over £150,000 to buy a substantial part of

Light snowfall on a forest track high above Abriachan

the **Abriachan Forest**. At the time, it was the largest community forest in Scotland, and it has been developed with public access and conservation foremost. A network of walking and cycling trails has been established, as well as a car park complete with a picnic site, an eco-toilet and plenty of information. Interesting features just off the course of the Great Glen Way include Loch Laide and the Caiplich Prehistoric Settlement. Visitors can become Friends of the Abriachan Forest Trust, and receive a newsletter keeping them in touch with developments. Pick up a leaflet in the forest or check the website www.abriachan.org.uk for full contact details.

Keep straight ahead and the track leaves the forest, with a view of little **Loch Laide** to the right. Cross a minor road and go through a kissing gate to follow a narrow, but clear and obvious gravel path. This path rises gently up a moorland slope dotted with trees, meandering and clipping the corner of a forest. Numerous signs point to the right, where an **eco-campsite** also offers a café just off-route. As the path approaches the whitewashed house of Woodend, it turns right and runs up to a kissing gate and a minor road, next to a sign for Caiplich Farm.

Turn left and follow the road, where there are a couple of houses tucked away at **Tomachoin** and Rinuden. The road passes passes a huddle of houses at **Ladycairn**, then crosses a heathery slope where a number of Scots pines grow. Although the road is fenced, it crosses broad and open moorland covered with ling and bell heather. There are views northwards towards the sprawling slopes of Ben Wyvis, but these are lost once the road crosses a crest over 300m (985ft). The road crosses a stream, then a clear and obvious gritty path heads left, across open moorland on the slopes of **An Leacainn**. The path passes a number of stones carved with 'Dochgarroch' and later links with forest tracks just above **Blackfold**.

Continue as signposted along a track, then quickly turn right as marked through gates into clear-felled forest. A sign reminds walkers that they are following an old drove road, where cattle were driven from west to east, from the Highlands to Inverness. The route passes through ancient pinewoods that are being regenerated, and the sign also draws the attention of walkers to a nearby 'lek'. ◂

A lek is a site where rare black grouse traditionally gather at dawn during spring and autumn to perform noisy courtship displays. As a consequence, dogs should be kept under control.

Follow the track into the forest and turn left at a junction to stay on the main track. The forest floor is grassy, heathery and mossy, with areas of bilberry. The track meanders and undulates slightly near **Craig Leach**, passing a kissing gate before heading more noticeably downhill. Old drystone walls flank the drove road and the ruin of an old 'lairage', once used as a lodging by drovers, is passed just before a couple of prominent horse chestnut trees.

Moss, heather and bilberry grow thick on top of the flanking walls, and plenty of slender birch and rowan trees grow alongside, often obscuring the ranks of conifers beyond. After passing beneath power lines, look out to the right to spot some fine examples of Scots pines on **Dunain Hill**, and also look to the left, between the birch trees, to glimpse the waters of the **Beauly Firth**; a sure sign that this walk across Scotland is drawing to a conclusion.

Go through a kissing gate and follow a broader track downhill, but turn right at a track junction to pass a pylon and go through an old gateway. Walk out of the woods, turning left through a gate to cross a dam holding a pond in place. There is a view of Inverness in the distance, then as the path climbs a grassy slope, there are views of the former Creag Dunain Hospital closer to hand. Follow the path downhill to a gate and turn left down a track, passing a variety of trees, including stout beech and towering Scots pines. Bend right on the lower slopes, then turn left to pass between old and new buildings. Turn right and left to reach a main road called Forester's Way.

Built in 1864, **Creag Dunain** was originally a huge Victorian mental hospital. By all accounts, its management was progressive and doctors were willing to practise the latest forms of treatment on their patients. The building was later used as a

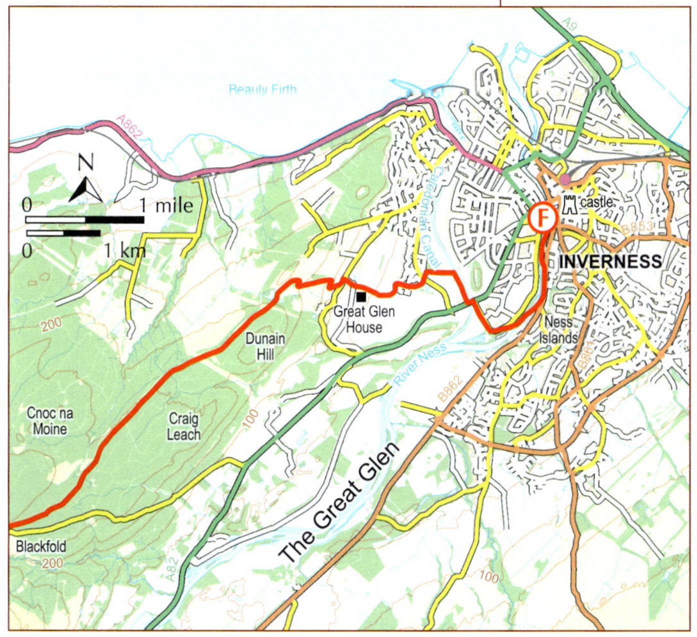

general hospital. In recent years it has been redeveloped for housing.

This is essentially an office block, but there are 'Paths for All' and other interesting publications available at reception. Energy-efficient and eco-friendly, it won an award for 'Sustainable Building of the Year' in 2006.

Turn left along Forester's Way, then turn right as signposted for the Great Glen Way, and note the **Great Glen House** to the right. ◂ Continue as marked and pick up a clear gravel path winding downhill between fields, with rampant hedgerows alongside. The path swings left beside some houses, then there is a right turn down through a broad and grassy space between houses. Cross a road to go through another grassy space, and drift left as marked to cross a road-end and go through an underpass beneath a busy road with bus stops.

Follow a paved path, then turn right alongside a golf course and follow a path along an embankment between the golf course and sports pitches. Steps lead up to the **Caledonian Canal**. Turn right to follow a tarmac track parallel, bearing in mind that this is actually running roughly in the direction of Fort William! Turn left across a swing

Great Glen House is an award-winning eco-building

bridge on the busy A82 road, then cross with care. There are buses along this road.

Follow the canal-side path only a short way, then head left and walk through two underpasses beneath a busy roundabout. Join a road and follow it past a car park and the Inverness Botanic Gardens. When the road turns left, head for a toilet block in a car park near Whin Park.

Turn left as marked along a tarmac path, then when the path runs alongside the **River Ness** turn right to cross a white suspension footbridge onto the **Ness Islands**. Turn left alongside the river again, then right across a curved footbridge, which has a small island in its middle. Keep right along another path, then when the island tapers out, turn right across another suspension footbridge. Turn left to walk alongside the **River Ness**, but turn right later to cross a short footbridge over a narrow water channel running parallel.

Turn left alongside the river and follow it into **Inverness**. The popular path is known as Ladies' Walk as far as a suspension footbridge, then it becomes Ness Bank. Watch out for a right turn away from the river, along an alley beside Ness Bank House. Climb up a few

Looking along the River Ness from Ness Islands towards the cathedral in Inverness

steps and turn left up the road called View Place to reach **Inverness Castle**.

> Castle Hill rises proudly above the River Ness and is obviously a strategic location. It may have been settled and fortified throughout history, but there was certainly a timber fort there in the 11th century. A stone fort was built in the 12th century, which was rebuilt in the 15th century. **Inverness Castle** was extensively damaged at the end of the Jacobite Rebellion in 1746. The neo-Norman castle, of well-dressed red sandstone, was built in 1834 as the Sheriff Court and still functions as such today. Outside the castle a statue of Flora MacDonald gazes towards the Great Glen. She was imprisoned in London for helping Bonnie Prince Charlie. Part of the building is equipped as the Castle Garrison Encounter and can be visited (tel 01463 243363).

The Great Glen Way finishes at a stone monument overlooking the River Ness and the later stages of the route. Spend a while looking back towards the Great Glen, then give some thought to how you will spend your remaining time in Inverness.

Behind Inverness Castle is the Castle Wynd, which leads down past toilets to the Town House and the High Street. Walkers will naturally find themselves exploring at least a small part of the city centre, even if they only want to head for the train or bus station. Those who stay overnight will have more time at their disposal and can enjoy further explorations of the city (see 'Last/First night: Inverness' in the Introduction).

THE GREAT GLEN WAY
NORTH TO SOUTH

The route starts with a short descent from Inverness Castle to the River Ness

STAGE 1

Inverness to Drumnadrochit

Start	Inverness Castle (NH 666 451)
Finish	Village Green, Drumnadrochit (NH 508 300)
Distance	30.5km (19 miles)
Total ascent	540m (1770ft)
Time	8hr
Terrain	Urban pathways through green spaces, followed by forest and moorland tracks and roads
Maps	OS Landranger 26, OS Explorer 416N, Harvey Great Glen Way
Refreshments	Plenty of choice in Inverness. Basic campsite café at Abriachan. Plenty of restaurants, cafés and take-aways in Drumnadrochit.
Public Transport	Local city bus services around Inverness. Regular daily Scottish Citylink buses link Inverness with Drumnadrochit and Fort William.

This is the longest stage on the Great Glen Way, and there is a fine view from Inverness Castle towards the Great Glen. Take care over route-finding through the city suburbs, where one green space after another leads the walker towards the countryside. The route actually drifts away from the Great Glen, following the course of an old drove road through an interesting remnant Scots pine forest. A road walk leads towards an eco-campsite near Abriachan, the only place this long day's walk could be broken. Abriachan Forest is managed by the local community, who have cleared, marked and signposted a network of trails. The area is proving popular with visitors and school parties, and a high point on the Great Glen Way is crossed around 380m (1245ft).

Drumnadrochit is reached at the end of the day, where the principal attractions are two rival exhibitions devoted to Loch Ness and its 'monster'.

Walkers starting at either the railway station or bus station in **Inverness** will have to negotiate the busy city streets for a few minutes to find **Inverness Castle**. This is prominently located on a green hill just behind the Town

House, overlooking the powerful flow of the River Ness. A stone monument marks the start of the Great Glen Way, and the route is marked throughout with signs bearing a 'thistle' logo.

Inverness Castle is the beginning or end of the Great Glen Way

Castle Hill rises proudly above the River Ness and is obviously a strategic location. It may have been settled and fortified throughout history, but there was certainly a timber fort there in the 11th century. A stone fort was built in the 12th century, which was rebuilt in the 15th century. **Inverness Castle** was extensively damaged at the end of the Jacobite Rebellion in 1746. The neo-Norman castle seen today, of well-dressed red sandstone, was built in 1834. Outside the castle a statue of Flora MacDonald gazes towards the Great Glen. She was imprisoned in London for helping Bonnie Prince Charlie. Part of the building is equipped as the Castle Garrison Encounter and can be visited (tel 01463 243363).

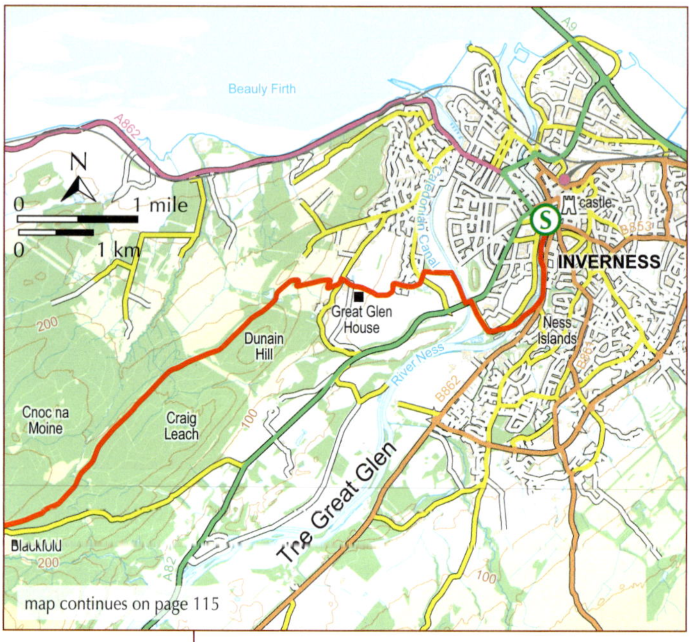

Walk down the road called View Place, and cross a busy road. Almost immediately, turn right down some stone steps and walk through an alley beside Ness Bank House, to reach the **River Ness**. Turn left along a popular riverside path, known as Ness Bank until it reaches a white suspension footbridge, where it becomes Ladies' Walk. Continue beside the river, then cross a short footbridge on the right, which spans a narrow water channel, then turn left to walk between the channel and the river. Turn right to cross a suspension footbridge onto the **Ness Islands**, then turn left and keep left. Later, cross a curved footbridge, which has a small island in its middle, and turn left to walk alongside the river again. Turn right over another suspension footbridge, then turn left to follow the river, and a narrow channel, to a toilet block near Whin Park.

Follow a road away from the river, passing alongside the Inverness Botanic Gardens and a car park. Head left as marked, walking through two underpasses beneath a busy roundabout. Keep right and follow a short stretch of canal-side path, turning left to follow the busy A82 road across a swing bridge on the **Caledonian Canal**. ▸

The A82 road has bus services.

Turn right to follow a clear tarmac track beside the canal, which actually leads back towards Inverness! However, there are steps down to the left, leading onto a path following an embankment between a golf course and sports pitches. Keep straight ahead and later turn left along a paved path, which goes through an underpass beneath a busy road with bus stops.

Walk past a road-end, then drift right across a grassy area as marked, looking for a grassy space between houses. Cross a road and walk gently up through another broader grassy space between houses. Turn left along a path behind some houses, then drift right as marked to follow a clear gravel path winding uphill between fields, with rampant hedgerows alongside. Follow the markers along a road, with the **Great Glen House** to the left, to reach a road junction. ▸ Turn left along the main road called Forester's Way, towards the former Creag Dunain Hospital, but turn right beforehand towards an old building, keeping left of it to pass between it and new buildings. Turn right and follow a path away from the last suburb of Inverness, into the countryside.

Great Glen House is essentially an office block, but there are 'Paths for All' and other interesting publications available at reception. Energy-efficient and eco-friendly, it won an award for 'Sustainable Building of the Year' in 2006.

Built in 1864, **Creag Dunain** was originally a huge Victorian mental hospital. By all accounts, its management was progressive and doctors were willing to practise the latest forms of treatment on their patients. The building was later used as a general hospital. In recent years it has been closed and redeveloped for housing.

The path bends left as it climbs, passing towering Scots pines and stout beech. Turn right at a gate to follow a clear path further uphill, overlooking the former Creag Dunain Hospital and Inverness. The path crosses a grassy slope and drops to cross a dam holding a pond in place. Go through a gate and turn right along a woodland track across the slopes of **Dunain Hill**. Go through an old gateway and past a pylon, then turn left up a broader track. Go through a kissing gate onto yet another track.

A lek is a site where rare black grouse traditionally gather at dawn during spring and autumn to perform noisy courtship displays. As a consequence, dogs should be kept under control.

A sign reminds walkers that they are following an old drove road, where cattle were driven from west to east, from the Highlands to Inverness. The route passes through ancient pinewoods that are being regenerated on **Craig Leach**, and the sign also draws the attention of walkers to a nearby 'lek'. ◂ Look out to the left to spot Scots pines, and to the right, between birch trees, to glimpse the waters of the **Beauly Firth**.

Pass under power lines and note slender birch and rowan trees growing alongside, often obscuring the ranks of conifers beyond. Moss, heather and bilberry grow thick on top of the old drystone walls that flank the track. Just after passing a couple of prominent chestnut trees, the ruin of an old 'lairage' is passed, once used by drovers. The track rises to a kissing gate, then meanders and undulates slightly without its flanking drystone walls. The forest floor is grassy, heathery and mossy, with areas of

An open moorland walk is enjoyed between Blackfold and Abriachan

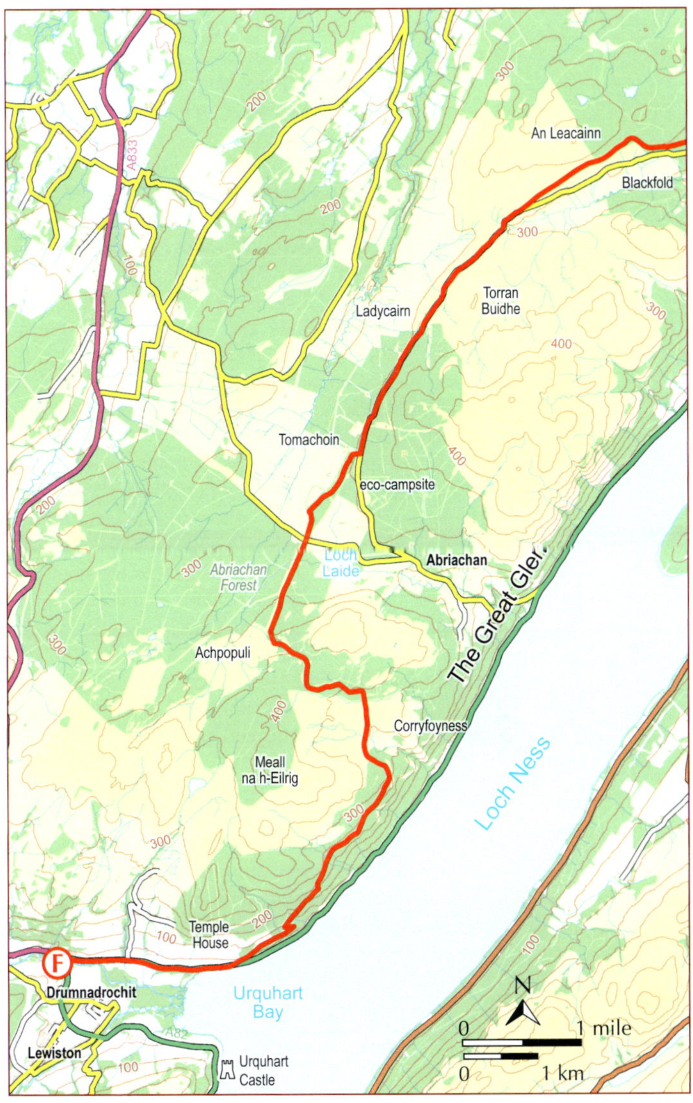
A833
An Leacainn
Blackfold
Torran Buidhe
Ladycairn
Tomachoin
eco-campsite
Loch Laide
Abriachan
Abriachan Forest
The Great Glen
Achpopuli
Corryfoyness
Meall na h-Eilrig
Loch Ness
Temple House
F
Drumnadrochit
Urquhart Bay
A82
Lewiston
Urquhart Castle
N
0
1 mile
0
1 km

bilberry. The track passes through a clear felled area, as well as through gates, where views begin to open up.

Cross a forest track just above **Blackfold** and pick up a gritty path that crosses open moorland on the slopes of **An Leacainn**, where there is ling and bell heather. The path passes a number of stones carved with 'Dochgarroch' and later descends gently to a minor road. Turn right to cross a stream; the road crosses a crest over 300m (985ft), with views northwards towards the sprawling slopes of Ben Wyvis. After crossing a heathery slope where a number of Scots pines grow, the road passes a huddle of houses at **Ladycairn**. The road passes through clear-felled forest where there are a couple of houses tucked away at **Tomachoin** and Rinuden. Watch out for a sign for Caiplich Farm, and go through a kissing gate on the right to leave the road.

A clear and obvious gravel path runs downhill and swings left in view of a white house called Woodend. Numerous signs point left, where an **eco-campsite** also offers a café, just off route. The path clips the corner of a forest and descends gently down a moorland slope dotted with trees, meandering before running straight to a kissing gate onto a minor road. Walk straight ahead along a forest track, with a view of little **Loch Laide** to the left. Also to the left, a little later, is access to a car park and a grass-roofed toilet block, along with plenty of information about the Abriachan Forest Walks.

Abriachan is only a small community of around 120 people, yet in the mid-1990s they managed to raise over £150,000 to buy a substantial part of the **Abriachan Forest**. At the time, it was the largest community forest in Scotland, and it has been developed with public access and conservation foremost. A network of walking and cycling trails has been established, as well as a car park complete with a picnic site, an eco-toilet and plenty of information. Interesting features just off the course of the Great Glen Way include Loch Laide and the Caiplich Prehistoric Settlement. Visitors can

One of many signs directing walkers off-route to an eco-campsite and café

become Friends of the Abriachan Forest Trust, and receive a newsletter keeping them in touch with developments. Pick up a leaflet in the forest or check the website www.abriachan.org.uk for full contact details.

The Great Glen Way is waymarked as usual, but signposts also point back to Inverness and ahead to Drumnadrochit. The track is still part of the old drove road that was followed earlier, and it leads straight up along a broad forest ride. Swing left to pass a building near **Achpopuli** and climb fairly steeply, levelling out on a high point around 380m (1245ft). The track meanders gently downhill and leaves the forest at a gateway.

Continue to descend a moorland slope dotted with birch trees. There are boggy hollows spiked with rushes, as well as heathery humps, and a view of isolated buildings at **Corryfoyness**. Go through a tall gate into another

A footbridge is crossed in a densely planted forest on the way from Corryfoyness to Drumnadrochit

forest, following a track that gradually moves closer towards Loch Ness. The first views over the loch are not particularly good, as the track descends gradually on a clear-felled slope. Views are lost as the track undulates, then suddenly gives way to a forest path.

The path runs downhill a short way, then crosses stepping stones over a small burn. Continue uphill, then downhill, then keep more or less level for a while. After passing through a more open area of grass and bracken, with birch trees, the path turns sharply left and right downhill. The path enters dense forest with no views;

little light reaches the forest floor, so only moss and wood sorrel grow alongside. Descend gradually to cross a footbridge, gaining a glimpse of Loch Ness before the path reaches a gate at the edge of the forest.

Follow the path across a grassy slope overlooking a stretch of **Loch Ness**, now featuring a view of Urquhart Castle. The path climbs through small gates, then enters woods and crosses a narrow access road that leads to Tychat. The path drops through more small gates and runs parallel to the main A82 road. There is another brief glimpse of Urquhart Castle across Urquhart Bay on Loch Ness. Follow a path around a tall fence to pass **Temple House**, then go down through a gate and follow the access road down to the main road. There is access on the other side of the road for **Urquhart Bay** harbour, for cruises on Loch Ness.

LOCH NESS

Loch Ness occupies a deep trough that has been filled with water ever since the end of the Ice Age, around 10,000 years ago, and it reflects enough light to brighten even the dullest days in the Great Glen. Six major rivers carry water into Loch Ness, from a part of the Highlands known for high rainfall, explaining why the River Ness flows so powerfully past Inverness. Here are some facts and figures to help appreciate its full extent:

- Catchment area: 1800km^2 (700 square miles)
- Surface area: 56km^2 (21.5 square miles)
- Length: 37km (23 miles)
- Width: 3km (2 miles)
- Shoreline length: 86km (53.5 miles)
- Volume: 7.5 cubic kilometres (1.8 cubic miles)
- Maximum depth: 230m (755ft)
- Surface level: 16m (52ft) above sea level

More astonishing facts include oft-repeated statements that the volume of water in the loch exceeds that of all the lakes and reservoirs in England and Wales, and is sufficient to immerse the entire population of the world!

John Cobb broke land and water speed records. In 1947 his land speed record stood a little short of 400mph (645kph). On 29 September 1952 he achieved a speed of 206mph (331kph) on Loch Ness, from Urquhart Bay. Unfortunately, his craft *Crusader* disintegrated and sank, taking Cobb's life, and the engine wasn't recovered for 50 years.

Turn right to follow the main road, keeping to the pavement on the right-hand side throughout, passing a couple of B&Bs to reach **Drumnadrochit**.

Drumnadrochit (Gaelic – *Druim na Drochaid*) is a busy little village with plenty to catch the attention of passing tourists. Two attractions vying for attention are Nessieland, beside the Loch Ness Hotel, open all year (tel 01456 450342, **nessieland.co.uk**), and the Loch Ness Centre & Exhibition at the Drumnadrochit Hotel, open all year (tel 01456 450573, **lochness.com**). There are entrance charges to both places. Whatever you want to know about Loch Ness and its 'monster', this is the place to take on board all the opinions, then you can make up your own mind. If nothing more than a 'Nessie' souvenir is required, a handful of gift shops around the village deal in the widest selection of products.

There is accommodation to suit every pocket, from hotels to guest houses and B&Bs, with an independent hostel in Lewiston and a campsite further along the road at Borlum. Most facilities are clustered round the village green at Drumnadrochit. There are toilets, bars, restaurants, cafés and take-aways. There are souvenir and gift shops. Regular daily Scottish Citylink buses link Drumnadrochit with Inverness and Fort William. Cruises on Loch Ness are also available (www.lochness-cruises.com).

STAGE 2A

Drumnadrochit to Invermoriston (high-level)

For 1:25K route map see booklet pages 26–32.

Start	Village Green, Drumnadrochit (NH 508 300)
Finish	Glenmoriston Arms Hotel, Invermoriston (NH 420 168)
Distance	22.5km (14 miles)
Total ascent	580m (1900ft)
Time	5hr 45min
Terrain	Ascent to a moorland road. Forest tracks and upland moorland paths with some short, steep slopes.
Maps	OS Landrangers 26 and 34, OS Explorer 416S, Harvey Great Glen Way
Refreshments	Café at a pottery at Grotaig. Invermoriston has a hotel with a bar/restaurant and one other café.
Public Transport	Regular daily Scottish Citylink buses link Invermoriston and Drumnadrochit with Inverness and Fort William

On leaving Drumnadrochit, walkers have to decide whether to make a detour to visit Urquhart Castle, or console themselves by studying a floral model of the castle on the village green. There are two options for linking Drumnadrochit and Invermoriston, but a decision doesn't need to be made until halfway through the day. The high-level option should be open at all times, but in really bad weather it might be wise to take the low-level route (Stage 2B). Bear in mind that a pottery at Grotaig offers a tearoom, and there might be roadside snacks nearby, but otherwise there are no refreshments until Invermoriston is reached at the end of the day. The highest point on the Great Glen Way is reached on the slopes of Creag Dhearg. Later, there is an option to switch to the low-level route by walking down a forest track to Alltsigh. Despite the route running high and being just outside the forest, there are no views of Loch Ness towards the finish because the hills of Meall na Sròine and Creag nan Eun are in the way.

Invermoriston is a tiny village, which can be explored easily in the evening. It is wise to book lodgings in advance, although it is a simple matter to catch a bus elsewhere in search of accommodation.

Follow the busy A82 road out of **Drumnadrochit**. The road passes through a roundabout to reach the neighbouring village of **Lewiston**, which has a small range of facilities. Cross the River Coiltie and turn right at a picnic area, as signposted for the Clunebeg Estate. ◂

Alternatively follow the path beside the main road, straight ahead to visit Urquhart Castle, then return to this junction later.

Follow the minor road straight ahead to reach a big sign for the Clunebeg Estate, and continue walking along a clear track. Although the track runs level alongside the bouldery River Coiltie, densely packed trees usually screen the river from view. Any houses seen on the far side are part of the village of Lewiston. Admire tall oaks and beech

URQUHART CASTLE

Urquhart Castle is 2km (1.25 miles) off-route, or 3.25km (2 miles) from Drumnadrochit, perched on Strone Point overlooking Loch Ness. It can be reached safely on foot as there is a path beside the busy A82 road, and Scottish Citylink buses serve both Drumnadrochit and the castle. The situation is splendid and it is a renowned place for those keeping a lookout for the Loch Ness Monster! Once one of the largest castles in Scotland, Urquhart Castle's sprawling ruins take time to explore. A visitor centre offers a thorough grounding in its construction and history, plus a café. Urquhart Castle is open all year, and there is an entrance charge (tel 01456 450551).

A Bronze Age promontory fort once stood on Strone Point, and there were other defensive structures on the site before Urquhart Castle was built in the 13th century. Its history is one of intense conflict, in which English and Scots alternately occupied it, with William Wallace and Robert the Bruce each holding the property for a time. Buchan, son of Robert II, held the castle from 1390, ruling with brutal force, and frequently robbing churches. In the 15th and 16th centuries the MacDonalds launched raids on the castle, which was later held by the Grants. The bulk of the damage to the castle was done with explosives in 1692, which prevented it becoming a Jacobite stronghold in subsequent years.

Visitors cross a wooden gangway across a defensive ditch, and pass through a gatehouse. However, in the past, most people approaching the castle would have done so through a watergate from Loch Ness. The centrepiece of the Urquhart Castle is a stout and impressive tower house, but be sure to take note of the complex arrangement of the ruined defensive walls that surround the site. The best vantage point is of course from the top of the tower house.

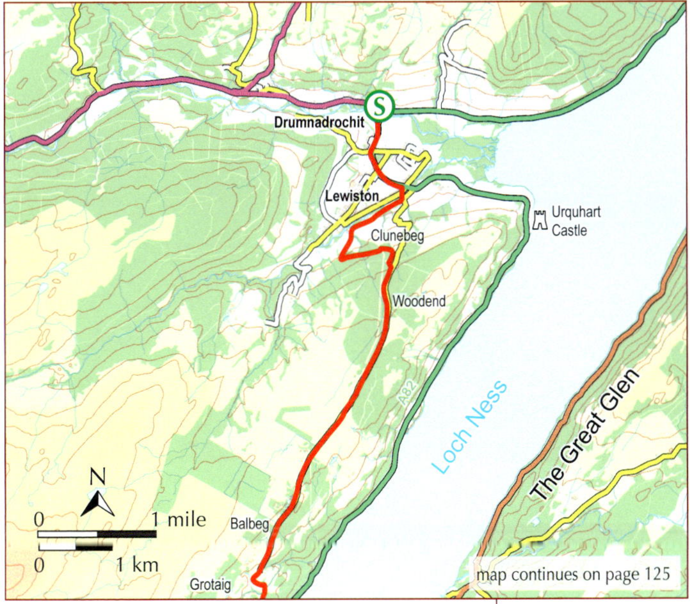

trees alongside the track up to Clunebeg House then follow a waymarked path straight ahead from Clunebeg Lodge B&B. The path swings left as it climbs across a slope of fine oaks and bracken, and there are views back towards Drumnadrochit. Go through a gate and cross a footbridge into dense forest, where there is later a brief glimpse of Drumnadrochit to the left. The path turns right and runs up to a gate on a track, where a left turn leads quickly up to another gate and a minor road.

Turn right as signposted for the Great Glen Way, climbing steeply up past a house called **Woodend**. The road climbs at a gentler gradient and later leaves the forest. A path runs parallel, off to the right, as the road undulates across heather moorland around 250m (820ft). The road has to be followed again, between swathes of rough grassland and improved pasture. Gorse flanks the road as it descends a boggy moorland slope, later passing the

The route follows a path from Grotaig, high above Ruskich Wood

Ancarraig lodges access. Use another path running parallel to the road, and look ahead to see the humped hills of Meall Fuar-mhonaidh and Creag Dhearg. There are occasional glimpses of Loch Ness while passing isolated houses and farms on the way to **Balbeg**, finally dropping to a car park, then watch for the Great Glen Way turning left through a gate. ◂

Keeping straight ahead leads, in less than 200m, to the Loch Ness Clay Works pottery and Walker's Café at Grotaig.

Walk down a track and cross a concrete bridge over Grotaig Burn. The track runs through a field, passing through patchy woodlands, then below a fort on the little hill of Dùn Scriben. Enter forest and follow a convoluted path through gates while running parallel to a track.

The path climbs away from the track and there are occasional views of Loch Ness. Note how the forest edges are softened by birch. The undulating path generally rises and joins a track in the forest above **Ruskich Wood**. Follow the track past **Lòn na Fola** and later cross a bridge over a waterfall. Keep walking to reach a junction of tracks, where the high-level and low-level routes part. Keep right (the low-level route – Stage 2B – turns sharp left downhill).

The track rises across a clear-felled and replanted slope, where occasional Scots pines have been left standing tall, among abundant rosebay willowherb. The track reaches a stone-built windbreak, where views across Loch Ness feature the remote Monadh Liath range rolling southwards into the distance. Turn right before reaching the windbreak to follow a waymarked path up the forested slope. The path climbs steeply at times and occasionally uses stone steps.

The path rises from the forest and easily traverses the rugged slopes of **Creag Dhearg**. The highest point on the Great Glen Way is reached, around 415m (1360ft), and another stone-built windbreak is passed, with a fine view of Loch Ness. The path winds downhill and features a few stone steps at one point. The rustic **Troll Bridge** is crossed, perched above a waterfall. Cross

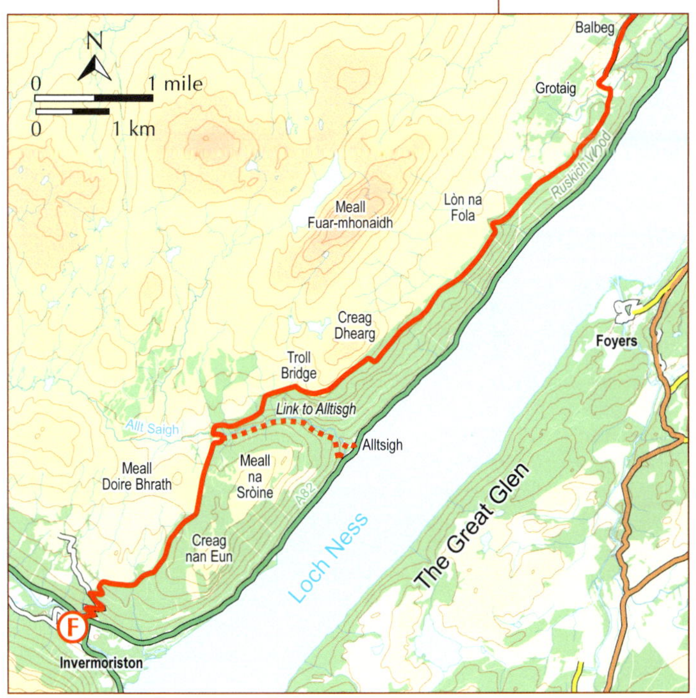

The track can be followed straight ahead and downhill for 2km (1.25 miles), reaching the low-level route at Alltsigh, close to the Lochside Hostel and bus services.

another footbridge later, while following the path just outside the forest, beside a tall deer fence.

Wind further downhill, back into the forest to join a track. Follow the track, which later swings left over a concrete bridge spanning **Allt Saigh**. ◂ Turn right as marked up a clear path, later passing a couple of stone slabs that flank the path like old gateposts. Pass the little hill of **Meall Doire Bhrath**, around 330m (1080ft), and note a curious sculpture on the right, The Viewcatcher, where tree branches have been woven into a circle, mounted on a stone plinth.

THE SEVEN MEN OF GLEN MORISTON

The date was 27 July 1746, when Bonnie Prince Charlie was on the run after the crushing defeat at the Battle of Culloden. Pursued by 'Butcher' Cumberland, and with a bounty of £30,000 on his head, Charles had not eaten for two days and was clad in rags by the time he reached Glen Moriston. Coming upon a crude hut and ravenously hungry, he was warned by his companions not to seek food or shelter in case he was recognised. Charles declared 'I had better be killed like a man than starved like a fool', and made his way to the hut. The seven men inside were mere outlaws, and one of them recognised him, but to their credit, they spurned the chance to claim the bounty and risked their lives to feed and shelter him. Meanwhile, on the road through Glen Moriston, an Edinburgh merchant named Roderick MacKenzie, who bore a passing resemblance to the Bonnie Prince, was shot at by troops. As he died he declared, 'Alas, you have killed your prince', and this ruse was sufficient to buy enough time for Charles to be smuggled out of the country.

Invermoriston (Gaelic – *Inbhir Mor Eason*) has only a few facilities, but at the end of the day these prove most welcome. The Glenmoriston Arms Hotel is very prominent. It was originally a drovers' inn, dating from 1740, and the oldest parts are around the bar and reception area. Johnson and Boswell stayed there while planning a trip to the Hebrides in 1773. There are a few B&Bs in and around the village, as well as the Invermoriston Community Shop, the Clog and Craft Shop, and further along the Skye Road, the Glen Rowan café. Toilets are available inside the Glenmoriston Millennium Hall, when open. Regular daily Scottish Citylink buses link Invermoriston with Inverness and Fort William, as well as the Isle of Skye.

The path reaches a turning space at the end of a track. Follow the track straight ahead, through partly clear-felled forest. Later, turn right down another path and cross a footbridge over a stream. The path winds uphill, with stone steps where it gets steeper. Old birch trees are dotted around on the slopes outside the forest. When the path descends, it follows a drystone wall, with the forest left and a field right. When the lower corner of the wall is reached, turn left through the forest to reach a track. The high-level route re-joins the low-level route at this point.

The high-level route descends through forest and woods above Invermoriston

Turn right to follow the track, crossing a bridge over a stream to join a road. ▶ Turn sharp left down the road and cross another bridge over the same stream. Dense conifers once flanked the road, but these have been felled, giving way to birch, oak, beech and sycamore, with a holly understorey. The steep and narrow road zig-zags past Craik na Dav B&B, reaching a junction with the A887. Turn left to pass the Clog and Craft Shop, where a milestone warns 'Last Clog Shop before Skye – 52 miles'. The little village of **Invermoriston** lies directly ahead.

Just before crossing the stream, a steep and winding gravel path offers a short-cut down to a road.

For 1:25K route map see booklet pages 26–32.

STAGE 2B

Drumnadrochit to Invermoriston (low-level)

Start	Village Green, Drumnadrochit (NH 508 300)
Finish	Glenmoriston Arms Hotel, Invermoriston (NH 420 168)
Distance	23.5km (14.5 miles)
Total ascent	590m (1935ft)
Time	5hr 30min
Terrain	Ascent to a moorland road. Forest tracks and paths with some short, steep slopes.
Maps	OS Landrangers 26 and 34, OS Explorer 416S, Harvey Great Glen Way
Refreshments	Café at a pottery at Grotaig. Invermoriston has a hotel with a bar/restaurant and one other café.
Public Transport	Regular daily Scottish Citylink buses link Invermoriston and Drumnadrochit with Inverness and Fort William

On leaving Drumnadrochit, walkers have to decide whether to make a detour to visit Urquhart Castle, or console themselves by studying a floral model of the castle on the village green. There are two options for linking Drumnadrochit and Invermoriston, but a decision doesn't need to be made until halfway through the day. Before making firm plans to follow the low-level route please note that it might sometimes be closed for timber harvesting. Check in advance on the Great Glen Way website, and if the route is closed switch to the high-level option (Stage 2A). The low-level route is easier, but it is also slightly longer.

Most of the day's walk is spent close to Loch Ness, with only occasional views, but this will change as more and more areas are clear-felled. Later, there is an option to switch to the high-level route by walking up a forest track from Alltsigh, otherwise stay on the low-level route all the way to Invermoriston.

Follow the busy A82 road out of **Drumnadrochit**. The road passes through a roundabout to reach the neighbouring village of **Lewiston**, which offers a pharmacy/

post office and Co-op, followed by a roundabout. Cross the River Coiltie and turn right at a picnic area, as signposted for the Clunebeg Estate. ▸

Alternatively, follow the path beside the main road, straight ahead to visit Urquhart Castle, then return to this junction later.

Urquhart Castle is 2km (1.25 miles) off-route, or 3.25km (2 miles) from Drumnadrochit, perched on Strone Point overlooking Loch Ness. It can be reached safely on foot as there is a path beside the busy A82 road, and Scottish Citylink buses serve both Drumnadrochit and the castle. The situation is splendid and it is a renowned place for those keeping a lookout for the Loch Ness 'monster'! Once one of the largest castles in Scotland, Urquhart Castle's sprawling ruins take time to explore. A visitor centre offers a thorough grounding in its construction and history, plus a café. Urquhart Castle is

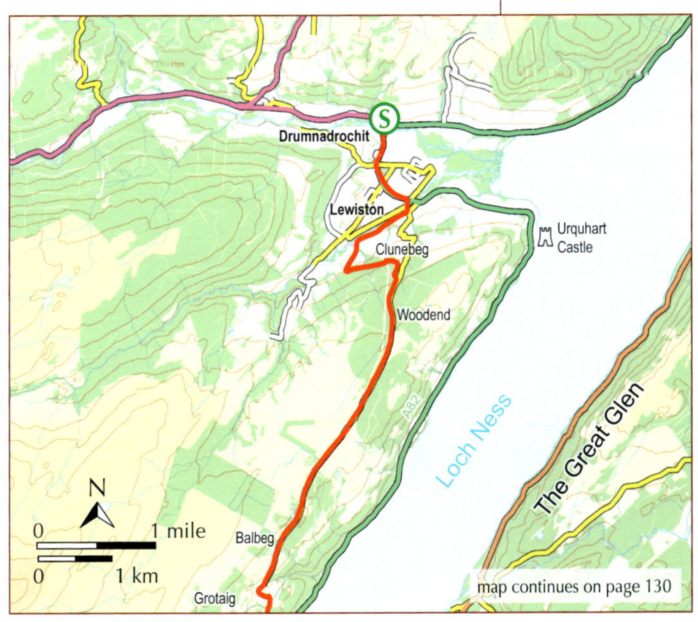

open all year, and there is an entrance charge (tel 01456 450551). For more information see Stage 5B.

Follow the minor road straight ahead to reach a big sign for the Clunebeg Estate, and continue walking along a clear track. Although the track runs level alongside the bouldery River Coiltie, densely packed trees usually screen the river from view. Any houses seen on the far side are part of the village of Lewiston. Admire tall oaks and beech trees while following the track up to Clunebeg House and follow a waymarked path straight ahead from Clunebeg Lodge B&B. The path swings left as it climbs across a slope of fine oaks and bracken, and there are views back towards Drumnadrochit. Go through a gate

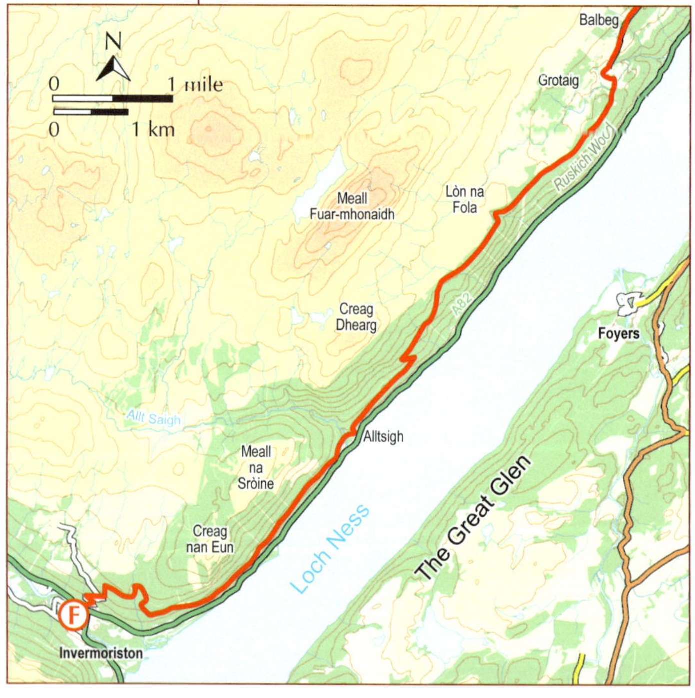

and cross a footbridge to enter dense forest, with a brief glimpse of Drumnadrochit to the left later. The path turns right and runs up to a gate on a track, where a left turn leads quickly up to another gate and a minor road.

Turn right as signposted for the Great Glen Way, climbing steeply up past a house called **Woodend**. The road ascends more gently and later leaves the forest. A path runs parallel, to the right, as the road undulates across heather moorland around 250m (820ft). The road has to be followed again, between swathes of rough grassland and improved pasture. Gorse flanks the road as it descends a boggy moorland slope, later passing the Ancarraig lodges access. Use another path running parallel, and look ahead to see the humped hills of Meall Fuar-mhonaidh and Creag Dhearg. There are occasional glimpses of Loch Ness while passing isolated houses and farms on the way to **Balbeg**, finally dropping to a car park, then watch for the Great Glen Way turning left through a gate. ▶

Walking straight ahead leads, in less than 200m, to the Loch Ness Clay Works pottery and Walker's Café at Grotaig.

Walk down a track and cross a concrete bridge over Grotaig Burn. The track runs through a field, passing through patchy woodlands, then below a fort on the little hill of Dùn Scriben. Enter forest and follow a convoluted path through gates, parallel to a track.

The path climbs away from the track and there are occasional views of Loch Ness. Note how the forest edges are softened by birch. The undulating path generally rises and joins a track in the forest above **Ruskich Wood**. Follow the track past **Lòn na Fola** and later cross a bridge over a waterfall. Keep walking to reach a junction of tracks, where the low-level and high-level routes part. Turn sharp left downhill (the high-level route – Stage 2A – keeps right).

The track descends and later makes a sharp right turn, descending further. Later, the track bends quickly left and right as it continues its descent. Another sharp left and right turn are made, while views through the Great Glen are lost as the track passes tall conifers. Simply keep walking downhill to reach a track junction at **Alltsigh**.

At the junction, turning left leads quickly to the busy A82 road beside Loch Ness, where turning

A view of Loch Ness from the rugged garden in front of the Lochside Hostel at Alltsigh

right leads to the **Lochside Hostel** and a bus stop. The hostel has splendid views across the loch.

Those who don't need to detour to Alltsigh can keep straight along a forest track as marked, crossing a concrete bridge over a rocky gorge with a waterfall and beautiful trees. A diligent search will reveal an old pack-horse bridge. Climb steeply, passing a track junction, then follow an undulating track fringed with broom. Keep straight ahead at a track junction beside a rock cutting, climbing gently for a while and passing a slope of gorse bushes. A bend is reached where there is a good view-point revealing the length of Loch Ness, but also turn and admire the fine variety of trees stacked against the cliffs of **Creag nan Eun**. Later, while climbing uphill, a post draws attention to the 'Stone Cave', said to have been built to offer shelter to a washerwoman on her frequent journeys between Alltsigh and Invermoriston. It still offers splendid shelter. Continue uphill at a gentle gradient, with occasional glimpses of Loch Ness, then turn right to ascend a narrow and bendy forest path as marked, to reach another forest track.

Turn left to follow the track, then left at a nearby junction as marked, but also consider turning right to see a signpost for a viewpoint. This short detour reveals a narrow path winding up a slope covered in ling and bell heather to reach the crude 'Stone Seat' where there is a fine view over **Loch Ness**. The village of Invermoriston, despite being close to hand, is completely hidden from view. Retrace steps to the junction. Follow the track uphill to another junction, then turn left and go through a tall gateway. Follow the track across a concrete bridge over a stream. The track swings left, then right, then while crossing a crest, a thinner part of the plantation reveals some of the former heather cover and low rocky outcrops. The

One of several vigorous streams crossed by the trail

track makes a gentle descent among closely packed trees. The high-level route re-joins the low-level.

Just before crossing the stream, a steep and winding gravel path on the left offers a short-cut down to a road.

Follow the track onwards, crossing a bridge over a stream to join a road. ◂ Turn sharp left down the road and cross another bridge over the same stream. Dense conifers once flanked the road, but these have been felled, giving way to birch, oak, beech and sycamore, with a holly understorey. The steep and narrow road zigzags past Craik na Dav B&B, reaching a junction with the A887 road. Turn left to pass the Clog and Craft Shop, where a milestone warns 'Last Clog Shop before Skye – 52 miles'. The little village of **Invermoriston** lies directly ahead.

THE SEVEN MEN OF GLEN MORISTON

The date was 27 July 1746, when Bonnie Prince Charlie was on the run after the crushing defeat at the Battle of Culloden. Pursued by 'Butcher' Cumberland, and with a bounty of £30,000 on his head, Charles had not eaten for two days and was clad in rags by the time he reached Glen Moriston. Coming upon a crude hut and ravenously hungry, he was warned by his companions not to cook food or shelter in case he was recognised. Charles declared 'I had better be killed like a man than starved like a fool', and made his way to the hut. The seven men inside were mere outlaws, and one of them recognised him, but to their credit, they spurned the chance to claim the bounty and risked their lives to feed and shelter him. Meanwhile, on the road through Glen Moriston, an Edinburgh merchant named Roderick MacKenzie, who bore a passing resemblance to the Bonnie Prince, was shot at by troops. As he died he declared, 'Alas, you have killed your prince', and this ruse was sufficient to buy enough time for Charles to be smuggled out of the country.

Invermoriston (Gaelic – *Inbhir Mor Eason*) has only a few facilities, but at the end of the day these prove most welcome. The Glenmoriston Arms Hotel is very prominent. It was originally a drovers' inn, dating from 1740, and the oldest parts are around the bar and reception area. Johnson and Boswell stayed there while planning a trip to the Hebrides in 1773. There are a few B&Bs in and around the village, as well as the Invermoriston Community Shop, the Clog and Craft Shop, and further along the Skye Road, the Glen Rowan café. Toilets are available inside the Glenmoriston Millennium Hall, when open. Regular daily Scottish Citylink buses link Invermoriston with Inverness and Fort William, as well as the Isle of Skye.

STAGE 3A

Invermoriston to Fort Augustus (high-level)

For 1:25K route map see booklet pages 22–26.

Start	Glenmoriston Arms Hotel, Invermoriston (NH 420 168)
Finish	Caledonian Canal Centre, Fort Augustus (NH 379 092)
Distance	12.5km (7.75 miles)
Total ascent	710m (2330ft)
Time	3hr 15min
Terrain	Forest tracks and upland moorland paths with some short, steep slopes
Maps	OS Landranger 34, OS Explorer 416S, Harvey Great Glen Way
Refreshments	Plenty of bars, restaurants, cafés and take-aways around Fort Augustus
Public Transport	Regular daily Scottish Citylink buses link Invermoriston and Fort Augustus with Inverness and Fort William

There are two options for linking Invermoriston with Fort Augustus. The high-level option should be open at all times, but in really bad weather it might be wise to take the low-level option (Stage 3B). In good weather it isn't particularly difficult, and some walkers might add it to the following day's walk (Stage 4) if they are trying to cover the Great Glen Way in a hurry. Alternatively, the afternoon could be spent exploring Fort Augustus, or taking a short cruise on Loch Ness in order to gain a greater appreciation of its vastness.

The high-level route of the Great Glen Way climbs above the forested northern slopes of Loch Ness, allowing much more wide-ranging views than are gained from the low-level option.

Leave **Invermoriston** by following the main A82 road downhill to cross the River Moriston, then turn right along a minor road. However, note the ravaged remains of Telford's Bridge spanning the river, and the splendid Moriston Falls that spill beneath it.

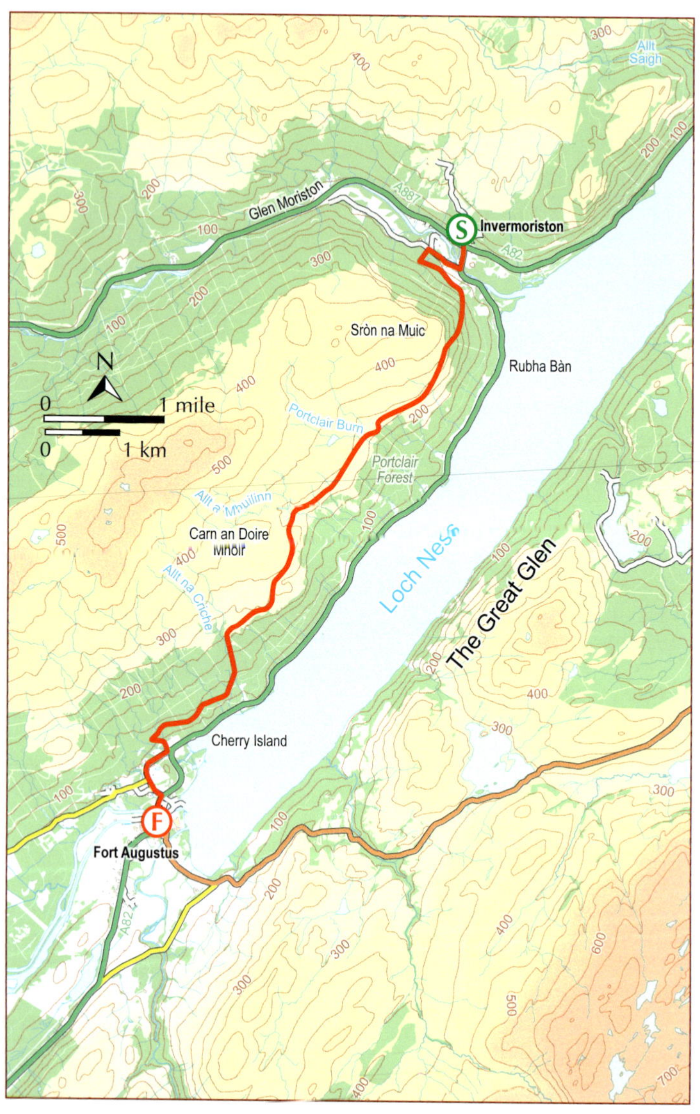
Allt Saigh
Glen Moriston
A887
Invermoriston
A82
Sròn na Muic
Rubha Bàn
N
0
1 mile
0
1 km
Portclair Burn
Portclair Forest
Allt a' Mhuilinn
Carn an Doire Mhoir
Allt na Criche
Loch Ness
The Great Glen
Cherry Island
Fort Augustus
A82

The ramshackle remains of **Telford's Bridge**, also known as the Old Bridge, could be crossed in preference to the main road bridge, but take care as the masonry is in a bad state of repair. Despite being nothing more than a standard double-span stone arch, its construction spanned several years from 1805 until 1813, owing to a 'languid and inattentive contractor' and 'idle workers'. The bridge is one of more than a thousand associated with Telford.

The minor road leads to Dalcataig, but the Great Glen Way suddenly turns left up a winding path on a clear-felled slope. Just before reaching a forest track, turn left as marked along an older track running parallel. Pass big beech trees, birch and alder, rather than conifers. The old track and the forest track join later. The high-level route runs straight up a path (the low-level route – Stage 3B – runs straight ahead along the forest track).

The path climbs, quickly crossing another forest track, becoming steeper as it winds up the forested slope,

A path climbs a clear-felled slope from Glen Moriston

occasionally featuring stone steps. Emerge from the forest below the rugged face of **Sròn na Muic**. The path traverses the slope above the forest, passing a stone bench and later crossing a couple of footbridges. Briefly touch the edge of the forest, descend to pass beneath a power line, and cross another footbridge. The path surface is firm, with good drainage, while the moorland supports grass, heather and bog myrtle.

Cross another two footbridges close together, where there are waterfalls on **Portclair Burn**. Continue traversing across the rugged moorland slopes above the forest, crossing a couple more footbridges. Descend into a valley to cross a footbridge over the **Allt a' Mhuilinn**. The path winds as it climbs from the valley, reaching a stone-built windbreak shelter on a shoulder of **Carn an Doire Mhòir**, around 315m (1035ft), where there are fine views of Loch Ness.

From the high-level route there are views across Loch Ness to Beinn a' Bhacaidh

The path continues with good views, winding and undulating, with a few stone steps leading up and down. Pass another viewpoint around 225m (740ft), then follow the path downhill as it eventually drops into the forest. There are vigorous little waterfalls alongside as the path

winds down to a forest track. Turn right and cross a bridge over a waterfall on the **Allt na Criche**, then turn left down another path, passing more waterfalls.

The path reaches a junction with a forest track on the Allt na Criche Trail. Turn right to follow the track gently downhill, reaching a junction where the high-level route and low-level route re-join. Keep right to follow the forest track uphill, pausing at a noticeboard overlooking the head of **Loch Ness**, above **Cherry Island**.

There is only one island in Loch Ness; the diminutive **Cherry Island** near Fort Augustus, which is actually an ancient man-made island dwelling, or *crannog*.

Continue up the track and cross a bridge. Later, turn left down a path on a steep slope covered in tall, stately pines. Cross a footbridge at the foot of the slope to reach a road at Three Bridges. Turn right and follow the narrow road past a few B&Bs, reaching a junction. ▶

A right turn at the junction, for Jenkins Park and Auchterawe, leads to the Great Glen Way Rangers' base.

Follow the road straight ahead, which is Bunoich Brae, passing Morag's Lodge, an independent hostel. Turn right down a tarmac path, short-cutting past a nearby road junction. Turn right to follow the busy A82, reaching the Caledonian Canal Centre in **Fort Augustus**.

FORT AUGUSTUS

The earliest settlement at Fort Augustus (Gaelic – *Cill Chuimein*) was founded in the 6th century by monks from Iona, led by St Cumin. Precious little else is recorded about the place until, in the aftermath of the Jacobite Rising of 1715, a fort was constructed on the site now occupied by the Lovat Hotel. When General Wade built a military road through the area in 1726, the fort was moved to where the Abbey now stands. Fort Augustus was named after William Augustus, Duke of Cumberland, and was destroyed at the beginning of the Jacobite Rising of 1745. 'Butcher' Cumberland had it rebuilt while engaged in a brutal campaign to suppress the Highland clans. In 1876 the site was given to the Benedictines who built the Abbey, vacating it in 1997. The Abbey has since been redeveloped and there is no longer any public access.

The bustling tourist village of Fort Augustus is halfway along the Great Glen Way. It offers plenty of accommodation, from luxury glamping, hostel and humble B&Bs to fine hotels. There is an ATM at the Londis store, a post office and a choice of food and gift shops, several bars, restaurants, cafés, take-aways and toilets. There are regular daily bus services to Fort William and Inverness. A variety of cruises on Loch Ness are also available. The Caledonian Canal Centre is worth a visit.

'Scottish Highlander' is a European Waterways barge, seen here passing through Fort Augustus

STAGE 3B

Invermoriston to Fort Augustus (low-level)

Start	Glenmoriston Arms Hotel, Invermoriston (NH 420 168)
Finish	Caledonian Canal Centre, Fort Augustus (NH 379 092)
Distance	12km (7.5 miles)
Total ascent	320m (1050ft)
Time	3hr
Terrain	Forest tracks and paths with some short, steep slopes
Maps	OS Landranger 34, OS Explorer 416S, Harvey Great Glen Way
Refreshments	Plenty of bars, restaurants, cafés and take-aways around Fort Augustus
Public Transport	Regular daily Scottish Citylink buses link Invermoriston and Fort Augustus with Inverness and Fort William

There are two options for linking Invermoriston with Fort Augustus. Before making firm plans to follow the low-level option, please note that it might sometimes be closed for timber harvesting. Check in advance on the Great Glen Way website, and if the route is closed, then switch to the high-level option (Stage 3A). This is a short day, and some walkers might add it to the previous day's walk (Stage 2) if they are trying to cover the Great Glen Way in a hurry. Alternatively, the afternoon could be spent exploring Fort Augustus, or taking a short cruise on Loch Ness in order to gain a greater appreciation of its vastness.

The low-level route of the Great Glen Way often runs close to Loch Ness, but the forested slopes usually shield it from view, so walkers see less of it than they might imagine.

Leave **Invermoriston** by following the main A82 road downhill to cross the River Moriston, then turn right along a minor road. However, note the ravaged remains of Telford's Bridge spanning the river, and the splendid Moriston Falls that spill beneath it.

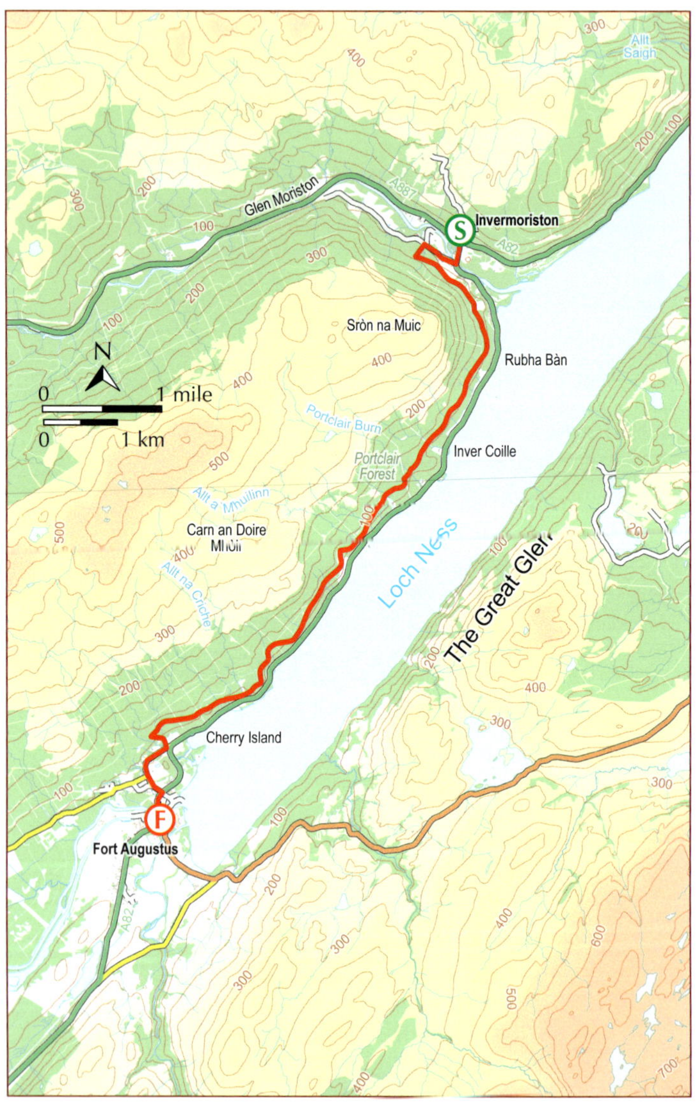

Allt Saigh
Glen Moriston
A887
Invermoriston
A82
Sròn na Muic
Rubha Bàn
N
0
1 mile
0
1 km
Portclair Burn
Portclair Forest
Inver Coille
Allt a' Mhuilinn
Carn an Doire Mhòir
Allt na Criche
Loch Ness
The Great Glen
Cherry Island
Fort Augustus
A82

The Glenmoriston Arms Hotel was a drover's inn, dating from 1740

The ramshackle remains of **Telford's Bridge**, also known as the Old Bridge, could be crossed in preference to the main road bridge, but take care as the masonry is in a bad state of repair. Despite being nothing more than a standard double-span stone arch, its construction spanned several years from 1805 until 1813, owing to a 'languid and inattentive contractor' and 'idle workers'. The bridge is one of more than a thousand associated with Telford.

The minor road leads to Dalcataig, but the Great Glen Way suddenly turns left up a winding path on a clear-felled slope. Just before reaching a forest track, turn left as marked along an older track running parallel. Pass big beech trees, birch and alder, rather than conifers. The old track and the forest track join later. The low-level route continues straight ahead, past a track junction (the high-level route – Stage 3A – climbs straight uphill).

The track enjoys a brief view of Loch Ness as it swings right to leave **Glen Moriston**, crossing a crest and running downhill. A broader track is reached at a junction, so keep right, in effect straight ahead, to climb steeply.

The River Moriston and Falls of Moriston can be explored from Invermoriston

A campsite at Inver Coille is marked off-route, down to the left.

The gradient eases and there are eventually good views of Loch Ness from a clear-felled slope. A gentle descent leads across a concrete bridge over a small waterfall, losing the views and crossing a dip in the track. ◀ Cross a concrete bridge over **Portclair Burn**, climb gently, then there are more views across Loch Ness, taking in the hill of Beinn a' Bhacaidh rising from the far shore. Descend gently into tall forest, where a concrete bridge spans a waterfall on the **Allt a' Mhullinn**. The track climbs over a gentle rise where there is a stone-slab seat; views both ways along Loch Ness seem endless, as well as stretching across the loch to the rugged hill of Beinn a' Bhacaidh.

Follow the undulating track, enjoying good views over a slope of young trees. Descend gradually among tall trees and keep straight ahead at a junction. There is a slight dip in the track, then a descent among tall conifers, with margins of heather, bilberry, mosses, ferns and wood sorrel. Pass a gate and avoid a right turn as the track descends and bends. The lower woods are mixed, with some fine oaks and birch, then the track swings left to cross a tumbling stream at **Allt na Criche**, almost reaching the busy main road.

Just before the road turn right through a gate and follow another track uphill. Plenty of birch trees grow among the conifers, and a junction is reached where the low-level and high-level routes re-join. Walk straight ahead to follow the forest track uphill, pausing at a noticeboard overlooking the head of **Loch Ness**, above **Cherry Island**.

There is only one island in Loch Ness; the diminutive **Cherry Island** near Fort Augustus, which is actually an ancient man-made island dwelling, or *crannog*.

Continue up the track and cross a bridge. Later, turn left down a path on a steep slope covered in tall, stately pines. Cross a footbridge at the bottom to reach a road at Three Bridges. Turn right and follow the narrow road past a few B&Bs, reaching a junction. ▸

A right turn at the junction, for Jenkins Park and Auchterawe, leads to the Great Glen Way Rangers' base.

Follow the road straight ahead, which is Bunoich Brae, passing Morag's Lodge, an independent hostel. Turn right down a tarmac path, short-cutting past a nearby road junction. Turn right to follow the busy A82, reaching the Caledonian Canal Centre in **Fort Augustus**.

A footbridge spans a stream near the first houses at Fort Augustus

FORT AUGUSTUS

The earliest settlement at Fort Augustus (Gaelic – *Cill Chuimein*) was founded in the 6th century by monks from Iona, led by St Cumin. Precious little else is recorded about the place until, in the aftermath of the Jacobite Rising of 1715, a fort was constructed on the site now occupied by the Lovat Hotel. When General Wade built a military road through the area in 1726, the fort was moved to where the Abbey now stands. For more information see Stage 3A.

The bustling tourist village of Fort Augustus is halfway along the Great Glen Way. It offers plenty of accommodation, from luxury glamping, hostel and humble B&Bs to fine hotels. There is an ATM at the Londis store, a post office and a choice of food and gift shops, several bars, restaurants, cafés, take-aways and toilets. The Great Glen Rangers have an office in the forest at Auchtertawe, not far from Fort Augustus (see Appendix A). There are regular daily bus services to Fort William and Inverness. A variety of cruises on Loch Ness are also available. The Caledonian Canal Centre is worth a visit.

'Fingal' is a Caledonian Discovery barge, seen here passing through the locks at Fort Augustus

STAGE 4

Fort Augustus to Laggan Locks

For 1:25K route map see booklet pages 17–22.

Start	Caledonian Canal Centre, Fort Augustus (NH 379 092)
Finish	Laggan Locks (NN 286 963)
Distance	17.5km (10.75 miles)
Total ascent	40m (130ft)
Time	4hr 30min
Terrain	A clear and firm canal-side track leads to Aberchalder. Another firm track continues beside Loch Oich, then a canal-side path leads to Laggan.
Maps	OS Landranger 34, OS Explorer 400, Harvey Great Glen Way
Refreshments	Restaurant off-route from the Aberchalder Swing Bridge. Bar and café at Laggan Locks.
Public Transport	Regular daily Scottish Citylink buses link Fort Augustus and Laggan with Inverness and Fort William

This is a splendid day's walk, where the walls of the Great Glen rise closer to hand and there are often views of the high mountains further beyond. The Great Glen Way climbs up a steep flight of five locks as it follows the Caledonian Canal away from Fort Augustus. A lovely stretch of the canal gradually rises to Aberchalder, where it is worth making a slight detour to admire the Bridge of Oich. The summit level of the canal is at Loch Oich, which is passed while walking parallel to a stretch of General Wade's military road, while following an old railway trackbed. Richly wooded slopes are protected as a nature reserve on the way to North Laggan, where facilities are very limited. A short stroll along the Caledonian Canal completes the day's walk.

Leave Fort Augustus via the Caledonian Canal Centre, on the A82 road beside a swing bridge. Climb past a flight of locks on the way out of town. Note that the Great Glen Way and cycle route 78 follow almost the same course to Fort William.

An attractive bend on the Caledonian Canal between Kytra Lock and Cullochy Lock

Walkers ascend a flight of five canal locks through Fort Augustus. At the bottom is the **Caledonian Canal Centre**, which tells the story of the canal, its history, construction and use. The centre also incorporates a café and accommodation. Open daily, 9am–5pm, with free entry, tel 01463 725581.

After passing the top lock, the canal gradually bends to the left and views of Fort Augustus are lost. A covered overspill weir allows excess water to fall into the **River Oich**, and there are glimpses of the river from time to time, as both the canal and river run parallel. The canal passes a power line and bends gradually to the right. A fine row of pine trees grows along the opposite bank. Hazel trees are abundant along the bank being followed, and tall pines flank the canal on both sides at **Kytra Lock**. ◂

A basic 'Trailblazer Rest' campsite is available.

After passing Kytra Lock an overspill weir has to be crossed, and this could mean wet feet if there is excess

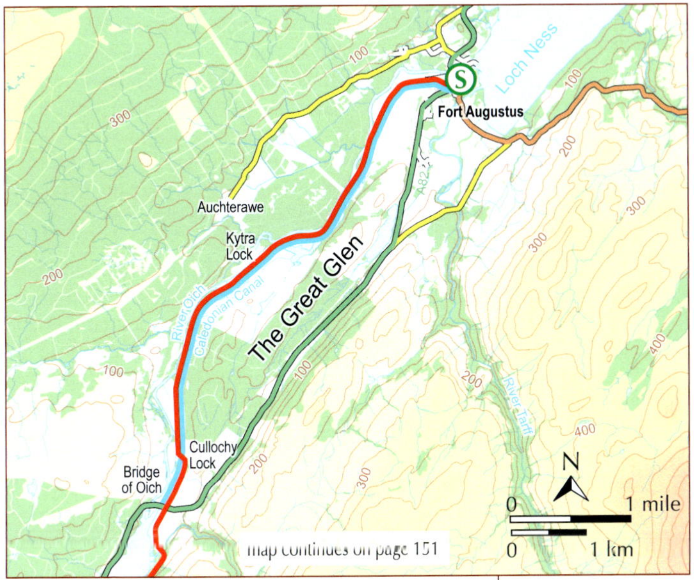

water in the canal, although this would be a very rare occurrence. The canal broadens considerably where a small loch was incorporated into its course. Later several particularly tall and graceful birch trees are passed. When **Cullochy Lock** is reached, cross over the lock gates to pick up and follow a track on the other side of the canal. Look across the water to spot a large overspill weir to the River Oich. A clear track runs beside the canal to reach the **Aberchalder Swing Bridge** and A82. ▸ See the 'Invergarry Link' (Stages 4A/5A) for details of an alternative route.

A restaurant and a B&B can be found by following the main road towards Fort Augustus, but they lie over 1km (0.5 mile) off-route and traffic can be very busy.

Cross the road and follow a path alongside the canal, where a mown grassy patch close to boat moorings offers a basic wild campsite. Later, go through a gate to continue near the shore of Loch Oich. Go through another gate and turn right to cross an old railway bridge over the Calder Burn. The Great Glen Way continues along the resurfaced trackbed of an old railway.

Loch Oich is the smallest of the three lochs linked by the Caledonian Canal. It measures 6.5km (4 miles) in length and is only 0.5km (0.3 miles) across at its widest point. Loch Oich's greatest depth is 40.5m (133ft), but it had to be deepened at both ends to accommodate traffic using the Caledonian Canal. The surface level of the loch is 32m (105ft), which is also the summit level for the canal.

The railway trackbed has been converted into a footpath and cycle route and is clear and obvious throughout. Follow it onwards, through a rock cutting and through a tunnel. Look down to the right to spot an old track running parallel, which is General Wade's military road.

The trackbed continues easily across a steep, wooded slope, overlooking a meadow as it passes the isolated **Leitirfearn Cottage**. ◀ The trackbed runs onwards beside Loch Oich, and the ruins of Invergarry Castle might be seen on the far shore. The woodlands are vividly green and are managed as a nature reserve. The track proceeds along the shore.

A very basic 'Trailblazer Rest' campsite is available. A key for the toilet needs to be obtained in advance from the Caledonian Canal office.

Leitirfearn Forest Nature Reserve features a lush, damp, vibrantly green woodland: a mix of ash, birch, elm and hazel. The steep slopes support cushions of moss and delicate ferns, as well as flowers in spring and fungi in autumn. It has the appearance of a jungle, yet it has been cut back twice to accommodate a road and railway. General Wade pushed a road through the woods around 1725, while the Invergarry and Fort Augustus Railway Company opened a line here in 1903. Both routes fell from favour, the road switching to the other side of the loch and the railway being abandoned in 1946.

The trackbed eventually bears a short length of railway line, beside the partly restored Invergarry Station. The track drops a short way to a gate, leading onto the narrow tarmac access road for the **Great Glen Water Park**.

The **Invergarry and Fort Augustus Railway Museum** (www.invergarrystation.org.uk) is being developed adjacent to the water park. A section of railway track has been restored.

There are several wooden holiday chalets here, and some of them can be hired to serve as a base while walking the Great Glen Way, commuting to and from each stage by bus. Turn left to avoid the park and follow the quiet road to a junction with the busy A82 road. ▸

Cross over the road with care near the Laggan Swing Bridge. Follow a path through an area of bracken above the Caledonian Canal. Pass broom, gorse and brambles while

The Well of the Seven Heads Coffee & Take-away is over 1km (0.5 mile) away and the road to it can be very busy.

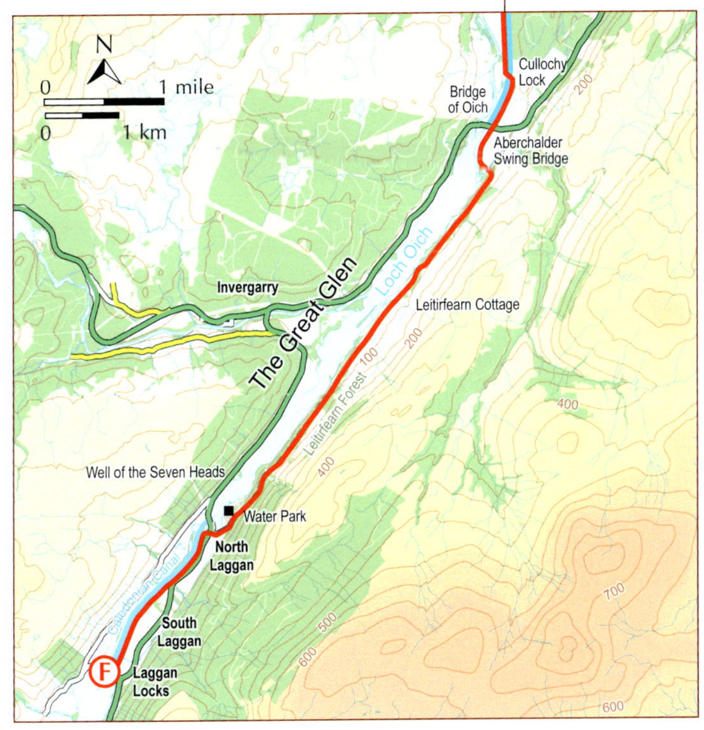

A path follows the Caledonian Canal from Loch Lochy, past Laggan, to Loch Oich

passing high above a mooring stage, then cross a footbridge over a canal feeder, the Allt an Lagain. There is access on the left to the A82, not far from the Great Glen Hostel in **North Laggan**. Take care if following the road there.

Rhododendron and broom are common beside the canal. The path broadens to a track and passes a slope of pine trees. Pass the *Eagle* barge and bar/restaurant, and follow the canal-side embankment, keeping left of a cottage to reach the double lock at **Laggan Locks**. Nearby facilities are limited to a café kiosk and a wild campsite.

A conflict known as the '**Battle of the Shirts**' took place at Laggan in the 16th century. The seeds were sown, as was often the case among Highland clans, with a perceived insult. Ranald Galda, of Clanranald, had been reared among the Frasers, and when he returned to his home a feast was prepared by way of welcome. As seven oxen were slaughtered, Ranald remarked that a few hens would have been sufficient, thus spurning the hospitality of his hosts. They called him 'Ranald of the Hens' and said that he could return to the Frasers if he didn't like it.

It was an uncomfortably hot day in 1544 when 300 Frasers faced a combined force of 600 MacDonalds and Camerons to settle the score at Laggan. Both sides had to put aside their hot and heavy woollen plaids and fight each other wearing long undershirts; hence the name 'Battle of the Shirts'. Neither side scored a victory, since the carnage was so great that only four Frasers and eight of their opponents were left standing at the conclusion of the battle.

LAGGAN

Laggan (Gaelic – *Lagan*) is a sprawling settlement with no clear centre. South Laggan is the area near Laggan Locks, while North Laggan is closer to the Laggan Swing Bridge, over 2km (1.25 miles) away. Facilities are limited to the Great Glen Hostel and Forest Lodge B&B. A café kiosk and a wild campsite are available below the locks. The *Eagle* is a converted Dutch barge that operates as a floating bar restaurant above Laggan Locks, and the next nearest restaurant is back at the Great Glen Water Park. Regular daily Scottish Citylink buses link Laggan with Fort William, Fort Augustus and Inverness.

For 1:25K route map see booklet pages 10–17.

STAGE 5

Laggan Locks to Gairlochy

Start	Laggan Locks (NN 286 963)
Finish	Gairlochy Bottom Lock (NN 176 842)
Distance	19km (12 miles)
Total ascent	300m (985ft)
Time	5hr
Terrain	Canal-side path, minor roads, forest tracks and clear, firm paths
Maps	OS Landranger 34, OS Explorer 400, Harvey Great Glen Way
Refreshments	The *Eagle* bar/restaurant and a café kiosk at Laggan Locks.
Public Transport	Regular daily Scottish Citylink buses link Laggan with Inverness, Fort Augustus and Fort William. Schooldays-only Shiel Buses linking Gairlochy, Spean Bridge and Fort William, which will divert to Achnacarry on request to the driver.

Most of the day is spent on the northern shore of Loch Lochy, on forest tracks running parallel to the shore, and there is no exit from these until Clunes is reached. The slopes are often well wooded or forested, and timber harvesting and replanting ensures that over time, different places will feature different views. Detours from the Great Glen Way can be considered around Achnacarry, either to see St Ciaran's Church, tucked away in the woods, or to visit the Clan Cameron Museum. This is essentially Cameron country (or at least it became so after the Camerons concluded a 350-year feud against the MacIntoshes!).

Bear in mind that Gairlochy offers only a wild camping area, with all other facilities being off-route. During school termtime there are limited Shiel Buses linking Gairlochy with Spean Bridge and Fort William, but be sure to check their timetables carefully. Alternatively, ask in advance if your accommodation provider is able to offer pick-ups and drop-offs.

Cross the lock gates over the canal at **Laggan Locks**. Walk between cottages to pick up and follow a cause-way road, crossing boggy ground beside **Cean Loch**. Pass some wooden lodges, then turn left at a road junction where the Invergarry Link joins from the right. Follow the road ahead until it crosses a bridge near **Kilfinnan Farm**. Turn right to follow a clear track uphill from the farm, enjoying views over the head of Loch Lochy. The gradient eases and the track keeps to the right as it passes the access for the Highland Lodges.

Go through a tall gate and continue straight ahead, reaching a junction of tracks near a communication mast, where a left turn is made down a forest track, almost exclusively flanked by birch. The track continues close to the shore of **Loch Lochy** and the trees are remarkably mixed, with conifers, alder and birch.

Laggan Locks is where the Caledonian Canal exits or enters Loch Lochy

The level of **Loch Lochy** was raised 3.65m (12ft) during the construction of the Caledonian Canal. Its surface level is now 28.5m (94ft) above sea level, and its maximum depth is 40.5m (133ft). The loch is just short of 16km (10 miles) in length and only once exceeds 1.5km (1 mile) in width. It is said to be inhabited by a monster known as 'Lizzie', no doubt related to 'Nessie'.

Just off-route, beside the loch near the ruins of Glas-Dhoire, is a basic 'Trailblazer Rest' campsite. A key for the toilet needs to be obtained in advance from the Caledonian Canal office.

Occasionally, the Great Glen Way Rangers station themselves at the Forest School and welcome the opportunity to have a chat with walkers.

Climb steeply uphill a short way from the shore and cross a bridge over the **Allt Glas-Dhoire**, walking among tall trees with no views. ◂ The track runs through younger forest where there is a margin of alder scrub, then another area of mature forest before crossing a bridge over the **Allt Glas-Dhoire Mór**. On the next gentle ascent and descent, clear-felling allows good views across the loch, but these are lost as the track climbs through more mature forest, passing another gateway before descending gently. The track rises uphill, then later passes a gateway and small waterfall on the Allt na Molaich. The track undulates past commercial conifers, as well as self-seeded alder and birch scrub, along with bracken, brambles and tufts of heather.

The track runs parallel to the shore of Loch Lochy until it swings right and goes through a tall gate to reach a car park. Continue past a couple of houses and wooden cabins, one of latter being the Clunes Forest School, arkaig.org. ◂

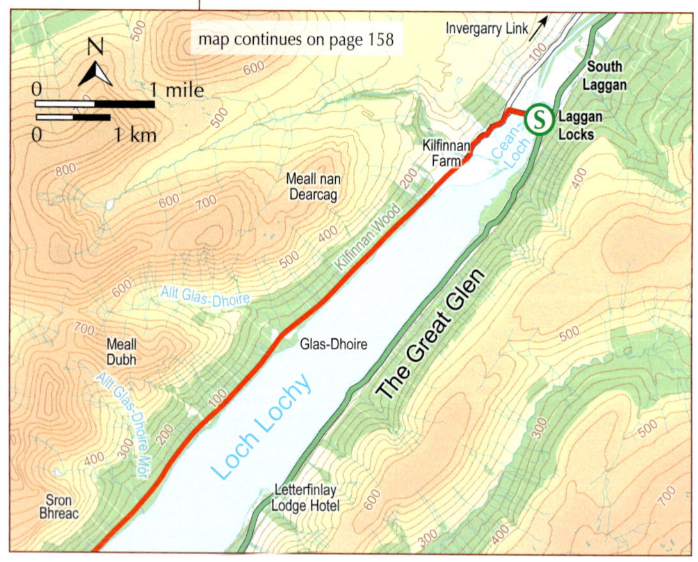

Turn left along the B8005 road at **Clunes**, passing modest forestry houses and a large white house. Continue along the road as the land near Loch Lochy is very wet and boggy, supporting profuse growths of bog myrtle. A fine variety of trees grace the shores of the loch, so that the area is rather like an arboretum. The most striking conifers are the giant redwoods, or sequoias, while the most impressive deciduous trees are the copper beeches. Continue along the road, crossing a bridge over the River Arkaig at **Bunarkaig**, where you reach a cluster of houses. ▸ Just up the road, another sign at a gateway invites visitors to make a detour to the **Clan Cameron Museum** at Achnacarry.

The Great Glen Way follows a long and easy forest track from Laggan to Bunarkaig

A short detour could be made to St Ciaran's Church, in a quiet woodland setting. Watch out for a sign showing the way along a track.

If you are a Cameron – and that includes members of nearly seventy 'sept' or sub-branch families! – then you should feel obliged to make a detour to the **Clan Cameron Museum**. The Museum, housed in a whitewashed 17th-century croft, is open each afternoon from April to mid-October, 11am–3pm. There should be a notice by the gates on the B8005 road if the museum is open. There is an entrance charge (tel 07900 217975, www.clancameronmuseum.co.uk and www.clan-cameron.org).

Follow the **B8005 road** until a left turn is waymarked down a clear gravel path, gradually descending across a slope of gnarled oaks, slender birch, beech and alder. The path wanders along the shore of Loch Lochy and crosses two footbridges as it rounds a small bay. Later, the path drifts away from the shore to cross a footbridge over the Allt Coire Choille-rais. Densely packed conifers

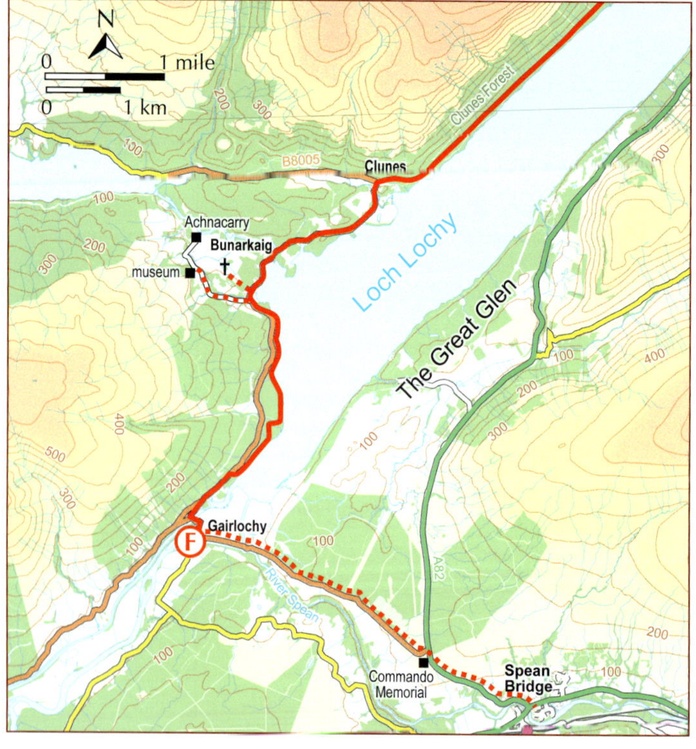

CLAN CAMERON

The Clan Cameron has a long association with the Great Glen. Originally, there were three families – the McMartins of Letterfinlay, the McGillonies of Strone and the McSorlies of Glen Nevis. The first Chief of the combined families was Donald Dubh, born around 1400, and the most recent is Donald Andrew John Cameron of Lochiel, the 28th Chief. Never shy of battle, the Camerons were described as 'fiercer than fierceness itself'. Their rallying cry was 'Sons of the hounds, come hither and get flesh!' The Camerons moved from Tor Castle to Achnacarry around 1660, and visitors will appreciate the attractions of the location, an easily defended mountain fastness with sheltered pasture.

The 19th Chief, the 'Gentle Locheil' supported Bonnie Prince Charlie in 1745, and in giving support, ensured that many other clans rallied to the cause. Despite early military success, the Prince's forces were soundly beaten at Culloden and Charles was lucky to escape with his life. In retribution for Locheil's support, the Duke of Cumberland destroyed the original timber-built Achnacarry House in 1746, and Locheil fled into exile. The current stone-built Achnacarry House dates from 1802, and the Clan Cameron has distinguished itself by raising generations of soldiery for the Queen's Own Cameron Highlanders. Achnacarry House was occupied by the military for most of World War 2, when it was the Commando Basic Training Centre, featuring one of the most gruelling military training regimes in the world.

allow little light to reach the ground, but birch trees fringe the loch shore. Later, the path passes fine beech trees, where bright green moss thrives, covering boulders and fallen tree trunks. Cross a footbridge and follow the path onwards, and look out for a prominent little lighthouse and signs that indicate where the **Caledonian Canal** leaves the loch. The path climbs steeply from the shore and reaches the B8005 road again.

Cross over and follow the path as it undulates across a forested slope, just above the road. The path joins the road just before a junction, where forking left leads down to a swing bridge over the Caledonian Canal at **Gairlochy**.

GAIRLOCHY

Gairlochy (Gaelic – *Gèarr Lòchaidh*) has won, or come runner-up, in the 'Waterway Length Competition' on several occasions. Note that Gairlochy isn't a village, but merely a scattering of houses, and if anything can't be obtained in the locality, then it is necessary to move far off-route.

Basic camping is permitted near Gairlochy Top Locks, but a key for the toilet at the canal lock must be obtained in advance from the Caledonian Canal office. The nearest lodgings are a hotel and guest house located towards the far end of the B8004 road, near the Commando Memorial. Any further facilities are well off-route at Spean Bridge. Shiel Buses run a very limited schooldays-only service linking Gairlochy with Spean Bridge and Fort William. The nearest taxi service operates from Fort William.

SPEAN BRIDGE

Spean Bridge (Gaelic – *Drochaid Aonachain*) is 6km (4 miles) away from Gairlochy. The High Bridge, built by General Wade in 1736, was the first bridge to span the rocky gorge beside the village. The West Highland Railway, built to serve Fort William from 1889, was equipped with a station at Spean Bridge. Outside the village, at a junction with the Gairlochy road, is the celebrated Commando Memorial, dating from 1952.

There are a few accommodation options around Spean Bridge, including hotels. There is a post office shop, with an ATM inside, as well as a restaurant, café and take-away. Regular daily Scottish Citylink bus services run to and from Fort William, Fort Augustus and Inverness. Stagecoach Highland buses run to and from Fort William, while schooldays-only Shiel Buses link Spean Bridge with Fort William and Gairlochy. Trains run to Fort William and Glasgow. Some accommodation providers in Spean Bridge offer lifts to and from Gairlochy, if given due notice.

INVERGARRY LINK

The Invergarry Link allows walkers to vary their journey along the Great Glen Way by passing through the village of Invergarry, instead of walking along the southern shore of Loch Oich. Invergarry offers slightly more in the way of lodgings and facilities than are found along the main route. However, using the link route shortens the distance from Fort Augustus on Stage 4 by 4km (2.5 miles), while the distance to Gairlochy on Stage 5 is increased by 7.5km (4.75 miles). Overall, using the Invergarry Link means walking 3.5km (2.25 miles) more than the main Great Glen Way route, with 250m (820ft) of extra ascent.

STAGE 4A

Fort Augustus to Invergarry

Start	Caledonian Canal Centre, Fort Augustus (NH 379 092)
Finish	Invergarry (NH 307 011)
Distance	13.5km (8.25 miles)
Total ascent	190m (625ft)
Time	3hr 30min
Terrain	Minor roads, forest tracks and paths
Maps	OS Landranger 34, OS Explorer 400, Harvey Great Glen Way
Refreshments	Restaurant off-route from Aberchalder Swing Bridge. Hotel/bar restaurant in Invergarry.
Public Transport	Regular daily Scottish Citylink buses link Invergarry with Fort William, Fort Augustus and Inverness

After climbing beside a fine flight of locks to leave Fort Augustus, a level track runs beside the Caledonian Canal. Once the main road is reached at the Aberchalder Swing Bridge, it is worth making a detour to inspect the older, elegant Bridge of Oich. Afterwards, the Invergarry Link parts from the main Great Glen Way, to use forest paths and tracks. After climbing and traversing a forested slope, there is a short descent to Invergarry. Limited lodgings and bus services are available, while the Glengarry Heritage Centre lies off-route.

Follow the route description for Stage 4 as far as the **Aberchalder Swing Bridge**. Use the safe pedestrian path across the bridge, then cross over the road to follow the pavement running parallel. By all means make a short diversion to study the **Bridge of Oich**, returning to the main road afterwards.

An older bridge was swept away in devastating floods during 1849, when the embankment of the Caledonian Canal was also breached. Five years elapsed before a new bridge was built, by a brewer-turned-engineer called James Dredge, from Bath. The **Bridge of Oich** looks like a slender suspension bridge, but was actually patented as a 'double cantilever', built on the 'taper principle'. The supporting chains gradually diminish as they spread outwards from the stout granite pillars that support them, and hold very little weight in the middle of

map continues from page 151

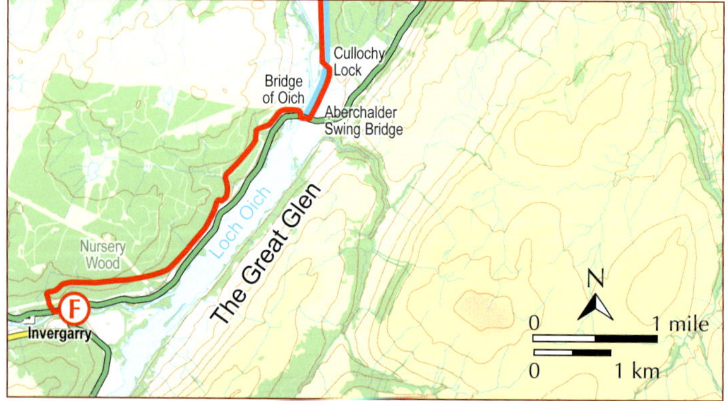

The Well of the Seven Heads is just off-route on the Invergarry Link, overlooking Loch Oich

the bridge. Apparently, if the bridge was ever severed in the middle, it would remain standing. The Bridge of Oich carried traffic until 1932, but the busy A82 road now crosses a more solid-looking stone bridge nearby.

A gravel path rises from the road and later makes a loop across a clear-felled slope. The path crosses a bridge, rises and falls, and follows a power line through a broad forest ride. When the path joins a track just above the main A82 road, turn right and follow the track, later rising to a junction. Keep left and there is a view down to the roof of the Invergarry Power Station. Keep following the track past **Nursery Wood**, and on a gentle downhill stretch, watch for a path off to the right. Follow it, and it later crosses back over the track.

A path drops downhill, passing conifers and rhododendron bushes, then tall oaks and rhododendron bushes, winding down to a telephone kiosk beside the

The Invergarry Hotel overlooks the River Garry on a link route from the Great Glen Way

A87 road at **Invergarry**. Turn left to pass a block of houses and the Invergarry Hotel to reach a junction with the main A82 road.

Invergarry (Gaelic – *Inbhir Garadh*) offers a small range of lodgings, including hotel, B&B and independent hostel. A short way along the Fort Augustus road, a filling station has a handy shop, with a B&B nearby. Regular daily Scottish Citylink buses link Invergarry with Fort William and Inverness. Check opening times in advance for the Glengarry Heritage Centre, which can be visited free of charge (tel 01809 501424, **glengarryheritagecentre.com**).

STAGE 5A

Invergarry to Gairlochy

Start	Invergarry (NH 307 011)
Finish	Gairlochy Bottom Lock (NN 176 842)
Distance	26.5km (16½ miles)
Total ascent	400m (1310ft)
Time	6hr 30min
Terrain	Minor roads, forest tracks and paths
Maps	OS Landranger 34, OS Explorer 400, Harvey Great Glen Way
Refreshments	Take-away at the Well of the Seven Heads
Public Transport	Regular daily Scottish Citylink buses link Invergarry with Fort William, Fort Augustus and Inverness

After leaving Invergarry by road, forest tracks lead uphill, gaining one good view of Loch Oich. A gradual descent leads to a road, where it is easy to detour off-route to the Well of the Seven Heads and a take-away. An easy road walk takes the Invergarry Link to a road junction, where it re-joins the main Great Glen Way. The rest of the day is spent walking beside Loch Lochy.

A break in the forest cover allows a view of Loch Oich between Invergarry and Aberchalder

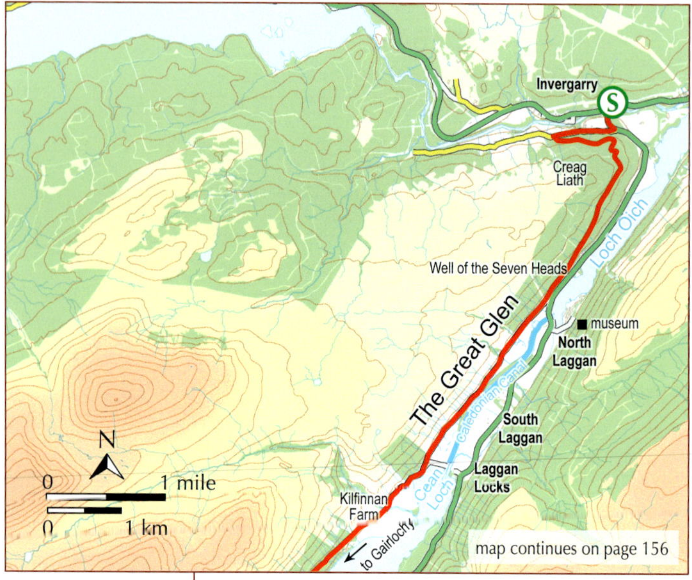

A take-away and the Well of the Seven Heads monument lie 750m further along the road.

To leave **Invergarry**, turn right along the main A82 road, and follow the pavement across a bridge over the River Garry. Turn right along a narrow road, passing the Saddle Mountain Hostel and a couple of houses. Turn left up a forest track, which quickly swings left as it climbs. At a higher level, it swings right and passes a picnic table around 130m (425ft), where there is a view of **Loch Oich**. The track undulates gently, passes a couple of junctions and descends gently to return to the A82 road. ◂

The Well of the Seven Heads marks an historic and bloody act of retribution. On 25 September 1663, Alexander MacDonald, Chief of Keppoch, and his brother Ranald were killed by seven others during a clan dispute. While most of their kinsfolk seemed content to let the matter rest, Iain Lom, the Keppoch Bard, called for revenge, enlisting the support of MacDonald of Glengarry and Sir James MacDonald of Sleat. After two years, the seven culprits were tracked down to Inverlair, where they were slain and beheaded. The severed heads were washed in a well beside Loch Oich, then displayed at Invergarry Castle before being taken to Gallows Hill in Edinburgh on 7 December 1665. The Well of the Seven Heads is now enclosed in stone and bears a monument crowned with seven unhappy-looking heads, surmounted by a hand holding a dagger. The tale of murder and revenge is carved around all four sides in English, Gaelic, French and Latin.

Turn right and follow the path parallel to the road, later turning right again up a narrow minor road. The road rises gently, undulates as it passes a few houses, then descends gently to a junction with another road. The Invergarry Link re-joins the main route of the Great Glen Way here.

Follow the Stage 5 route description from here to Gairlochy.

The Bridge of Oich can be inspected by making a short detour at Aberchalder

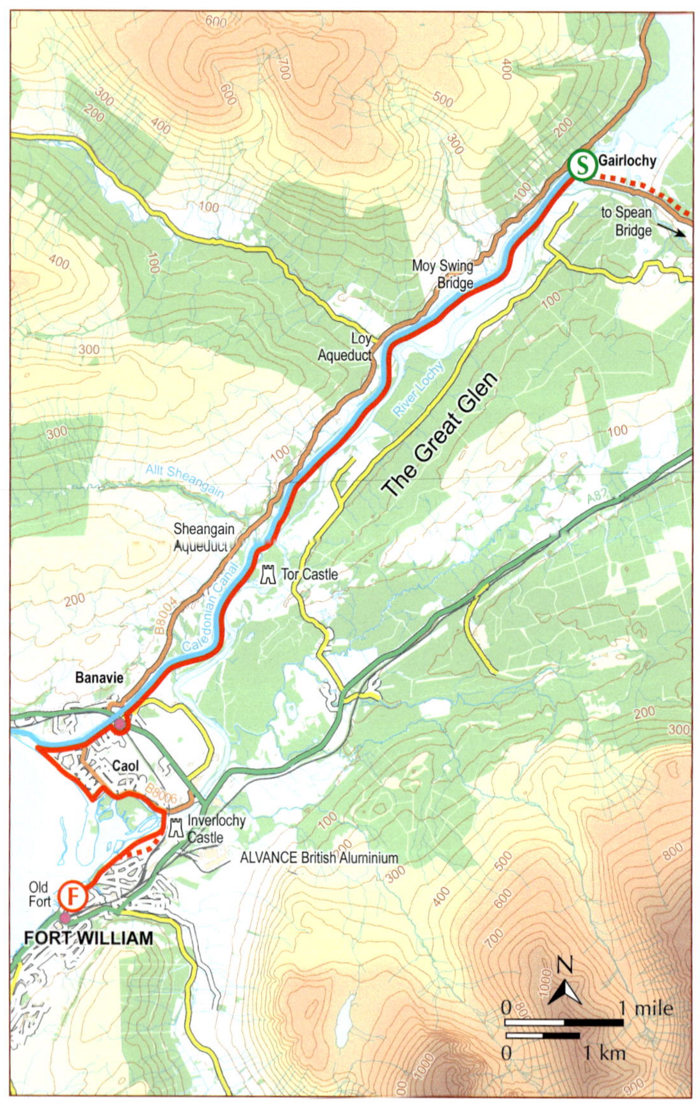
Gairlochy
to Spean Bridge
Moy Swing Bridge
Loy Aqueduct
River Lochy
The Great Glen
Allt Sheangain
Sheangain Aqueduct
Tor Castle
Caledonian Canal
B8004
A82
Banavie
Caol
B8006
Inverlochy Castle
ALVANCE British Aluminium
Old Fort
FORT WILLIAM
N
0
1 mile
0
1 km

STAGE 6

Gairlochy to Fort William

Start	Gairlochy Bottom Lock (NN 176 842)
Finish	Railway station, Fort William (NN 105 742)
Distance	17km (10.5 miles)
Total ascent	10m (35ft)
Time	4hr 30min
Terrain	Long, clear canal-side track, followed by low-level paths, tracks and roads near the coast
Maps	OS Landranger 41, OS Explorers 392 and 400, Harvey Great Glen Way
Refreshments	Bar and restaurant at Banavie. Shops and bars at Corpach. Shops and take-aways at Caol. Plenty of bars, restaurants and cafés around Fort William.
Public Transport	Shiel Buses run a limited schooldays-only bus service linking Fort William, Gairlochy and Spean Bridge. Shiel Buses also link Banavie, Corpach and Caol with Fort William, and run most of the town services around Fort William. Trains between Fort William, Banavie and Corpach, as well as to Spean Bridge and Glasgow.

Most of this final stage is on a long and narrow 'island', flanked on one side by the Caledonian Canal and on the other by the River Lochy. This is an easy day's walk, descending in stages while following a clear canal-side track past locks. A series of roads, tracks and paths run close to the coast on the way to Fort William.

Facilities increase as the route progresses, and Fort William offers the largest concentration of lodgings and other services encountered since the start of the Great Glen Way in Inverness.

Leave **Gairlochy** and its swing bridge by following a track past Gairlochy Bottom Lock. The track drops a little, then crosses an overspill weir and enjoys a fine view of the broad and shingly River Lochy. Looking ahead you can

For 1:25K route map see booklet pages 6–10.

see Ben Nevis rising majestically from the further reaches of the Great Glen. Tall beech trees grace the canal-side, and later, on the far bank, a knoll bearing distinctive pine trees is an old burial ground. Also look across the canal to spot an inflowing stream, then reach the attractive **Moy Swing Bridge**.

The **Moy Swing Bridge** simply allows the farmer from Moy to drive tractors and trailers down to his riverside meadows. Canal traffic, meanwhile, relies on a keeper to open and close the bridge on demand. However, the bridge is not mechanised, and only one half can be opened manually at a time; hence the need for a small boat so that the keeper can row across and open the other half. Basic camping, with no facilities, is permitted on grass beside a cabin.

Continue along the track; views across small meadows near the River Lochy are later closed off as trees flank the canal-side. Further along, the canal crosses the **Loy Aqueduct** over the River Loy.

To see the **Loy Aqueduct** properly turn sharp left on a downward track well after crossing over it, then retrace your steps afterwards. It is a splendid structure; the River Loy flows through a large central arch, while smaller arches on either side allow passage for man and beast.

The track later crosses an overspill, where excess water flows down into the River Lochy. Look across the canal to see a knoll crowned with a few pine trees, which is another old burial ground. The track rises then falls gently, passing abundant birch trees on the little hill of Druim na h-Atha, then a cottage. Continue enjoying the variety of trees alongside, and look across the water to spot a stream feeding water into the canal.

It is quite possible to cross the **Sheangain Aqueduct** without noticing, but take a few minutes to have a proper look at it.

Use a narrow path to descend from the embankment to gain a view of the three arched tunnels. Two carry water from the **Allt Sheangain**, while the third covers a stone-paved passage for man and his animals.

Not far from the Sheangain Aqueduct, **Tor Castle** overlooks the River Lochy. It was built by the MacIntoshes, who vacated it towards the end of the 13th century. Some time later it was occupied by the Camerons, sparking a feud between the two clans that spanned some 350 years, continuing even after the Camerons abandoned the property in 1660 and went to settle in Achnacarry. There is a B&B near the castle.

The canal curves gently left and right and for brief periods there are no signs of habitation, while a splendid variety of trees flank both banks; follow the track onwards, passing through a gate beside tall pines. Banavie Top Jetty is reached. Walk downhill in stages alongside the celebrated stepped locks known as Neptune's Staircase to reach the busy A830 at Banavie Swing Bridge.

The Soldier's Bridge runs parallel to a railway bridge near the ruins of Inverlochy Castle

A broad path accompanies the Caledonian Canal from Corpach to Banavie

Neptune's Staircase is an inspired name for the tightly packed series of eight canal locks at Banavie. The arrangement is difficult to see in its entirety, and the best views are those seen in the aerial shots used for postcards. Canal cruisers can pass from top to bottom in about ninety minutes, including the road and rail swing bridges at the bottom, but the time taken can almost double if craft pass through in the other direction at the same time.

Banavie (Gaelic – *Banbhaidh*) is a little village with only a few facilities. The Moorings Hotel, a couple of guest houses and a hostel are available, along a with canal-side restaurant and ice cream shop. There are regular daily bus and train services to and from Corpach and Fort William, as well as a schooldays-only service back to Gairlochy.

Cross the busy A830 road with care and turn left to pass **Banavie Station**. Turn right at a junction, over a level crossing, and continue along the road almost as far as a little pub restaurant called The Lochy. Head right up a path, as directed, to reach the Caledonian Canal again. Continue straight along the broad gravel track, flanked on the right by grassy, flowery waterside banks, with tall beech trees on the left often obscuring views of Caol. (Note that a cycleway on the left offers a short-cut directly to the shore of Loch Linnhe.) The canal describes a broad and graceful curve to the right, later passing an overspill, where excess water flows down into Loch Linnhe. When the Corpach Double Lock is reached, the Great Glen Way turns left down a path, but walkers might wish to continue to the nearby terminus of the **Caledonian Canal** at the Corpach Basin and explore the village of Corpach too.

CORPACH

Corpach (Gaelic – *A' Chorpaich*) is an interesting little village, well worth a visit, overlooking the western sea terminus of the Caledonian Canal. There is public access to the Corpach Sea Lock and Corpach Basin, where boats may be moored while they wait for a favourable tide. The Narrows nearby are dominated by a huge sawmill, which chews up trees from the surrounding forests. A popular attraction for those with an interest in geology is 'Treasures of the Earth', which focuses on mines, minerals, gemstones and fossils. Open February and March 10am–4pm; April, May, June, September and October 10am–5pm; July and August 10am–6pm. Limited opening in winter (01397 772283, treasuresoftheearth.co.uk). There is an entrance charge.

Corpach has a couple of bunkhouses and B&B establishments. The Co-op store has a post office inside and an ATM outside. Toilets are available in the Kilmallie Hall, when open, while canal users have access to toilets near the canal office. The Tradewinds pub offers meals. There are regular daily bus and train services to and from neighbouring Banavie and Fort William.

Step down from the stout embankment of the **Caledonian Canal**, following a path across a footbridge below the overspill weir. Walk along a coastal path hemmed in between the shore of Loch Linnhe and a sports pitch, continuing along a broad path through a coastal green, parallel to Erracht Drive in the village of **Caol**.

Caol (Gaelic – *Caol Loch Abar*) is a village close to The Narrows, where Loch Linnhe turns a right-angle corner and becomes known as Loch Eil. There are a couple of shops, pubs and take-aways, a post office, toilets and regular daily bus services to and from neighbouring Fort William, Corpach and Banavie.

INVERLOCHY CASTLE

The Comyns were a powerful Scottish family with two branches, the Red Comyns and the Black Comyns. The Red Comyns built Inverlochy Castle (Gaelic – *Inbhir Lòchaidh*) in 1280 and surrounded it with a moat connected to the River Lochy. The four-square thick stone walls are protected by drum towers at each corner, the largest being Comyn's Tower. There was probably a timber-built Great Hall inside the walls. The castle is always open and there is no entrance charge.

The Red Comyns and Black Comyns supported John Balliol's claim to the Scottish throne, and therefore attracted the enmity of Robert the Bruce. The MacDonalds supported Bruce, and in 1297 their vessels engaged Comyn vessels off Inverlochy, resulting in the sinking of two ships. The Comyns were later defeated in battle at Inverurie in May 1308, and Bruce granted Inverlochy Castle to the MacDonalds.

In the 15th century the MacDonalds were often in conflict with the Stuarts, who sat on the Scottish throne. Following a MacDonald raid on Inverness, James I sent a force commanded by the Earl of Mar to Inverlochy in 1431. As the army camped by the river they were picked off by MacDonald bowmen from the strategic hill of Tom na Faire, losing a thousand men. In 1645 there was another battle, this time between the Royalist army of Charles I, led by the Marquis of Montrose (with MacDonald support), and a Covenanting force led by the Marquis of Argyll (with Campbell support). Again, the strategic hill of Tom na Faire was put to good use by the Royalists; despite their smaller force they suffered only 20 casualties, while their opponents suffered 1500.

Following the construction of a fort at Fort William in the late 17th century (see below), Inverlochy Castle fell from favour. Military might was further consolidated when General Wade built a road from Fort William to Fort Augustus, passing Inverlochy Castle and completed in 1727. The castle was abandoned and was used by the Invergarry Ironworks from 1729 to 1736 as a store for pig iron.

Walk to the end of the coastal path, then turn left along Glenmallie Road. Turn right at a junction to follow the **B8006**, Kilwallie Road, which soon bends left to run parallel to the **River Lochy**. Walk along a shared footpath and cycleway beside a flood defence wall, re-joining the road at a bus stop. Follow the road gently uphill towards a railway bridge and turn right to cross the Soldier's Bridge. This long footbridge, opened in 2018 to replace a wooden structure, runs parallel to a railway bridge over the river. Stepping down from the bridge, consider making a detour beneath the railway line to visit the nearby **Inverlochy Castle**.

Cross a bridge over the tailrace stream flowing from the ALVANCE British Aluminium works. ▸ Turn right to pick up and follow a path into a field, drifting left away from the tailrace. Follow the riverside path past a sports pitch, then continue across a rushy meadow. Enter woodland and follow the path across a couple of small footbridges. Alder trees tend to screen both the river and the Inverlochy suburbs of Fort William from sight. Turn left,

At peak high tides, there is an alternative route straight ahead through the suburbs.

Neptune's Staircase is a series of eight canal lock gates and a swing bridge at Banavie

then right to cross a bridge over the River Nevis. Ben Nevis rises far inland to the left, while the waters of Loch Linnhe are nearby.

Briefly follow a road past a few houses, then follow a clear path alongside a 'shinty' pitch (shinty is a popular Gaelic sport that resembles hockey). The path reaches a busy roundabout beside McDonald's restaurant in Fort William. Keep right to walk round the roundabout and reach the ruins of the **Old Fort**, where a few low walls stand above the shore of Loch Linnhe. A stone monument marks the end of the Great Glen Way.

The original '**Old Fort**' was a timber structure, built by General Monck to house 250 men. He referred to it as 'the fort of Inverlochy' in 1654, when writing to advise Oliver Cromwell of its completion. A stone fort was constructed in 1690 by General Mackay, housing 1000 men and defended by 15 guns. It was named in honour of King William, a member of the Dutch House of Orange, who fought a decisive battle against King James in that year. William ruled Britain jointly with his wife, Mary, the daughter of James II of Scotland. General Gordon attacked the fort during the 1715 rebellion, then in 1746 Sir Ewen Cameron attacked it. The fort was largely dismantled and the land bought by the West Highland Railway Company in 1889. They pushed a railway through the site, leaving only the small portion of the original walls seen today, which includes a sally port. The original stone-arched gateway to the fort was rebuilt and now serves as the entrance to a small graveyard off the busy Belford Road in Fort William.

To walk from the Old Fort into town, the best way is to double back to McDonald's restaurant, then cross a road and walk across Morrison's supermarket car park to reach the railway station or bus station. There is immediate access to the centre of **Fort William** by way of an underpass (see 'First/Last Night: Fort William' in the Introduction).

APPENDIX A

Useful information

Great Glen Way

Great Glen Way Rangers
Auchterawe
Fort Augustus
Inverness-shire PH32 4BT
tel 01320 366633
greatglenway@highland.gov.uk

Great Glen Way official website
www.highland.gov.uk/greatglenway

Scottish Outdoor Access Code
www.outdooraccess-scotland.scot

Caledonian Canal

Caledonian Canal Office
Seaport Marina
Muirtown Wharf
Inverness IV3 5LE
tel 01463 725500
www.scottishcanals.co.uk/visit/canals/visit-the-caledonian-canal

Public Transport

Traveline Scotland
tel 0871 200 2233
www.travelinescotland.com
Up-to-date information about trains, buses or ferries (smartphone app available).

Inverness Airport
tel 01667 464000
www.hial.co.uk/inverness-airport

Cross Country Trains
www.crosscountrytrains.co.uk

Avanti West Coast trains
www.avantiwestcoast.co.uk

LNER
www.lner.co.uk

ScotRail
www.scotrail.co.uk

FlixBus
www.flixbus.com

National Express
www.nationalexpress.com

Scottish Citylink
www.citylink.co.uk

Shiel Buses
www.shielbuses.co.uk

Stagecoach
www.stagecoachbus.com

Caledonian Discovery Cruises
www.caledonian-discovery.co.uk

European Waterways
www.europeanwaterways.com/destination/scotland

Cruise Loch Ness
www.cruiselochness.com

Accommodation

See Appendix B for a Great Glen Way accommodation list, and it is also worth checking online sites such as www.airbnb.co.uk and www.booking.com

Visit Scotland
www.visitscotland.com

Hostelling Scotland
www.hostellingscotland.org.uk

Scottish Independent Hostels
www.scottish-hostels.com

Baggage Transfer

Loch Ness Travel
tel 01463 832566
www.lochnesstravel.com

Ticket to Ride
tel 01463 419160
www.tickettoridehighlands.co.uk

Piggyback Baggage Transfers
tel 01687 460167 or 07909 640987
www.piggybackbaggagetransfers.com

Tourist Information
www.visitscotland.com

Tourist Attractions
West Highland Museum
Fort William
tel 01397 702169
www.westhighlandmuseum.org.uk

Treasures of the Earth
Corpach
tel 01397 772283
treasuresoftheearth.co.uk

Clan Cameron Museum
Achnacarry
tel 07900 217875
www.clancameronmuseum.co.uk

Caledonian Canal Centre
Fort Augustus
tel 08700 500208
www.scottishcanals.co.uk/events/host-your-own-event/event-spaces/caledonian-canal-centre

Urquhart Castle
Drumnadrochit
tel 01456 450551
www.historicenvironment.scot/visit-a-place/places/urquhart-castle

Nessieland
Drumnadrochit
tel 01456 450342
nessieland.co.uk

Loch Ness Exhibition Centre
Drumnadrochit
tel 01456 450573
lochness.com

Inverness Museum and Art Gallery
Inverness
tel 01463 234353
www.highlifehighland.com/inverness-museum-and-art-gallery

Emergency Services
For police, ambulance, fire, mountain rescue or coastguard, dial 999 or 112.

APPENDIX B

Accommodation along the route

Location	Name	Type	Tel	Web	Comments
Fort William There is plenty of accommodation in Fort William, and this is just a central selection.					
	Premier Inn	hotel	0333 777 7268	www.premierinn.com	
	Imperial Hotel	hotel	01397 702040	www.sgehotelgroup.com/imperial	
	Travelodge	hotel	0871 984 6419	www.travelodge.co.uk/hotels/565/Fort-William-hotel	
	Ossian's Hotel	hotel	01397 700857		
	The Alexandra Hotel	hotel	01397 702241		
	Berkeley Guest House	B&B/Guesthouse	01397 701185	https://berkeleyguesthouse.co.uk	
	MacLean Guest House	B&B/Guesthouse	01397 703083	www.macleanhouse.co.uk	
	Craig Nevis Guest House	B&B/Guesthouse	01397 702023	https://craignevis.co.uk	

hotel · B&B/Guesthouse · self catering · campsite · hostel

Location	Name	Type	Tel	Web	Comments
	Fort William Backpackers		01397 700711	https://fortwilliambackpackers.com	
	Guisachan Guest House		01397 703797	https://guisachanguesthouse.co.uk	
	Bank Street Lodge		01397 700070	www.bankstreetlodge.co.uk	En suite rooms. No breakfast.
	1 Caberfeidh		07534 3[illegible]2100	https://travellingsindre.com/no-1-caberfeidh-uk	
	6 Caberfeidh B&B		01397 7[illegible]3755	www.booking.com	
	Constantia House B&B		01397 7[illegible]2893		
	Stobahn Guest House		01397 7[illegible]2790		
Glen Nevis (off-route)	Ben Nevis Guest House		01397 708817	www.bennevisguesthouse.co.uk	
	Brevins Guest House		01397 701412	www.thebrevins.co.uk	
	Achintee Farm		07497 082820	www.achinteefarm.com	
	Ben Nevis Inn		01397 701227	www.ben-nevis-inn.co.uk	Bar and restaurant
	Glen Nevis Youth Hostel		01397 702336	www.hostellingscotland.org.uk/hostels/glen-nevis/	Breakfast available. Licensed café bar.
	Glen Nevis Campsite		01397 702191		Camping and various self-catering options. Restaurant and bar on site.

Location	Name	Type	Tel	Web	Comments
Lochyside	Cuil Na Sithe		01397 702267	https://cuil-na-sithe-bed-breakfast.highlandshotelspage.com/en/	
Caol	Failte Mhor Guest House		07301 224933	https://failtemhor.co.uk/	
Corpach	Smiddy Bunkhouse & Blacksmith's Hostel		01397 772467	https://snowgoosecentre.co.uk/accommodation/blacksmiths-bunkhouse/	
	Travee B&B		01397 772262	https://travee.co.uk/	
	Heather's B&B		01397 773744		
Banavie	Culacrick B&B		07920 760240	www.booking.com	
	The Moorings Hotel		01397 772797	www.moorings-fortwilliam.co.uk	
	Chase the Wild Goose Hostel		07563 049068	www.chasethewildgoosehostel.co.uk	
	Seanivan		07799 137734		
	Treetops B&B		01397 772496	www.treetopsfortwilliam.co.uk	
	Braeburn Guest House		01397 772047	https://braeburnfortwilliam.co.uk	
	Ben Nevis Manor		07391 826499	www.booking.com	
Tor Castle	Torcastle House		01397 701633	www.torcastlebandbfortwilliam.co.uk	
Moy Bridge	Very basic campsite with no facilities				

Location	Name	Type	Tel	Web	Comments
Gairlochy	Basic campsite at Gairlochy Top Locks				
Spean Bridge (off-route)	Old Pines Hotel		01397 712324	www.oldpines.co.uk	
	Coinachan Guest House		01397 712417		
	Braelea		07771 331015		
	Rosebank Guest House		07944 645157	https://rosebankguesthouse.scot/	
	Inverour Guest House		01397 7 2213	www.inverour.co.uk	
	Riverside Lodge Gardens		01397 7 2702		
	Spean Lodge		07779 3-0110	https://speanlodge.com/	
	Smiddy House		01397 7-2335	www.smiddyhouse.com	
Glas-Dhoire	Very basic 'Trailblazer Rest' campsite				
South Laggan	Basic campsite at Laggan Locks				
	Forest Lodge Guest House		01809 5C1219	www.forestlodgeguesthouse.co.uk	Offer evening meals
	Great Glen Hostel		01809 5C1430	www.greatglenhostel.com	Half board (breakfast & dinner) available
Leitirfearn	Very basic 'Trailblazer Rest' campsite				

Location	Name	Type	Tel	Web	Comments
Invergarry	Saddle Mountain Hostel		01809 507240	https://saddlemountainhostel.scot	
	Invergarry Hotel		01809 50[illegible]206	www.invergarryhotel.co.uk	
	Glengarry Castle Hotel		01809 50[illegible]254	www.glengarry.net	
	Nursery Cottages		01809 501285	www.nurserycottageinvergarry.co.uk	
	Glen Albyn Lodge		01809 501348	https://highlandlodgegreatglen.co.uk	You rent the whole place
Glengarry (off-route beyond Heritage Centre)	Rokeby Manor		01397 704250	www.blacksheephotels.com/rokeby-manor	
	Ardgarry Farm B&B		01809 501226	www.ardgarryfarm.co.uk	
	Faichemard Farm Campsite		01809 501314	https://campsite.faichemard.scot/	
Aberchalder Swing Bridge	Very basic campsite with no facilities				
Aberchalder (off-route)	Lundie View B&B		07599 1[illegible]4884	https://lundieviewbnb.co.uk	
Kytra Lock	Very basic 'Trailblazer Rest' campsite				

Location	Name	Type	Tel	Web	Comments
Fort Augustus	Caledonian Canal Centre and Lock Chambers		01463 725581	www.scottishcanals.co.uk/events/host-your-own-event/event-spaces/caledonian-canal-centre	No catering facilities, apart from in the bothies
	Bank House B&B		01320 366755	www.visitlochness.co.uk	
	Lorien House B&B		01320 366576	www.lorien-house.co.uk	
	Kings Inn B&B		01320 365406	https://kings-inn-bb.highlandshotel-spage.com/en	
	Abbey Cottage B&B		01320 310524	https://abbeycottagelochness.co.uk	
	Richmond House Hotel		01320 333221	www.richmondhousehotel.com	
	Caledonian Hotel		07803 926513	https://caledonianhotelfortaugustus.weebly.com/	
	Oaklands B&B		01320 366487	www.oaklandslochness.uk	
	White House B&B		01320 366561		

Location	Name	Type	Tel	Web	Comments
	Conifers B&B		01320 36[illegible]758		
	Kettle House B&B		01320 36[illegible]408	www.kettlehouselochness.co.uk	
	Carn A Chuilinn B&B		07872 54[illegible]172	http://carnachuilinn.co.uk	
	Suardal B&B		07470 38[illegible]871		
	Loch Ness Guest House		01320 96[illegible]101	www.lochnessguesthouse.com	
	Sonas B&B		01320 36[illegible]291		
	Appin House		07902 8[illegible]3692	www.booking.com	
	Morag's Lodge Hostel		01320 36[illegible]289	https://moragslodge.com	Self-catering kitchen and breakfast and meals available
	Nessdecker		07712 5[illegible]9626	www.nessdecker.co.uk	
	Rose Cottage B&B		07860 8[illegible]3245	https://rosecottagefortaugustus.co.uk	
	Thistle Dubh B&B		01320 36[illegible]380	www.thistle-dubh.co.uk	
	The Inch Hotel		01456 45[illegible]900	www.inchhotel.com	
Inver Coille					
(from low-level route only)	Inver Coille Campsite		01320 3[illegible]1224	www.inver-coille.co.uk	Camping and glamping

Location	Name	Type	Tel	Web	Comments
Invermoriston	Glenmoriston Arms Hotel		01320 35[illegible]206	https://glenmoristonarms.co.uk/index.php	
	Bracarina House B&B		01320 35[illegible]279	www.bracarinahouse.co.uk	Evening meals available
	Darroch View B&B		01320 35[illegible]388	www.booking.com	
	Bracadale B&B		01320 35[illegible]258		
	Craik na Dav		01320 35[illegible]277	www.craik-na-dav.com	
Alltsigh (low-level route only)	Lochside Hostel		01320 35[illegible]274	https://lochsidehostel.com	Breakfast available. Shop.
Clunebeg	Clunebeg Lodge B&B		01456 45[illegible]097	www.clunebeglodge.com	
Borlum (off-route)	Loch Ness Bay Camping		01456 45[illegible]544	https://lochnessbaycamping.co.uk/camping/	

Location	Name	Type	Tel	Web	Comments
Lewiston	Loch Ness Inn		01456 450991	www.staylochness.co.uk	
	Bunillidh		07713 606308	www.booking.com	
	Glen Rowan Guest House		01456 450232		Temporarily closed
	Seilebost B&B		01456 45[illegible]278		
	Balmridge House B&B		07799 08[illegible]251	www.balmridgehouse.co.uk	
	Loch Ness Backpackers Lodge		01456 450807	www.lochness-backpackers.com	
	Aslaich B&B		07813 80[illegible]969	https://aslaich.uk/	
	Woodlands Guest House		07422 66[illegible]489	https://woodlands-lochness.co.uk	
	Kilmore Farmhouse B&B		01456 450524	www.kilmorefarmhouse.co.uk	
	Loch Ness B&B		07833 94[illegible]486	www.booking.com	
	Benleva Hotel		01456 450080	http://benleva-hotel.highlandshotels.net/en/	

Location	Name	Type	Tel	Web	Comments
Drumnadrochit	The Glen B&B		01456 450279	www.lochness-theglen.com	
	Fiddlers Rest B&B		01456 450223	www.oakdalerooms.co.uk	
	Morlea B&B		01456 450495	https://morleabedandbreakfast.co.uk/	
	Greenlea B&B		01456 450645	www.greenlea-drumnadrochit.co.uk	
	Bridgend House		07711 497831	www.bridgendhouse.co.uk	
	Loch Ness Hostel		07773 160260	www.1lochnesshostel.co.uk	
	Loch Ness Drumnadrochit Hotel		01456 450218	https://lochnessdrumnadrochit.cobb-shotels.com/	
	Loch Ness Lodge Hotel		01456 450342	https://lochness-hotel.com/	
	Glenkirk B&B		01456 450802	www.lochnessbandb.com	
	Kilmichael House B&B		01456 450703	www.kilmichaelhouse.co.uk	
Abriachan	Camping Pod Heaven		mob 07570 862151	https://campingpodheaven.com/	Glamping and camping
	Eco-Campsite		01463 861462		

Location	Name	Type	Tel	Web	Comments
Inverness There is plenty of accommodation in Inverness, and this is just a central selection	Premier Inn		0333 3213256	www.premierinn.com	
	Bught Caravan Park & Campsite		01463 235920	www.invernesscaravanpark.com	
	Cavell House B&B		01463 232850	www.cavellguesthouseinverness.co.uk	
	Corbies Rest Guest House		01463 235557	https://corbiesrest.com/	
	Moray Park Guest House		01463 233528	https://moraypark.co.uk/	
	Talisker B&B		01463 235221	www.scotland-inverness.co.uk/talisker	
	Macrae Guest House		01463 243658		
	The Glenmoriston Town House Hotel		01463 223777	www.glenmoristontownhouse.com	
	Glen Mhor Hotel		01463 234308	www.glen-mhor.com	
	BazPackers Hostel		01463 717663	www.bazpackershostel.co.uk	

Location	Name	Type	Tel	Web	Comments
	Wychway Guest House		01463 239299		
	Castle View Guest House		07775 733191	https://castleviewguesthouseinverness.com/	
	Inverness Student Hotel		01463 235556	www.booking.com	
	The Kings Highway		01463 251800	www.jdwetherspoon.com/hotels/the-kings-highway/	
	Royal Highland Hotel		01463 231926	www.royalhighlandhotel.co.uk	
	MacDougall Clansman Hotel		01463 713702	www.invernesscentrehotel.co.uk	
	Youth Hostel		01463 23[illegible]771	www.hostellingscotland.org.uk/hostels/inverness	
	Seaport Marina				Basic campsite

APPENDIX C

Timeline history

The following timeline history is biased in favour of events that took place in the Great Glen and the Highlands of Scotland, at the expense of events that took place around Edinburgh or the Scots/English border.

7500BC	Mesolithic hunter-gatherers made their way along the Highland coast, carrying simple stone tools and pots. They left little trace of their passing, except where they settled long enough to create 'middens' (rubbish dumps of bones and shell fragments).
3000BC	Neolithic migration through Scotland, with the construction of chambered cairns. The 'Fortingall Yew' sprouted around this time and probably remains the oldest living tree in Europe.
300BC	During the Iron Age, Celtic tribes from southern Scotland and Ireland migrated northwards, building forts (duns) and stone towers (brochs)
AD43	Emissaries were sent from the Orkney Islands to make contact with Claudius during the Roman conquest of Britain. A tribe living in the Great Glen was named the Caledones at this time; the name was later used to describe almost all the tribes living in the Highlands of Scotland.
AD84	The battle of Mons Graupius, thought to be in the Grampian, or Moray, region. Agricola led four legions of Roman soldiers into battle against the native Caledonii, who were led by Calgacus. Although the Romans won the battle, they were never able to subdue the Highlanders, and withdrew southwards. The Romans were impressed by the hardy nature of the tribes, while Tacitus said they had red hair and large limbs.
AD122	Hadrian's Wall was constructed across northern England
AD142	The Antonine Wall was constructed across central Scotland
AD250	The 'Scots', who were an Irish tribe, began to conduct raids along the western seaboard of Scotland
AD297	A Roman writer, Eumenius, was the first to mention the Picts by name, although it is thought they were already well established in the land
AD367	The Scots, Saxons and Franks came into greater contact with the Picts as they worked their way into Scotland
AD392	St Ninian introduced Christianity to the far south of Scotland at Whithorn
AD400–500	The legendary Pictish warrior Cruithne was said to have ruled over much of Scotland for 100 years. On his death, each of his seven sons ruled over part of his kingdom. Around AD500, the Western Highlands were already under Scots control, while Fergus established the kingdom of Dalriada, based around Argyll and the islands. The Picts found themselves pushed more to the north and east of Scotland.
AD563	St Columba was exiled from Ireland and settled on Iona

AD565 St Columba travelled through the Great Glen and is credited with seeing the Loch Ness 'monster' on his way to Inverness. He met the Pictish king Brude and duelled with his magician Briochan. Around this time, there were essentially four distinct civilisations in Scotland: the northern Picts and southern kinsmen; the Scots of Dalriada; the Britons in central Scotland, with the Saxons and Angles further south. This situation led to a period of conflict and strife. Cumin, a follower of Columba, established a monastic settlement in the middle of the Great Glen.

AD603 King Aedan of Dalriada united the Scots and Picts in an attempt to drive the Angles southwards into Northumbria. He was defeated in battle.

AD657–85 Bridei, a Pictish ruler, attacked the Argyll capital of the Scots and subdued them, and later launched an assault against the expanding Northumbrian kingdom, leading to a short period of Pictish domination in Scotland

AD706–24 The Pictish ruler Neachtan worried about religious authority and banished Christian monks from his kingdom. However, he later relented and joined a religious community.

AD731–61 Oengus Mac Fergus became the first king of both the Picts and the Scots, although he was unable to take the kingdom of Strathclyde. After his death, the Scots dissociated themselves from Pictish rule.

AD780 Invaders from Scandinavia appeared in small numbers

AD789–820 A series of rulers, some Pictish and some Scots, ensured that the two kingdoms were basically unified throughout this period

AD839 Increasing numbers of Norse invaders caused huge problems. The Picts and Scots united, but were defeated by the invaders, leaving the two kingdoms severed from each other.

AD842–48 Kenneth Mac Alpin, king of the Scots at Dalriada, moved to Scone and took with him the Lia Fáil, or Stone of Destiny, now known as the Stone of Scone. This ancient stone, reputedly carried by the Celts from Scythia to Ireland, and thence to Scotland, was always associated with the coronation of kings. With its aid, and much political and physical manoeuvring, Mac Alpin became the first true King of the Scots. The official language was Gaelic, as the Pictish language and culture quickly expired. However, Norse influence remained strong throughout the region.

AD850 Kenneth Mac Alpin conducted a series of raids on Northumbria

AD900 Constantin II attempted to absorb Norse settlers into the emerging kingdom of Scotland

1005–34 Malcolm II achieved Scottish unity and expelled the English

1040 Duncan, heir of Malcolm, was killed by Macbeth, but not in the manner described by Shakespeare

1057 Macbeth was killed by Malcolm III, who took the throne and instituted the royal House of Canmore

1093 Death of St Margaret, founder of the modern city of Edinburgh, and wife of Malcolm III

1124–53	David I introduced Norman culture to Scotland and built several abbeys in southern Scotland, including Jedburgh, Kelso, Melrose and Dryburgh
1156	Somerled, progenitor of the great clans MacDonald and Ranald, led a force against the Norse and became ruler of old Dalriada, although the islands remained nominally under Norse control
1263	The Norse relinquished control over the Hebrides after the Battle of Largs
1280	Inverlochy Castle was built by the Comyns at the foot of Ben Nevis
1290	The Scots queen Margaret, also known as the 'Maid of Norway', died on her way to marry Edward, son of Edward I of England. The Scots asked Edward I to decide who should rule Scotland out of a total of 13 claimants. Edward chose John Balliol, a man he could easily control.
1297–1305	William Wallace led a violent campaign against the English, and was eventually captured and executed
1306–29	Robert the Bruce strove to gain the Scottish throne. During this campaign he was supported by the MacDonalds, and gave them Inverlochy Castle in 1308. After the defeat of Edward II at Bannockburn, the Treaty of Northampton recognised Scottish sovereignty.
1368	Edinburgh Castle was built
1371–90	Robert II founded the royal House of Stewart. The king was often in conflict with the barons, as well as occasionally at war with the English.
1400	Birth of Donald Dubh, who became the first chief of the Clan Cameron, often in dispute with their Great Glen neighbours the MacIntoshes
1431	The MacDonalds had raided Inverness, so James I sent a force commanded by the Earl or Mar to Inverlochy. The MacDonalds defeated them in the First Battle of Inverlochy.
1472	Orkney and Shetland passed from Norse to Scottish control
1488–1515	The Highlands received little interference during the reign of James IV, and the king was eventually killed in war against the English at Flodden
1542	James V was defeated in battle by Henry VIII at Solway Moss
1544	The Battle of the Shirts took place at Laggan in the Great Glen
1560–87	A time of political and religious strife. In 1560 Mary, Queen of Scots, travelled from Catholic France to Calvinist Scotland and married Lord Darnley in 1565. He was murdered in 1567, and Mary married the Earl of Bothwell, resulting in her expulsion from Scotland. Imprisoned by her father's cousin Elizabeth I, Mary was executed in 1587.
1603	As Elizabeth I died without an heir, Mary's son, James VI of Scotland, was also crowned James I of England, although the Scottish and English parliaments remained separate. Political and religious strife continued.
1638–43	Both the Scottish and English parliaments rebelled against the rule of Charles I. The authority of Charles had already been challenged by the National Covenant in Scotland, and this led to Presbyterianism becoming the leading faith in Scotland. England descended into Civil War.

1645	During the Second Battle of Inverlochy, the Civil War gave long standing rival clans a chance to settle differences. The Marquis of Montrose, with MacDonald support, fought on the Royalist side. A Covenanting force, led by the Marquis of Argyll with Campbell support, fought on the Parliamentarian side. The Royalists won, but retribution was swift and terrible.
1649–52	Following the execution of Charles I, Oliver Cromwell was made Lord Protector. He initiated a bloody campaign to clear the Scottish Highlands of Royalist support.
1654	A wooden fort was built by General Monck, and referred to as 'the fort of Inverlochy', following the abandonment of Inverlochy Castle nearby
1660	The Restoration of the Monarchy. Charles II was invited back to England and the Covenanters were persecuted throughout Scotland. The Camerons abandoned Tor Castle and moved to Achnacarry.
1663–65	The 'Keppoch' murders, and the fierce retribution that resulted in the beheading of seven murderers at Inverlair, commemorated at the Well of the Seven Heads in the Great Glen
1688–89	James VII of Scotland (and II of England) was ousted from the throne in favour of his daughter Mary, and her husband William of Orange. James's supporters were known as 'Jacobites' and were defeated at the Battle of Killiecrankie. Presbyterianism was re-established in Scotland.
1690	General Mackay replaced 'the fort of Inverlochy' with a stone fort, which he named Fort William, in honour of the new king
1692	Urquhart Castle was rendered unusable. Highlanders who refused to support the king were slaughtered at the infamous Massacre of Glencoe.
1707	The Scottish and English parliaments were united during the reign of Queen Anne
1714	With the death of Queen Anne, George I, descended from a daughter of James VI of Scotland, was crowned king, inaugurating the Hanoverian succession
1715	The First Jacobite Rebellion, following which a fort was established in the middle of the Great Glen
1725	General Wade began constructing roads through the Highlands
1726	The first plans for the Caledonian Canal through the Great Glen were drawn, but nothing was achieved on the ground
1736	General Wade built the High Bridge over a gorge at Spean Bridge
1745–46	The Second Jacobite Rebellion, led by 'Bonnie Prince Charlie', who was a grandson of James VII of Scotland. Following initial surprising victories, his army of Highlanders pushed as far south as Derby. Charles would have pressed on to London, but for the counsel of his advisers. However, once he turned back towards Scotland, the Duke of Cumberland pursued the Scots to bloody defeat at Culloden, and wreaked havoc through the Great Glen. Charles was lucky to be able to escape with his life, aided at the end by Flora MacDonald. The fort in the middle of the Great Glen was rebuilt and named Fort Augustus after the 'Butcher' Duke of Cumberland.

1788	The death of 'Bonnie Prince Charlie' in Rome. (Interestingly, an early 19th-century monument raised in the Vatican in honour of the last of the Stuarts was partly funded by the Hanoverian King George IV.)
1790	The Forth and Clyde Canal was opened through central Scotland
1800	The beginning of the brutal 'Highland Clearances' led to the massive depopulation of the Highlands, with much farmland turned over to sheep pasture. While some people moved elsewhere in Scotland, most were forced to emigrate to North America.
1803–22	The Caledonian Canal was cut through the Great Glen. Tourism in the area began to develop apace.
1837	Coronation of Queen Victoria
1842–46	Railways finally linked London with Glasgow and Edinburgh. Fort William was lit using oil lamps.
1848	Queen Victoria purchased the Balmoral Estate in the Highlands
1849	The Potato Famine hit the Highlands particularly hard, leading to one final clearance of the poorest part of the population from the land
1854	The Bridge of Oich was constructed by James Dredge at Aberchalder
1855	The Inverness and Nairn Railway was opened
1864	The Creag Dunain Hospital opens near Inverness
1876	The site of Fort Augustus was given to the Benedictines, who built an abbey there
1883	A pony track was constructed from Glen Nevis to the summit of Ben Nevis
1886	Foundation of the Scottish Home Rule Association
1889	The West Highland Railway reaches Fort William
1895	The development of a hydroelectric plant leads to electric lighting for Fort William
1901	The death of Queen Victoria
1903	The Invergarry and Fort Augustus Railway was opened, but was never extended through the Great Glen to Inverness as originally planned
1928	The Foundation of the Scottish National Party
1931	The British Aluminium (later Alcan) plant opened near Fort William, powered by an extensive hydroelectric scheme
1934	First photograph of the Loch Ness 'monster' published, leading to an influx of visitors and the further development of the tourist trade
1940–45	During World War 2, Commandos were based at Achnacarry House, enduring one of the world's toughest training regimes
1946	The Inverness and Fort Augustus Railway was closed
1952	Queen Elizabeth, the Queen Mother, unveiled the Commando Memorial above Spean Bridge
1953	Coronation of Queen Elizabeth II

The Clan Cameron Museum is off-route at Achnacarry (Stage 2, S–N; Stage 5, N–S), but is worth a visit if you can spare the time

1964	The Forth Road Bridge was opened near Edinburgh. The Scottish Pulp and Paper Mill was opened near Fort William.
1970	The North Sea oil industry was developed, leading to increased prosperity in some parts of the Highlands
1973	The United Kingdom joined the Common Market
1979–2000	Scotland voted in two referenda on the issue of devolution, involving many years of debate, resulting in the election of a Scottish parliament
2000	Inverness was granted a city charter
2002	The Great Glen Way was officially opened by Prince Andrew, Earl of Inverness
2003	The Land Reform (Scotland) Act came into force, clarifying and guaranteeing rights of access to the Scottish countryside
2014	Work is completed on new high-level stretches of the Great Glen Way. A referendum posed the question 'Should Scotland be an independent country?', with 55.3% of voters against and 44.7% of voters for.
2015	In the General Election, an overwhelming number of Scottish National Party candidates were elected
2020–21	Lockdowns due to Covid meant that no-one walked the Great Glen Way for periods of several weeks
2022	Death of Queen Elizabeth II at Balmoral Castle
2023	Coronation of King Charles III

APPENDIX D

Gaelic–English glossary

The oldest place names in the Great Glen are Gaelic, since the language of the Picts has been lost. Gaelic thrives in the Highlands, and road signs throughout the region are often bilingual. Gaelic place names appear in abundance on maps, and they are often highly descriptive of landscape features.

Gaelic	English
abhainn	river
allt	stream
ard	high
ath	ford
auch	field
bal/bally	township
bàn/bhàn	white
beag/bheag	small
bealach	pass/col
ben/beinn/bheinn	mountain
biorach	pointed
breac/bhreac	speckled
buidhe	yellow
caisteal	castle
caol	narrow
caorach	rowanberry
carn	cairn
cioch/ciche	breast
cir/chir	comb/crest
clachan	farm/hamlet
cnoc	small hill
coille	wood
coire/choire	corrie
creag	crag
dearg	red
donn	brown
dubh	black
dun	fort
eas	waterfall
eilean	island
fada/fhada	long

Gaelic	English
fionn	fair
gaoithe	wind
garbh	rough
gearr	sharp
glais	stream
glas/ghlas	grey
gleann	glen/valley
guala	shoulder
inbhir	confluence
innis	island/field
iolaire	eagle
lagan	hollow
leac	flat rock
leathan	broad
loch	lake
lochan	small lake
maol/mhaoile	bald
meall	rounded hill
mhuileann	mill
monadh	mountain
mór/mhór	big
mullach	summit
odhar	dappled
oighe	youth
reamhar	fat
righ	king
ruadh	russet
suidhe	seat
torr	small hill
uaine	green
uisge	water

NOTES

NOTES

NOTES

NOTES

NOTES

NOTES

The view from Inverness Castle, taking in the cathedral, River Ness and Dunain Hill

DOWNLOAD THE GPX FILES

All the routes in this guide are available for download from:

www.cicerone.co.uk/1127/GPX

as standard format GPX files. You should be able to load them into most online GPX systems and mobile devices, whether GPS or smartphone. You may need to convert the file into your preferred format using a conversion programme such as gpsvisualizer.com or one of the many other such websites and programmes.

When you follow this link, you will be asked for your email address and where you purchased the guidebook, and have the option to subscribe to the Cicerone e-newsletter.

www.cicerone.co.uk

LISTING OF CICERONE GUIDES

BRITISH ISLES CHALLENGES, COLLECTIONS AND ACTIVITIES

Great Walks on the England Coast Path
Map and Compass
The Big Rounds
The Book of the Bivvy
The Book of the Bothy
The Mountains of England and Wales:
Vol 1 Wales
Vol 2 England
The National Trails
Walking the End to End Trail
Cycling Land's End to John o' Groats

SHORT WALKS SERIES

15 Short Walks Hadrian's Wall
15 Short Walks in the Lake District: Keswick, Borrowdale and Buttermere
15 Short Walks in the Lake District: Windermere Ambleside and Grasmere
15 Short Walks Lake District: Coniston and Langdale
15 Short Walks in Arnside and Silverdale
15 Short Walks in the Ribble Valley
15 Short Walks in Nidderdale
15 Short Walks in Northumberland: Wooler, Rothbury, Alnwick and the coast
15 Short Walks in the Yorkshire Dales: Grassington, Skipton, Malham and Ilkley
15 Short Walks in the Peak District: Bakewell and the White Peak
15 Short Walks on the Malvern Hills
15 Short Walks in Cornwall: Falmouth and the Lizard
15 Short Walks in Cornwall: Land's End and Penzance
15 Short Walks in the South Downs: Brighton, Eastbourne and Arundel
15 Short Walks in the Surrey Hills
15 Short Walks on Dartmoor North: Okehampton and Chagford
15 Short Walks on Dartmoor South: Ivybridge and Princetown
15 Short Walks on Exmoor
15 Short Walks Winchester
15 Short Walks in Bannau Brycheiniog: Brecon Beacons
15 Short Walks in Pembrokeshire: Tenby and the south
15 Short Walks in Dumfries and Galloway
15 Short Walks in the Trossachs: Callander and Aberfoyle
15 Short Walks on the Isle of Mull
15 Short Walks on the Orkney Islands
15 Short Walks on the Shetland Islands

SCOTLAND

Ben Nevis and Glen Coe
Cycling in the Hebrides
Cycling the North Coast 500
Great Mountain Days in Scotland
Mountain Biking in Southern and Central Scotland
Mountain Biking in West and North West Scotland
Not the West Highland Way: A Mountain High Way
Scotland
Scotland's Best Small Mountains
Scotland's Mountain Ridges
Scottish Wild Country Backpacking
Skye's Cuillin Ridge Traverse
The Borders Abbeys Way
The Great Glen Way
The Great Glen Way Map Booklet
The Hebridean Way
The Hebrides
The Isle of Mull
The Isle of Skye
The Skye Trail
The Southern Upland Way
The West Highland Way
The West Highland Way Map Booklet
Walking Ben Lawers, Rannoch and Atholl
Walking in the Cairngorms
Walking in the Pentland Hills
Walking in the Scottish Borders
Walking in the Southern Uplands
Walking in Torridon, Fisherfield, Fannichs and An Teallach
Walking Loch Lomond and the Trossachs
Walking on Arran
Walking on Harris and Lewis
Walking on Jura, Islay and Colonsay
Walking on Mull, Coll and Tiree
Walking on Rum and the Small Isles
Walking on the Orkney and Shetland Isles
Walking on Uist and Barra
Walking the Cape Wrath Trail
Walking the Corbetts
Vol 1 South of the Great Glen
Vol 2 North of the Great Glen
Walking the Fife Pilgrim Way
Walking the Galloway Hills
Walking the John o' Groats Trail
Walking the Munros
Vol 1 Southern, Central and Western Highlands
Vol 2 Northern Highlands and the Cairngorms
Winter Climbs in the Cairngorms
Winter Climbs: Ben Nevis and Glen Coe

NORTHERN ENGLAND ROUTES

Cycling the Reivers Route
Cycling the Way of the Roses
Hadrian's Cycleway
Hadrian's Wall Path
Hadrian's Wall Path Map Booklet
The Coast to Coast Cycle Route
The Coast to Coast Map Booklet
The Coast to Coast Walk
Walking the Dales Way
The Dales Way Map Booklet
Walking the Pennine Way
Pennine Way Map Booklet

LAKE DISTRICT

Bikepacking in the Lake District
Cycling in the Lake District
Great Mountain Days in the Lake District
Joss Naylor's Lakes, Meres and Waters of the Lake District
Lake District Winter Climbs
Lake District:
High Level and Fell Walks
Low Level and Lake Walks
Mountain Biking in the Lake District
Outdoor Adventures with Children — Lake District
Scrambles in the Lake District —
North
South
Trail and Fell Running in the Lake District
Walking The Cumbria Way
Walking the Lake District Fells —
Borrowdale
Buttermere
Coniston
Keswick
Langdale
Mardale and the Far East
Patterdale
Wasdale
Walking the Tour of the Lake District

NORTH-WEST ENGLAND AND THE ISLE OF MAN

Cycling the Pennine Bridleway
Isle of Man Coastal Path
The Lancashire Cycleway
The Lune Valley and Howgills
Walking in Cumbria's Eden Valley
Walking in Lancashire
Walking in the Forest of Bowland and Pendle
Walking on the Isle of Man
Walking on the West Pennine Moors
Walking the Ribble Way
Walks in Silverdale and Arnside

NORTH-EAST ENGLAND, YORKSHIRE DALES AND PENNINES

Cycling in the Yorkshire Dales
Great Mountain Days in the Pennines
Mountain Biking in the Yorkshire Dales
The Cleveland Way and the Yorkshire Wolds Way
The Cleveland Way Map Booklet
The North York Moors
Trail and Fell Running in the Yorkshire Dales
Walking in County Durham
Walking in Northumberland
Walking in the North Pennines
Walking in the Yorkshire Dales: North and East
South and West
Walking St Cuthbert's Way
Walking St Oswald's Way and Northumberland Coast Path

DERBYSHIRE, PEAK DISTRICT AND MIDLANDS

Cycling in the Peak District
Dark Peak Walks
Scrambles in the Dark Peak
Walking in Derbyshire
Walking in the Peak District - White Peak East
White Peak West

WALES AND WELSH BORDERS

Cycle Touring in Wales
Cycling Lon Las Cymru
Great Mountain Days in Snowdonia
Hillwalking in Shropshire
Mountain Walking in Snowdonia
Offa's Dyke Path
Offa's Dyke Map Booklet
Scrambles in Snowdonia
Snowdonia: 30 Low-level and Easy Walks — North, South
The Cambrian Way
The Pembrokeshire Coast Path
The Pembrokeshire Coast Path Map Booklet
The Snowdonia Way
The Wye Valley Walk
Walking Glyndwr's Way
Walking in Carmarthenshire
Walking in Pembrokeshire
Walking in the Brecon Beacons
Walking in the Wye Valley
Walking on Gower
Walking the Severn Way
Walking the Shropshire Way
Walking the Wales Coast Path

SOUTHERN ENGLAND

20 Classic Sportive Rides
in South East England
in South West England
Cycling in the Cotswolds
Mountain Biking on the North Downs
Mountain Biking on the South Downs
The North Downs Way
The North Downs Way Map Booklet
The South Downs Way
The South Downs Way Map Booklet
The Cotswold Way
The Cotswold Way Map Booklet
The Ridgeway National Trail
The Ridgeway Map Booklet
The Thames Path
The Thames Path Map Booklet
The Two Moors Way
Two Moors Way Map Booklet
Walking the South West Coast Path
South West Coast Path Map Booklet
Vol 1: Minehead to St Ives
Vol 2: St Ives to Plymouth
Vol 2: St Ives to Plymouth
Vol 3: Plymouth to Poole
Suffolk Coast and Heath Walks
The Kennet and Avon Canal
The Lea Valley Walk
The Peddars Way and Norfolk Coast Path
The Pilgrims' Way
Walking Hampshire's Test Way
Walking in Essex
Walking in Kent
Walking in London
Walking in Norfolk
Walking in the Chilterns
Walking in the Cotswolds
Walking in the Isles of Scilly
Walking in the New Forest
Walking in the North Wessex Downs
Walking on Dartmoor
Walking on Guernsey
Walking on Jersey
Walking on the Isle of Wight
Walking the Dartmoor Way
Walking the Jurassic Coast
Walking the Sarsen Way
Walks in the South Downs National Park

ALPS CROSS-BORDER ROUTES

100 Hut Walks in the Alps
Alpine Ski Mountaineering Vol 1 — Western Alps
The Karnischer Hohenweg
The Tour of the Bernina
Trail Running — Chamonix and the Mont Blanc region
Trekking Chamonix to Zermatt
Trekking in the Alps
Trekking in the Silvretta and Ratikon Alps
Trekking Munich to Venice
Trekking the Tour du Mont Blanc
Tour du Mont Blanc Map Booklet
Walking in the Alps

FRANCE, BELGIUM, AND LUXEMBOURG

Camino de Santiago — Via Podiensis
Chamonix Mountain Adventures
Cycling London to Paris
Cycling the Canal de la Garonne
Cycling the Canal du Midi
Mont Blanc Walks
Mountain Adventures in the Maurienne
Short Treks on Corsica
The GR5 Trail
The GR5 Trail — Vosges and Jura
Benelux and Lorraine
The Moselle Cycle Route
Trekking in the Vanoise
Trekking the Cathar Way
Trekking the GR10
Trekking the GR20 Corsica
Trekking the Robert Louis Stevenson Trail
Via Ferratas of the French Alps
Walking in Provence — East
Walking in Provence — West
Walking in the Auvergne
Walking in the Brianconnais
Walking in the Dordogne
Walking in the Haute Savoie: North
Walking in the Haute Savoie: South
Walking on Corsica
Walking the Brittany Coast Path
Walking in the Ardennes

PYRENEES AND FRANCE/SPAIN CROSS-BORDER ROUTES

Shorter Treks in the Pyrenees
The Pyrenean Haute Route
The Pyrenees
Trekking the Cami dels Bons Homes
Trekking the GR11 Trail
Walks and Climbs in the Pyrenees

SPAIN AND PORTUGAL

Camino de Santiago: Camino Frances
Coastal Walks in Andalucia
Costa Blanca Mountain Adventures
Cycling the Camino de Santiago
Mountain Walking in Mallorca
Mountain Walking in Southern Catalunya
Spain's Sendero Historico: The GR1
The Andalucian Coast to Coast Walk
The Camino del Norte and Camino Primitivo
The Camino Ingles and Ruta do Mar
The Mountains Around Nerja
The Mountains of Ronda and Grazalema
The Sierras of Extremadura
Trekking in Mallorca
Trekking in the Canary Islands
Trekking the GR7 in Andalucia
Walking and Trekking in the Sierra Nevada
Walking in Andalucia
Walking in Catalunya — Barcelona
Girona Pyrenees
Walking in the Picos de Europa
Walking La Via de la Plata and Camino Sanabres
Walking on Gran Canaria
Walking on La Gomera and El Hierro

Walking on La Palma
Walking on Lanzarote and Fuerteventura
Walking on Tenerife
Walking on the Costa Blanca
Walking the Camino dos Faros
Portugal's Rota Vicentina
The Camino Portugues
Walking in Portugal
Walking in the Algarve
Walking on Madeira
Walking on the Azores

SWITZERLAND

Switzerland's Jura Crest Trail
The Swiss Alps
Tour of the Jungfrau Region
Trekking the Swiss Via Alpina
Walking in Arolla and Zinal
Walking in the Bernese Oberland — Jungfrau region
Walking in the Engadine — Switzerland
Walking in Ticino
Walking in Zermatt and Saas-Fee

GERMANY

Hiking and Cycling in the Black Forest
The Danube Cycleway Vol 1
The Rhine Cycle Route
The Westweg
Walking in the Bavarian Alps

POLAND, SLOVAKIA, ROMANIA, HUNGARY AND BULGARIA

The Danube Cycleway Vol 2
The High Tatras
The Mountains of Romania

SCANDINAVIA, ICELAND AND GREENLAND

Hiking in Norway —
North
South
Trekking the Kungsleden
Trekking in Greenland — The Arctic Circle Trail
Walking and Trekking in Iceland

SLOVENIA, CROATIA, SERBIA, MONTENEGRO AND ALBANIA

Hiking Slovenia's Juliana Trail
Mountain Biking in Slovenia
The Islands of Croatia
The Julian Alps of Slovenia
The Mountains of Montenegro
The Peaks of the Balkans Trail
The Peaks of the Balkans Trail
The Slovene Mountain Trail
Walking in Slovenia: The Karavanke
Walks and Treks in Croatia

ITALY

Alta Via
1 — Trekking in the Dolomites
2 — Trekking in the Dolomites
Day Walks in the Dolomites
Italy's Grande Traversata delle Alpi
Italy's Sibillini National Park
Ski Touring and Snowshoeing in the Dolomites
The Way of St Francis: Via di Francesco
Trekking Gran Paradiso: Alta Via 2
Trekking in the Apennines
Trekking the Giants' Trail: Alta Via 1 through the Italian Pennine Alps
Via Ferratas of the Italian Dolomites:
Vol 1
Vol 2
Walking in Abruzzo
Walking in Italy's Cinque Terre
Walking in Italy's Stelvio National Park
Walking in Sicily
Walking in the Aosta Valley
Walking in the Dolomites
Walking in Tuscany
Walking in Umbria
Walking Lake Como and Maggiore
Walking Lake Garda and Iseo
Walking on the Amalfi Coast
Walking the Via Francigena Pilgrim Route
Part 1
Part 2
Part 3
Part 4
Walks and Treks in the Maritime Alps

IRELAND

The Wild Atlantic Way and Western Ireland
Walking the Kerry Way
Walking the Wicklow Way

EUROPEAN CYCLING

Cycling the Route des Grandes Alpes
Cycling the Ruta Via de la Plata
The Elbe Cycle Route
The River Loire Cycle Route
The River Rhone Cycle Route

INTERNATIONAL CHALLENGES, COLLECTIONS AND ACTIVITIES

Europe's High Points
Pocket First Aid and Wilderness Medicine

AUSTRIA

Innsbruck Mountain Adventures
Trekking Austria's Adlerweg
Trekking in Austria's Hohe Tauern
Trekking in Austria's Stubai Alps
Trekking in Austria's Zillertal Alps
Walking in Austria
Walking in the Salzkammergut: the Austrian Lake District

MEDITERRANEAN

The High Mountains of Crete
Trekking in Greece
Walking and Trekking in Zagori
Walking and Trekking on Corfu
Walking on the Greek Islands — the Cyclades
Walking in Cyprus
Walking on Malta

HIMALAYA

8000 metres
Everest: A Trekker's Guide
Trekking in the Karakoram

NORTH AMERICA

Hiking and Cycling the California Missions Trail
Hiking the Pacific Crest Trail
The John Muir Trail

SOUTH AMERICA

Aconcagua and the Southern Andes
Hiking and Biking Peru's Inca Trails
Trekking in Torres del Paine

AFRICA

Climbing Toubkal
Kilimanjaro
Walking in the Drakensberg
Walks and Scrambles in the Moroccan Anti-Atlas

NEW ZEALANDAND AND AUSTRALIA

Hiking the Overland Track

CHINA, JAPAN AND ASIA

Annapurna
Hiking and Trekking in the Japan Alps and Mount Fuji
Hiking in Hong Kong
Japan's Kumano Kodo Pilgrimage
Japan's Kumano Kodo Pilgrimage
Trekking in Bhutan
Trekking in Ladakh
Trekking in Tajikistan
Trekking in the Himalaya

TECHNIQUES

Fastpacking
The Mountain Hut Book

MINI GUIDES

Alpine Flowers
Navigation

MOUNTAIN LITERATURE

A Walk in the Clouds
Abode of the Gods
Fifty Years of Adventure
The Pennine Way — the Path, the People, the Journey
Unjustifiable Risk?

For full information on all our guides, books and eBooks, visit our website:
www.cicerone.co.uk